SEP 24 2004

JEWISH
OF
PSYCHOANALYTIC
MOVEMENT

D0735490

SEP 24 2004

JEWISH ORIGINS OF THE PSYCHOANALYTIC MOVEMENT

Dennis B. Klein

The University of Chicago Press

Chicago & London

*Published by arrangement with Praeger Publishers
and Dennis B. Klein*

The University of Chicago Press, Chicago 60637
The University of Chicago Press, Ltd., London

© 1981 by Praeger Publishers
© 1985 by Dennis B. Klein
All rights reserved. Published 1985
Printed in the United States of America

94 93 93 92 91 90 89 88 87   5 4 3 2

Library of Congress Cataloging in Publication Data

Klein, Dennis B.
  Jewish origins of the psychoanalytic movement.

  Bibliography: p.
  Includes index.
  1. Psychoanalysis — History. 2. Jews — Intellectual
life — History. 3. Freud, Sigmund, 1856-1939. 4. Rank,
Otto, 1884-1939. I. Title.
BF175.K49 1985   150.19′5′09   84-28083
ISBN 0-226-43960-7 (paper)

CONTENTS

ACKNOWLEDGMENTS   vii

PREFACE, 1985   ix

INTRODUCTION   xi

Chapter

1   ASSIMILATION AND DISSIMILATION   1
    The Situation in Vienna   2
    Self-Determination   16
    A Jewish Task   28

2   FREUD AND THE PSYCHOLOGY OF MOVEMENT   40
    Godless, but Ethical — and German   42
    Encounter with Anti-Semitism   48
    Koller, Breuer, and the Society of Physicians   55

3   THE PREFIGURING OF THE PSYCHOANALYTIC
    MOVEMENT: FREUD AND THE B'NAI B'RITH   69
    Forging a Jewish Bond   69
    The B'nai B'rith in Vienna   75
    A New Forum for Movement   84

4   THE PSYCHOLOGY OF THE FOLLOWER: OTTO RANK   103
    The Art of Psychoanalysis   104
    Nietzsche as Surrogate Father   108
    A Radical Cure of Neurosis   118

5   CONCLUSION   138
    A Jewish Movement   138
    The Particular and the Universal   141

Appendix A   LECTURES FREUD PRESENTED TO
    THE B'NAI B'RITH, 1897-1917   155

Appendix B   OTTO RANK: A CHRONOLOGY   166

Appendix C   TRANSLATION OF OTTO RANK'S "DAS WESEN DES
              JUDENTUMS" ("THE ESSENCE OF JUDAISM")   170

Bibliography   174

Index   193

About the Author   199

ACKNOWLEDGMENTS

The people who made it possible for me to locate the essential documentary and unpublished material for this book were Ludwig Markovits, Ruth Meron, Sybil Milton and her colleagues at the Leo Baeck Institute (New York), and the staff at the Otto Rank Collection in the Special Collections Division of Columbia University. A Fulbright-Hays Fellowship funded the research.

For their intellectual and personal support, I am constantly grateful to William J. McGrath, Ernst and Hilde Federn, David Bronsen, Andrei S. Markovits, Abraham J. Karp, and Ruth Kimmerer. I would also like to thank H. L. Ansbacher for his special help in preparing the second edition of this book.

My deepest appreciation, and my growing love, goes to my parents, Jean and Harold Klein, my brothers Roger and Richard Klein and their families, and to my wife, Libby, and my son, Aaron.

ABOUT THE AUTHOR

Dennis B. Klein has published in the areas of European and Jewish history. His articles and reviews appeared in *New German Critique*, *American Historical Review*, *Journal of Modern History*, and *Jews and Germans from 1860 to 1933*, a collection of papers published in Germany. He has also written, on commission, a study about the American Jewish community during the 1930s and 1940s. Grants from the Spencer Foundation, the National Endowment for the Humanities, and the Memorial Foundation for Jewish Culture support his current research on problems in German and German-Jewish history from the late nineteenth century through the two world wars.

Dr. Klein has studied at Hobart College, the University of Rochester, the University of Vienna, and Harvard University. He has taught at the Melton Center for Jewish Studies of Ohio State University, Michigan State University, and New York University. Dr. Klein is Director of the Center for Holocaust Studies, under the auspices of the Anti-Defamation League.

PREFACE, 1985

When the outlines of this book first took shape some ten years ago, modern Jewish history was just becoming a separate field of study with its own interpretive perspectives. Certainly, before the late 1960s and early 1970s, historians had observed most of the important events marking the appearance of European Jews on the modern world-historical stage. What had changed, however, was the premise of modern Jewish historiography: Whereas historians once observed Jewish history largely as an aspect of European history — the European acceptance or rejection of Jews — historians now considered the internal and distinctive character of modern European-Jewish life. Perhaps the focus on Jews after the 1967 war, or a readiness to extend a glance backward, beyond the Holocaust, to the formative decades of emancipated Jewry, or a new awareness of ethnic and gender distinctions spurred this special interest in modern Jewish history.

After these ten to fifteen years, interest in modern Jewish history remains strong and seminal. That interest provided a seed for this book, making it possible to begin with the question, why, during its first four years, were all the members of the psychoanalytic movement Jewish, and then to show the quality and creative possibilities of their Jewish self-conceptions.

Psychoanalysis, the other of the twin themes in this book, also became the subject of renewed historical inquiry at the time when the idea for this book first took root. More a different angle of investigation than a definable field, the new criticism of psychoanalysis probed Freud's family secrets, challenging the protective idolatry around Freud and his movement. The fascination with Freud always existed, of course. And the psychoanalytic world-view, which postulates the hidden and intimate, but powerful, influences shaping human behavior and thought, continually demands clarification. Eventually, however, historians began to see psychoanalysis as springing from Freud's own family romance — the impact of Freud's father's death in 1896; Freud's transferential relationship with Wilhelm Fliess in the 1890s; his discovery of a family secret about his real mother; or his romantic desire for his sister-in-law, who moved in with the Freuds in 1895.

Another seed for this book lies within this revisionary climate, which still sets the tone for the historical interpretation of psychoanalysis. This climate of reinterpretation supplied a focus for the book on another intimate tie in Freud's life: the relationship he formed in 1897 with his "brothers" — his Jewish brothers in the fraternal society of B'nai B'rith. The movement of psychoanalysis is difficult to reconstruct without showing its basis in, and the quality of, a Jewish fraternal bond.

Four years after the publication of the first edition, the cumulative yield from the two broad historical perspectives outlined here underscores this book's most important conclusions. For all of its sovereign value, psychoanalysis may well not have achieved recognition if not for the perseverence of those who became its voice. Commitment to its ideas is surely part of the reason for this collective zeal. Another reason springs from the circumstances of Jewish life in anti-Semitic Vienna at the turn of the century, and especially the unusual blend of assimilation and dissimilation.

The concern of recent historiography with the integrity of "outsiders" and the intimacies of public figures has opened new lines of investigation. Toward making the argument in this book, those topics have provided a framework for responding to the inert discussion about the insignificance or oversignificance of the Jews in Freud's circle — a problem explored in some detail in the introduction. Without these new perspectives, a crucial piece of psychoanalytic history would not have surfaced.

Dennis B. Klein
New York, New York

INTRODUCTION

This book takes seriously Sigmund Freud's feeling for the movement of psychoanalysis and the constant remaking of this movement around Freud. As with the history of ideas generally, the history of psychoanalysis has been in part a history of suppressing or distorting the vital subjective or sectarian loyalties of individuals who are involved in developing and promoting nonsectarian, universal ideas. The psychoanalytic movement stands out as an intellectual endeavor that invites misrepresentation and confusion, for it exhibited considerable particularistic tendencies. First, the early analysts regarded themselves as an embattled, heroic elite, intolerant of the outside world, but determined, as if in combat, to advance their knowledge. Their intense feeling of moral superiority disposed them toward a cause — indeed, engaged them in a movement, which took the circle far beyond the usual bounds of a scientific effort.

Still more sectarian and particularistic was the remarkable predominance of Jews in the psychoanalytic circle. From its beginning in 1902 to 1906, all 17 members were Jewish. The full significance of this number lies again in the way they viewed themselves, for the analysts were aware of their Jewishness and frequently maintained a sense of Jewish purpose and solidarity. Freud's biographer and disciple, Ernest Jones, recognized that this feeling of positive Jewish pride formed the matrix of the movement in the psychoanalytic circle: As a spur to renewed independence, it tightened the bond among the members and powered their self-image of a redemptive elite.[1] So powerful were their Jewish self-conceptions that even after 1906, when Jones and other non-Jews entered the group, the feeling of a Jewish movement persisted.

The scholarship on the Jewishness of Freud and his colleagues (although in fact this scholarship is limited to Freud) has shown signs of fatigue in its overextended acrobatics of either disguising or magnifying the meaning and impact of the movement's unmistakable sectarian quality. Generally, this literature exemplifies a problem in a way of thinking about the distinction between the particular and the universal — to most, this distinction involves a fundamental contradiction. Jones is typical of those supporting psychoanalysis who cannot accept the Jewish attachments of the early analysts, seeing them as an impurity and as an interference in the psychoanalytic advancement of truth. Annoyed with the Jews in the circle for assuming an attitude of Jewish superiority, and a possible victim himself of mistrust between Jews and non-Jews, he consistently understated the positive value of Jewish pride in the movement or misrepresented its value in Freud's life. For example, Jones omitted Freud's expression of gratitude to "those of our faith" in a then-unpublished letter Freud had addressed to his fiancée in 1884.[2]

If the tendency to deny or underestimate the movement's Jewish content is strong, the opposite tendency, to exaggerate or overestimate it, is, for many, irresistible. Critics favoring the latter approach dig into the surface of the movement to uncover two deeper levels of Jewish activity: the level of motive in using psychoanalysis to foster Jewish interests, and the broader level of historical and social forces in Jewish life that instigate the self-interests of Jews. Although in this case, attention focuses on the Jewishness of the early analysts, it reduces psychoanalysis to a crypto-Jewish science, and, finally, to the historical Jewish need for entry into Western culture. This approach to the psychoanalytic movement comes out of a tradition in Jewish intellectual or cultural history that attempts to explain what it sees as the extraordinary creative impact of Jews on modern life. The most recent example of this kind of Jewish sociologism is Frederic Grunfeld's *Prophets Without Honour*. Grunfeld argues that for Jews emigrating from East Europe, the suddenness of the transition from isolated ghetto life to the freedom of the cosmopolitan West released a burst of creative energy and enthusiasm, and that their subsequent marginal existence as refugee intellectuals gave them a revolutionary perspective on life. A corollary of this argument links the homelessness of Jews with their natural predilection for innovation.[3]

For those studying the Jewish dimensions of Freud's circle, the psychoanalytic stress on hidden motivations apparently has given free rein to this search for a collective Jewish unconscious in the work of Jews. Since the inception of the movement, supporters and detractors alike have made competing claims in fathoming a Jewish spirit or intelligence in Freud's work.[4] But, regardless of how they have defined this spirit, so long as it resembles some aspect of psychoanalysis, they show no interest in understanding the analytic project itself. Rather, they use Freud's Jewishness for the ulterior purposes of either commending psychoanalysis as one more Jewish contribution to the modern world or discrediting it as one more subversive Jewish challenge to regnant moral convictions.

Only a scholarly detachment distinguishes the three recent, important investigations into Freud's Jewishness from this transparently ad hominem approach, for, in their studies, John Cuddihy, David Bakan, and Marthe Robert also reduce psychoanalysis to a Jewish program — the desire of Freud to facilitate the admission of Jews into Western culture.[5] Finding sufficient evidence of Freud's Jewish self-awareness, but not of a Jewish preoccupation, they invent rhetorical hypotheses about his Jewishness as ballast for disclosing or decoding the veiled psychoanalytic project of Jewish emancipation. These hypotheses float entirely outside historical reality, which explains their divergence from the Jewish sources of psychoanalysis.

In *The Ordeal of Civility,* Cuddihy places Freud much too close to the East European roots of his parents. He conveniently overlooks Freud's contempt for unassimilated Jews, arguing that from them, Freud understood the primitive, emotional thrust of premodern life. Cuddihy then brings to light Freud's "secret": In using the spontaneous but crude Ostjude as the model for the id, and the modern but overrefined bourgeois as the model for the superego, the founder of psychoanalysis worked out a scheme, stripped of provocatively explicit Jewish content, for reconciling the conflict between Jews and non-Jews. In Bakan's study, *Sigmund Freud and the Jewish Mystical Tradition,* Freud appears closer to the West, but still shows the positive influences of East European traditions. Bakan finds interesting parallels between psychoanalysis and the Kabbalah, but recklessly leaps to the conclusion that psychoanalysis is nothing more than "dissimulated" antinomian mysticism, an implicit Sabbatian apostasy of the rabbinic, legalistic tradition. In this view, Freud endeavored to transmit mystical thought, dressed up in psychoanalytic disguise because of the constant peril of anti-Semitic persecution, in order to encourage other East European descendants to embrace the freedoms of Western life.

Of the three studies, Robert's *From Oedipus to Moses: Freud's Jewish Identity* comes nearest to the truth in conveying Freud's desire for leaving the East behind, to participate fully in Western society. Robert correctly sees Freud as an assimilated Jew — that is, a Jew who recognized the distance still separating Jews from non-Jews, but who nevertheless adhered to the unifying humanist ideologies of the West that made divisiveness or disparity morally intolerable. But like Cuddihy and Bakan, she presumes that Jews like Freud were obsessed with the desire for integration, and therefore also interprets psychoanalysis as a symptom of urgent Jewish needs. According to Robert, psychoanalysis resolved Freud's personal dilemma of pursuing his ambitions in the West European world, without betraying his Jewish past by assimilating or submitting to Christian culture: As a rational and scientific theory, it neutralized the differences between Jews and non-Jews, in preparation for communication between the two sides.

In the view of traditional historians, psychoanalysis is seen as either a purely universal and human theory or, for those aware of its Jewish aspect, a piece of Jewish history. Each position has its merits, but each is prone to excess. Those who want to preserve the universality of psychoanalysis are bent on making the Jewish sources of the movement disappear. Those who want to bring out these sources are inclined toward obscurantism and provincialism. While the two groups differ over just how to deal with the manifestations of Jewishness in Freud's circle, they both make the same mistake: They do not see the active side of how the analysts themselves understood and used their Jewishness, and therefore miss the creative and human content of their sectarianism. Freud and his coworkers did indeed inherit a common Jewish past, which included the struggle for integration. But especially after 1880, when anti-Semitism intensified in Vienna and deepened Jewish sensitivities, they joined an increasing number of Jews who reinterpreted and manipulated the Jewish legacy of frustrated social integration, to articulate the more basic nineteenth century search for the cultural whole.

Revisionist historians restore the actors to the stage of deposited history by bringing out the subjective and the volitional in the historical process. In *Freud, Biologist of the Mind,* Frank Sulloway offers refreshing insight into the anatomy of the movement around Freud.[6] The psychoanalytic movement, he argues, rested on two pillars: the proprietary claim to originality, and the missionary self-image of heroic destiny. By establishing the facts that psychoanalysis originated not in Freud's self-analysis, but from a larger intellectual confluence, and stood not in hostile opposition to an unprepared world, but in self-imposed isolation, Sulloway makes clear that the movement emerged solely from the revolutionary minds of Freud, his disciples, and his biographers. He explains that analysts have frequently sought to substitute, for their actual place in the intellectual and social world of the time, a mythical reconstruction of history in order to convince themselves, and others, of their unique importance.

Though Sulloway focuses his analysis of the movement on what he calls its myth of origins and its myth of the hero, his argument fully applies to the Jewish myth-making process as well. Actually, it is the Jewish myth-making process that invigorated the analytic self-image of a missionary elite. Freud put the process to work throughout his most creative years, from his attack on the "Christian views" of the Viennese medical establishment,[7] marking an early step in his self-imposed isolation, to his identification with the Jewish prophet Moses, an archetype, for him, of ethical responsibility. Revisionism thus provides a necessary corrective to the shortsightedness of traditional history, which takes literally, as historical reality, Freud's inventive, metaphorical understanding of Jewish persecution and Jewish humanitarianism.

If Sulloway and other revisionist historians preserve the myth-making process, against a hardening into literalness, they nevertheless let it die another death: by neglect. Once they expose the subjective refashioning of history and the self-serving motives beneath the deliberate historical distortion — once, that is, they make the distinction between myth and reality — they proceed to call myth making false history, and therefore, to invalidate it. This is one conclusion Peter Gay draws in *Freud, Jews and Other Germans.* He denies the significance of Freud's Jewish consciousness, and of the Jewish consciousness of his contemporaries, dismissing the belief of Jews in their cleverness and their thirst for innovation as mere fantasy, a self-delusion.[8] Sulloway articulates the extent of this logic: The historian must reverse the process of myth in order to achieve a "mythless history."

Revisionist historians make a historical misjudgment about the psychoanalytic movement. They separate, once and for all, the myths of the psychoanalytic movement from its reality, when in fact the myths sever from reality only after 1908. From this point on, Freud realized that the movement, in danger of becoming a "Jewish national affair,"[9] must forgo its Jewish redemptive myth in order to secure for psychoanalysis a bona fide place in the international scientific community. However, before 1908, the myths and the movement were of the same piece. The present book enables an understanding of the Jewish attachment of the analysts in their work, of the particular in the universal, as well as of the universal in the particular. It not only recognizes the subjective content of their Jewish consciousness — their Jewishness by choice as well as by existence. It also shows the positive significance of the subjective in history, arguing that the Jewish self-images of Freud and his coworkers were catalytic in giving rise to the movement and in fortifying their creative perseverance. If the analysts' sense of their superiority and redemptive purpose supplied an impetus to their creative work, then their Jewish self-conceptions must be regarded as the real, and not merely fabricated, origins of psychoanalysis. By giving movement to their endeavors, the Jewish consciousness of Freud and his colleagues strengthened their confident independence, provided a basis for mutual encouragement, propelled the resolve for ambitious work, and gave substance to the conviction that they were fulfilling a revolutionary mission. This book therefore focuses on the formation and early-development period in psychoanalytic history, before, that is, the myths began to outlive their originating function.

To help clarify the development of these themes in the present work, a few preliminary distinctions are necessary. It goes without saying that, in disputing the traditional Jewish-historical approach to the psychoanalytic movement, this study cannot accept some of the general assumptions underlying traditional Jewish intellectual history. Least of all can it accept the notion of a Jewish contribution to German culture. The number of Jews in Vienna who, like the analysts, advanced their work as Jews was actually quite small. On this point, Bakan, Cuddihy, and Robert are more accurate than Grunfeld is in seeing a prevalent German or European loyalty among German Jewry. But the former three writers also take the part for the German-Jewish cultural whole, and therefore overlook the significant, if not widespread, Jewish withdrawal from the dominant culture and subsequent formation of a Jewish subculture. Traditional history is a victim of ironic revenge: Its tendency to see the Jews as a single, homogeneous whole, with characteristically Jewish experiences, comes at the expense of the rest, making for only a partial understanding of the Jewish involvement in European life. The Jews can become an abstraction which conceals and obscures the crucial differences among them, such as the diverse reactions to anti-Semitism that led some Jews anxiously to hasten their assimilationist efforts, and led others (fewer) to dissimilate and redefine their Jewishness.

Leaving aside the question of a Jewish element in German culture, this study looks, instead, at the contribution of only some Jews. Still, even as a minority, those Jews who affirmed their Jewishness reflect a larger part of modern Jewish history than their small numbers would at first indicate. By making explicit their Jewish distinctiveness, they both represented the common feeling of distance from Germans, which their Jewish contemporaries had felt as well, but suppressed, and also anticipated the ruptures that separated Jews from non-Jews after World War I. Indeed, even as a minority of Jews within the Jewish minority, their self-consciously Jewish participation in German culture says something about nineteenth century Central Europe, since their dissimilation from Germans, but not yet hopeless incompatibility with them, shows the heterogeneity of its social order.

But the chief reason for concentrating on a small minority of Jews is to understand a vital source of creativity in the psychoanalytic movement, and, perhaps, by showing the particular in the universal, an aspect of the creative process itself. In its focus on the analysts' subjective, Jewish loyalties, this study will not ignore the objective conditions of life for Jews in nineteenth century Vienna. Chapter 1 defines the historical boundaries of ascendant liberalism in Austria during the 1860s and 1870s, as well as the endemic character of Austrian anti-Semitism after 1880. It therefore brings out the range of possibilities for Jewish action and, in particular, sets the stage for the unprecedented reaction of dissimilation. The one conspicuous constant throughout this period was the desire of Jews for integration. This hope and vision entered into the Jewish anticipation of assimilation, as well as into the later, Jewish-national consciousness of universal redemption. Jews drew on basic Enlightenment ideas or on antiliberal, Nietzschean values to lend an aspect of authority to the desire for integration. It is therefore not difficult to understand why traditional historians see the desire for integration as a socially conditioned incentive.

However, the Jewish wish for integration is not reducible specifically to social needs. It was not even exclusively Jewish. Integration or universality was a moral ideology that exerted a powerful influence on nineteenth century historical beliefs generally. The meaning of Jewish integration must be understood in both of the ways assimilated Jews of this period understood it: as a reconciliation of hostile social differences that would directly benefit Jews, and as a unifying, universal, moral ideal that would benefit all humanity.

Moreover, in spite of its exertion on Jews, the ideology of the whole never forced or determined the same understanding of it or approach to it. Like other historical boundaries, it merely beckoned a response. Even in the psychoanalytic movement, which exhibited strong unity, the comprehension of the whole differed sharply. Freud was not as zealous as Otto Rank was for establishing a regenerative principle of the whole. Freud aimed at liberating humanity from repression and neurotic misery through an arduously uncompromising commitment to truth. Rank expressed impatience with theory and demanded a radical cure of neurosis. Correspondingly, Freud's and Rank's Jewish self-images differed as well: Rank saw his Jewishness as a condition of redemption; Freud saw it as a precondition, a preparation for the psychoanalytic task.

Yet, for all the internal differences in the movement, they are minor compared with the differences between the analytic and the pre-1880 Jewish view of the whole. Both Rank and Freud, as well as other analysts, were sensitive to the fracturing of life around them. They even took part in it, moving from

German deference to Jewish defiance as a strategy for combating the sources of conflict. Forward movement to the new order demanded, first, this one or these two steps backward from their discordant world. By contrast, before the polarization of the Austro-Hungarian Empire and the eruption of anti-Semitic rage, movement for Jews was centripetal. Assimilation was positive and hopeful. Assimilated Jews, and non-Jews as well, could look forward, almost without circumspection, to a new, integrated order.

So self-assured and so logically compelling is this world view of linear progress toward the whole that, in spite of the subsequent period of profound social disruptions, it survives to this day. But this world view is no longer appropriate. Ethnic, class, and national allegiances are too powerful to ignore. Nor are they necessarily the manifestations of hopelessly selfish interests. Whatever Jewish self-assertion contributed to the antagonistic climate in Vienna after 1880, its expression in the psychoanalytic movement makes clear that, in the postliberal period, sectarian loyalties not only are more realistic than love based on faith for all humanity, but also can invigorate and mobilize creative responses to a warring world.

NOTES

1. See Ernest Jones, *Free Associations: Memoirs of a Psycho-Analyst* (New York: Basic Books, 1959), 208-12.

2. Compare Ernest Jones, *The Life and Work of Sigmund Freud*, vol. 1 (New York: Basic Books, 1953), 160, with Sigmund Freud, *The Letters of Sigmund Freud 1873-1939*, ed. Ernst L. Freud, trans. Tania and James Stern (London: The Hogarth Press, 1961), 101-02.

3. Frederic V. Grunfeld, *Prophets Without Honour: A Background to Freud, Kafka, Einstein and Their World* (London: Hutchinson and Co., 1979). See also, Thorstein Veblen, "The Intellectual Pre-Eminence of Jews in Modern Europe," *Essays in Our Changing Order*, ed. Leon Ardzrooni (New York: A. M. Kelly, 1964); Charles Singer, "Science and Judaism," in *The Jews*, vol. 2, ed. Louis Finkelstein (New York: Harper and Brothers, 1960), esp. 1412-14; and Lewis Feuer, *The Scientific Intellectual* (New York: Basic Books, 1963), 301-2.

4. See, for example, A. A. Roback, *Jewish Influence in Modern Thought* (Cambridge, Mass.: Sci-Art Publishers, 1929), 171-97; and Victor von Weizsäcker, "Reminiscences," in *Freud and the 20th Century*, ed. Benjamin Nelson (New York: Meridian Books, 1958).

5. John Murray Cuddihy, *The Ordeal of Civility: Freud, Marx, Lévi-Strauss, and the Jewish Struggle with Modernity* (New York: Basic Books, 1974); David Bakan, *Sigmund Freud and the Jewish Mystical Tradition* (Princeton: Princeton University Press, 1958); Marthe Robert, *From Oedipus to Moses: Freud's Jewish Identity*, trans. Ralph Manheim (Garden City, N.Y.: Anchor Books, 1976).

6. Frank J. Sulloway, *Freud, Biologist of the Mind: Beyond the Psychoanalytic Legend* (New York: Basic Books, 1979).

7. See Sigmund Freud, *The Origins of Psycho-Analysis: Letters to Wilhelm Fliess, Drafts and Notes: 1887-1902*, ed. Marie Bonaparte, Anna Freud, and Ernst Kris, trans. Eric Mosbacher and James Strachey (New York: Basic Books, 1954), 55.

8. Peter Gay, *Freud, Jews and Other Germans: Masters and Victims in Modernist Culture* (New York: Oxford University Press, 1978), esp. 101.

9. Sigmund Freud and Karl Abraham, *A Psycho-Analytic Dialogue: The Letters of Sigmund Freud and Karl Abraham 1907-1926,* ed. Hilda C. Abraham and Ernst L. Freud, trans. Bernard Marsh and Hilda C. Abraham (New York: Basic Books, 1965), 34.

JEWISH ORIGINS
OF THE
PSYCHOANALYTIC
MOVEMENT

1

ASSIMILATION AND DISSIMILATION

When the Viennese author Arthur Schnitzler (1862-1931) wrote his celebrated novel *Der Weg ins Freie* (*The Road to the Open*) in 1908, he noted the contrast between Jews of his own day and Jews of the previous generation. "A Jew who loves his country, . . . I mean in the way my father did, with real enthusiasm for the [Austro-Hungarian] dynasty, is without the slightest question a tragic-comic figure. I mean . . . he belonged to that liberalizing epoch of the seventies and eighties when even shrewd men were overcome by the catch-words of the day. A man like that today would certainly appear merely comic."[1] Schnitzler was referring to Austria's brief but intense era of political liberalism, which, after only two decades of rule, began to draw to a close in the 1880s.[2] The patriotic enthusiasm of the Jews during this era reflected the widespread confidence in the extension and guarantee of rights to those outside the spheres of political and economic influence, traditionally controlled by the aristocracy and by Catholic clericalism. Denied the complete integration into society promised in their legal emancipation at the end of the previous century, Jews commonly supported and promoted the ideals of the constitutional era with uncommon zeal.

What exactly appeared comic to Schnitzler about Jews of the earlier generation? In *Professor Bernhardi,* a play written four years after *The Road to the Open,* he dramatized the heroic pursuit of justice and reason, with the same conviction he himself had expressed in the 1860s and 1870s, during the period

1

of his youth. "The so-called liberalism did not leave me unscathed," he noted at the time.[3] Jews like him shared the wish fulfilled in one of Freud's dreams, to return to this period of political liberalism.[4] It was not the ideals of their fathers' generation that seemed distant to Jews at the turn of the century, but the way their fathers embraced these ideals — "with real enthusiasm for the dynasty," as Schnitzler remarked, or with undaunted devotion to the basic principles of the Enlightenment, the ideological genesis of political liberalism. It was the eagerness of their optimism — and not only eagerness, but their patriotic and ethical zeal — that appeared comic to Jews who lived through the aftermath, the demise of political liberalism.

The contrast between the two ages was indeed significant. By the beginning of World War I, many Jews no longer relied on the state or on the self-evident truths of the Enlightenment, but took it upon themselves as Jews to realize these ideals. Yet, for all the differences, the age of political liberalism had an important influence on them. This period, the period of their youth, formed the values and aspirations of their mature lives. Even when such values were no longer catchwords, they were reluctant to surrender the desire for social integration. The contrast between this period and the next influenced their social and intellectual development as well. Reacting to the errors of their fathers and to their own disappointments, they became particularly sensitive to the method of preserving the ideals, that is, to the crucial importance of self-reliance or, more precisely, of Jewish self-assertion. However brief and comic the enthusiasms of the constitutional era may have been, the impact they had on Jews was immense.

THE SITUATION IN VIENNA

The basic democratic principles of the Enlightenment were never a real political option in the empire until the February Patent was decreed in 1861. Even the political momentum of the March days in the revolutionary year 1848 lasted only a short time. With the imperial patent of 1851, the Emperor Franz Josef rescinded all rights granted in 1849. Conditions which marked the political situation for most of the century were once again imposed. Moreover, the Concordat of 1855 recognized, as before, the alliance between the empire and the papal seat, thus reviving Catholic supremacy over cultural and political affairs. For the Jews of Vienna — at the time numbering 6,000, or barely 1 percent of the city's population, the reaction frustrated the feeling of anticipation created by the initial successes of the revolution. Officials subjected Jews and others outside the sphere of control to the scrutiny of the military police, as well as to economic and social restraints, making freedom of movement, possession of property, and choice of occupation more difficult. Freedom existed only in the realm of finance and in skillful journalistic efforts to evade the censor.[5]

The government established in 1861 under Anton von Schmerling (1804-93) was far from realizing the human liberties and constitutional rights of the enlightened liberal tradition, but it signaled new hope for the disenfranchised. Even more significant, perhaps, were the plans for the reconstruction of the imperial capital. With the declining influence of the absolutist regime — dramatized by the loss of territory to the Italian kingdom of Sardinia in the battle of Solferino in July 1859 — the medieval ramparts surrounding the old city were razed to allow for an impressive Ringstrasse with monumental structures for government and culture, thus hailing the coming reign of law and the arts. The visual change enhanced the confidence and sense of progress of the Viennese middle class. For Viennese Jewry, it was, moreover, a restatement of their legal emancipation from the medieval walls of the ghetto. This relationship between political liberalism and Jewish emancipation, rooted in their parallel development from the end of the eighteenth century on, was the basis of the interconnection between Jewish self-interest and social reform.[6]

As a consequence of this interconnection, the language most often used by Jews was that of the Enlightenment. For example, when reactionary forces threatened nascent constitutionalism, Jews commonly appealed to reason. Their enthusiastic support of the widely publicized Kuranda-Brunner case illustrates this well. Ignaz Kuranda (1812-84) was a leading exponent of liberalism in Germany and Austria. His newspaper, *Grenzboten,* published in Leipzig, became the intellectual center of liberalism in the Germany and Austria of the 1840s. Later, in Vienna, he edited the *Ostdeutsche Post.* At the beginning of the liberal era, Kuranda attacked another newspaper editor, Sebastian Brunner of the clerical *Weiner Kirchenzeitung,* for his ruthless defamation of the Jewish character. Brunner had charged that the Jewish religion encouraged the murder of Christians and the use of the victims' blood for ritual purposes. Though such invective had neither the authority nor the success of later anti-Semitic developments, his campaign disgraced the proponents of freedom and toleration. In May 1860, the two tried their respective viewpoints before the courts. "Just as we were the first to carry the banner of civilization as a people or nation or tribe," Kuranda declared, "so we are the last to knock at the portals of humanity asking for admittance and equality of rights. This is the due meaning of the present case. Dr. Brunner is the representative of a lost cause . . . in [his] fight against the general feeling for justice which is struggling for utterance." Kuranda shrewdly appealed to the growing popular and official hostility toward the reaction. The courts supported his position; Brunner, facing defeat, was forced to resign from his newspaper. Kuranda was elected, in the following year, to the Diet of Lower Austria and, in 1868, to the Reichsrat of the imperial government. Throughout the period of liberal rule, Kuranda played a leading role in liberal politics.[7]

He also held important positions in the Jewish community; shortly after the case, he was elected an administrative officer, and he served as its president from 1871 until his death in 1884.[8] This parallel recognition from politically liberal and Jewish circles shows their close ideological relationship. Religious leaders described Judaism as a legitimate voice of liberal ideals as well. One of the most articulate of these spokesmen was Adolf Jellinek (1821-93), chief rabbi of Vienna from 1865 until his death. In 1870, he said, with typical confidence, that Judaism "hallows and sanctifies the ideals of modern society, bringing to sick and confused humanity healing and recovery, peace and reconciliation."[9] Jellinek instructed observant Jews to recognize how the customs and laws furthered "the moral refinement of man." His biographer, Moriz Rosenmann, noted the rabbi's unyielding attempt at attributing universal meaning to the particular laws of Jewish religion.[10]

Jellinek's frequent contributions to *Die Neue Zeit,* a liberal newspaper that began publishing in 1861, indicate the strength of his belief in political liberalism. Events toward the end of the decade stimulated the sense of anticipation among Jews, to an unprecedented degree. In 1867, a new administration replaced the old liberals after the Prussian army had crushed Austrian forces in the struggle for hegemony over German Europe. In order to assure fidelity to the reduced and demoralized dynasty, the *Bürgerministerium* extended the rights and the franchise decreed in the February Patent. These legal acts and the new constitution, the *Staatsgrundgesetz* (December 21, 1867), were the most liberal steps ever taken in the history of the empire. The constitution provided for complete equality and justice before the law, freedom of faith and choice of occupation, and right of ownership and residence. The government immediately challenged the Concordat and attempted to free schools from ecclesiastical control. By 1871, when an abrasive church-state *Kulturkampf* threatened the unity of the nascent German Empire, the Austrian government broke the hold of the church over its people.[11] The strategy behind the enactment of this constitution worked for Jews. For all but the most orthodox Jews — in Vienna there were few — support for the state was unrestrained. In his study of liberalism in the Habsburg Monarchy, Georg Franz concluded that no social group supported the liberal government as vigorously, and attacked the forces of the reaction as bitterly, as the Jews.[12] Prominent Jewish businessmen were happy they could say what their ancestors could not, that they were free citizens in a free state.[13] Jellinek asserted, in the spirit of the day, "In line with the most vital interests, the Jews of Austria must adhere to the constitution and to the forces of liberalism."[14] Schnitzler recalled the confident outlook of his adolescent liberal views: These "idealized values were taken for granted from the start as fixed and uncontestable. In those days we thought we knew what was true, good, and beautiful; and all life lay ahead of us in grandiose simplicity."[15]

The state's promotion of political liberalism, as well as the fashionable appeal of Enlightenment ideals, in this constitutional era encouraged Jews to look forward to the day of their social acceptance and established political liberalism as the medium of their emancipation. Devotion to the state replaced devotion to Jewish existence, marking this a period of extreme Jewish assimilation. It was a period when Jews and non-Jews merged in their common support of liberal ideals. Only with the collapse of political liberalism and the cessation of this bilateral process, were Jews who continued to assimilate disgraced. But in the 1860s, and especially after 1867, assimilation was a function of the political aspirations of Jews and non-Jews alike. The process encouraged the consolidation of the empire, after its defeats to Sardinia and Prussia, and elevated the disenfranchised to politically equal status.

By supporting the liberal state and the ideals it fostered, Jews were favoring specifically the tradition of the Enlightenment, which aimed at leveling, rather than preserving, social differences. They joined in the efforts at achieving a secular and rational order, not a pluralistic one, and therefore neglected their vestigial Jewish loyalties, or subordinated them (made them private or instrumental) to the neutral, universal ideals of common human rights and common human freedom. To advance the cause for true social assimilation, Jellinek interpreted Jewish law so as to unite the faithful with non-Jewish society. For him, the fundamental nature of Judaism complemented the values and ideals of liberalism. Instead of being a religion of "petty externalities, unessential minutiae, [and] antiquated customs," he felt Judaism was a religion of "the spirit, of the heart, of the loving deed, of holiness, justice, freedom, charity and truth." He prefered the title "preacher" to "Rabbi," since he believed he served common religious interests, not just the isolated interests of Judaism.[16]

More specifically, adherence to political liberalism signified a strong allegiance to German culture and to the ruling minority of the Austrian-German bourgeoisie. The convergence of Jewish assimilation and political liberalism with the Austrian-German middle class was rooted in the imperial policies of Joseph II at the end of the eighteenth century. Like his *Toleranz-Edikt* (1782), which legally emancipated Jews in the empire, the effort at Germanizing political and cultural affairs reflected his intention of centralizing the imperial administration. The egalitarian effect of his policies, which included subordination of the church and the aristocracy to the state, appealed both to Jews and to Austrian Germans, thus forging their close political alliance. The government of Anton von Schmerling, Josephian in its centralized bureaucratic structure and liberal policies, revived German authority as well as the related German-Jewish alliance. Enfranchisement and other liberal decrees went hand in hand with the promotion of German interests in the empire.

The political phenomenon of German liberalism involved a fundamental contradiction between the neutral values of the Enlightenment and the self-serving interests of the ruling class. In his memoirs, Ernst von Plener (1841-1923), a leading liberal statesman, observed: The "fundamental ideal [of the February Patent] was, to be honest, the attempt to secure the historic and political position of the German nation, which, as is well known, does not constitute the majority of the population of Austria, but which through historic labor, education, prosperity and the burden of taxation towered above all others.[17] German liberals had a disproportionately large number of seats in the Reichstag. Even after 1867, they were the largest parliamentary faction.[18]

Because most Jews understood German liberalism as an instrument of social reform, they failed to perceive this contradiction of the liberal tradition. They revered the political and cultural position of the Germans as much as the liberal ideals of the Enlightenment. As Jacob Katz noted, Jewish assimilation was an ideology coupled with imminent social change,[19] and German liberalism traditionally, and at the beginning of the 1860s, was in the vanguard of a progressive political movement.

In government, the press, and the arts, Jews embraced German culture and German political ideals. Theodor Herzl (1860-1904), who came to Vienna from Budapest at the end of the liberal era, commented on the German culture of assimilated Jewry, and on the way Jews "attached themselves with all their heart to the German nation."[20] One publicist and politician, Heinrich Jacques, expressed this passion in a pamphlet published in the twilight of the reaction. Entitled *Denkschrift über die Stellung der Juden in Österreich* (*Memorial on the Status of the Jews in Austria,* 1859), it denounced the restrictions placed on Jews as intolerable and anachronistic in a time of change and national fermentation. For the sake of the fatherland, he implored, Austria ought to lead Jews "toward patriotic activity in the development of property, agriculture, mining and manufacture." He felt this required only the legal recognition of the Jews as citizens of the state, for, in spite of the treatment of the Jews by Austrian officials, their loyalty to the state remained as firm as it was during the time of nationalist awakening at the end of the previous decade. He believed that Jews had been so faithful to the cause of "German freedom" that they were willing to die for it even if they failed to achieve their emancipation. Jacques's claim of selfless patriotism was, of course, an overstatement, since he was, after all, pleading for the legal recognition of Jews. However, by overstating the case, he indicated the extent of Jewish fidelity to the German cause.[21]

Jellinek was even more direct than Jacques in expressing the patriotism of Jews. In 1877, he declared, "With regard to their background, [Jews] are inclined to the German nationality, they sympathize with a grandly conceived Austria based on a strong centralized government."[22] What is interesting about this remark, beyond its corroboration of strong Jewish support of German liberalism, is the moment when Jellinek made it. He defended German authority as the last stronghold of the liberal tradition in Austria, despite its increasing negligence in discharging its public responsibilities, and its imminent defeat during the national electoral campaign of 1879. Toward the end of this decade, the conflict between the German desire for power and its liberal image became more and more visible. The liberal government neglected other national groups in the empire, especially the Czechs, with their unique cultural and national traditions, the Slavs to the south, and Italian irredentists. Moreover, the government ignored the interests of the lower middle class, labor, and agriculture. Scandals, political corruption, and the crash of 1873 exposed the narrow economic and political interests of the upper German bourgeoisie and its ideological hypocrisy.

So firm was the loyalty of Jews that they continued to identify with German liberalism through this period of its undemocratic rule and the following years of its political isolation. We "cannot forget that it was the central parliament . . . that voted for the Bill of Rights [in 1867]," Jellinek exhorted in 1883.[23] Like so many others, he preferred recalling the government of the constitutional period to supporting the subsequent administration of Count Taaffe, for the Iron Ring of Taaffe's ministry was made up of the traditional enemies of Austrian Jewry — clericals, the aristocracy, and conservative Slavs, Poles, and Czechs. With suffrage extension beyond the German middle class, from 1882 on, and with the subsequent growth of popular parties, the liberal platform remained viable only in Vienna, though even there, its influence declined rapidly after the mid-1890s.[24] Viennese Jews could still look to the local German left, but just as attractive to them as political representation were the noble ideals of liberalism. Not only did Jellinek look back to the constitutional government, but he sympathized with the "grandly conceived" Austrian *Rechtsstaat.*

Because Jews adhered so rigorously to the liberal tradition, their German-Jewish identity and assimilationist aspirations survived the decline of political liberalism and of German middle-class supremacy. Almost all Viennese newspapers representing the interests of Jews continued to support the monarchy and the Enlightenment ideals in the 1880s and 1890s, as they did during the constitutional era.[25] One journalist, Daniel Spitzer (1835-93), whose feuilletons, or literary essays, appealed to the large Jewish reading audience of Vienna's major liberal newspaper, the *Neue Freie Presse,* constantly used the unifying principles of liberal ideology as his critical perspective of national and social conflicts within the empire. His reliance on the catchwords and the satirical, punitive tone of his articles made him, in the eyes of many, the *Gewissen Wiens,* the conscience of Vienna.[26] Schnitzler recalled how "rationalistic" he himself was at the time. Like Spitzer, he denounced national conflicts, believing that "original hatred between nations was non-existent," and objected to his military obligation (1882-83), insisting upon the "illiberality" of compulsory duty.[27] During the early 1880s, he and Herzl belonged to the liberal and German national student society, the *Akademische Lesehalle.*[28]

Though German-liberal tenacity helped to stabilize Jewish existence in the decades before World War I, it also had the opposite effect. During the 1860s and 1870s, when the constitutional government embodied and made visible the promise of liberal ideals, Jews like Jacques could proclaim the cause of German freedom in harmony with political and social reality. Jews commonly regarded Schiller and Goethe not only as "the flower of the true German spirit," but as a practical source of inspiration for the current day.[29] But continued attachment to a position of declining or isolated influence after 1880 — a position that, even in Vienna, became increasingly vulnerable to popular disfavor — made their assimilation more tenuous. Many Jews not only lost touch with rising political forces, but suffered humiliation as outsiders. As a consequence,

Jews found it awkward or difficult to achieve social acceptance. Frequently, they avoided situations that tended to distinguish them as Jews, feeling embarrassment or shame when such situations arose. Intermarriage, name changing, and conversion were commonplace. They would also alter their appearance to hide superficial differences. Recalling his visit to Vienna in the late 1890s, the noted German author Jacob Wassermann (1873-1933) remarked, "The German Jews among whom I lived had accustomed me to more polished manners, a less conspicuous demeanor." Herzl confirmed the observation: "The Jews, who have so long been condemned to a state of civic dishonor, have, as a result, developed an almost pathological hunger for honor."[30]

Nothing threatened the process of assimilation, or isolated assimilated Jewry, as much as the anti-Semitic movement in Austria. As it developed, it exacerbated existing national and social tensions. Even worse, it attacked Jews directly. Jews throughout Western and Central Europe reacted with dismay to the emergence of illiberal and anti-Semitic forces in their countries. But nowhere did assimilation seem more elusive than in Austria. Even in Paris, during the turbulent 1890s, when the trial of the Jew Alfred Dreyfus unleashed an anti-Semitic response that severely divided the city, most native Jews minimized the significance of the affair and retained faith in the longevity of liberal ideals. Hoping the disturbance would fade away, they preferred to remain silent and as inconspicuous as possible.[31] Jews in the Wilhelmine Empire, disturbed by anti-Semitic developments there, affirmed their attachment to German culture all the more, rather than moderating the assimilation. Some, like the philosopher Ernst Cassirer, optimistically believed anti-Semitism was something Germans were likely to outgrow, while others stressed their hyphenated identities as German-Jews, or their prefaced identities as *Nurdeutsche* or *Kulturdeutsche* as opposed to Teutonic or anti-Semitic Germans. As Gershom Scholem recently observed, the assimilation of German Jews was so intense that Jews often believed that they adhered to German culture more faithfully than did the Germans themselves.[32]

This kind of response to anti-Semitism was not without parallel in Austria. Jews regarded Brunner's campaign as eccentric. Even the sustained attack against the "godlessness and greed" of German Jews that Karl Freiherr von Vogelsang (1818-90) waged in the mid-1870s, in the pages of the Catholic conservative newspaper *Vaterland,* left most Jews undisturbed. Since anti-Semitism during the constitutional era appeared only in clerical and conservative circles as an instrument of retaliation against prevailing anti-clerical and liberal forces, Jews dismissed such hostility as tasteless atavism.[33] For two decades, and especially during the 1870s, Austrian Jews, like French and German Jews, enjoyed the guardianship of political liberalism and a national political consensus.

After 1880, the situation of Austrian Jews began to diverge from the situation of their counterparts in France and Germany. The strong French revolutionary ideal encouraged French Jews to ignore native social conflict and, therefore, to assume that anti-Semitism was a foreign imposition, an unfortunate interruption of French life. The liberal tradition in Austria was, by comparison, new and untried. By 1890, Austrian Jews no longer felt confident that liberalism could withstand the anti-Semitic threat. The German political effort to consolidate the nascent empire led many Jews there to regard anti-Semitism as a harmless, or at most an annoying, distraction. German Jews believed that the authorities would not tolerate, for long, this retrogressive movement.[34] The political consolidation in Germany contrasted sharply with the fragmentation in the multinational Hapsburg realm. By the 1890s, social cleavage was deep, marked by the Czech movement for Bohemian autonomy, Catholic loyalty to Rome, pan-Slavism, irredentism in Italian Austria, and German nationalism. Such conditions not only failed to inhibit the spread of anti-Semitism, but allowed anti-Semitism to become a characteristic or normal part of Austrian social and political life. Because of the weak liberal tradition and the intensive, internecine struggle for sovereignty or hegemony, Austrian Jews lacked the cultural and political alternatives that legitimated or enhanced the Jewish desire to assimilate in France or Germany. To the Jews of Austria, anti-Semitism became an insurmountable obstacle.

Paradoxically, the growth of the divisive phenomenon of Austrian anti-Semitism was in part the result of the liberal government's declaration of democratic reforms. Constitutional statutes renewing the 1848 grants of residential, property, and trade rights encouraged thousands of Jews in the eastern part of the empire — Galicia and Hungary — to leave the oppressive conditions of impoverishment and local political intolerance for the economically advanced imperial capital. The influx of *Ostjuden* into Vienna, and specifically into the city's second district, the Leopoldstadt (where Freud and Rank lived for many years), was never as great as it was in the 1860s. The height of the migration occurred in the years immediately after the 1867 constitutional ratification. By the end of the decade, 17,541 Jews had come from the East, raising the Jewish population from 6,217 in 1859 to 40,227, a jump from 1.3 to 6.1 percent of the total population.[35]

Certain distinctive cultural characteristics augmented this specter of immigrant Jewry — a meager style of dress, an indigenous manner of speech, and a display of provincial and religious customs. This massive and alien presence incited existing, but, to this point, largely latent, prejudices against Jews. As economic conditions grew worse in the 1870s, and especially after the 1873 crash, this highly exposed immigrant Jewish population appeared as competitors, and were vilified as "intruders" by the discontented *Mittelstand* and university students. "Who are the peddlers?" cried one craftsman at an 1880 meeting of artisans protesting Jewish competition. "They are mainly Polish, Hungarian, and fugitive Russian Jews." Two years later, the artisan movement crystallized into an organized campaign against Jews, with the formation of the *Österreichische Reformverein* (Austrian Reform Association).[36]

As national and social polarization deepened within the empire, anti-Jewish intolerance intensified. At the end of the 1870s, the focus of the hostilities increased to include Jews from the West as well as from the East. This shift from cultural to racial anti-Semitism initially came from within the German nationalist movement. Organized in the late 1860s by the young and radical segment of the German-Austrian middle class, the movement, at first, criticized the narrow economic and political base of the Austrian liberal ruling class, supported the progressive German Empire, and affirmed the rich, national, and organic tradition of German culture. Many Jews, including Freud, belonged to the active student movement, the *Leseverein der deutschen Studenten Wiens* (Reading Society of the German Students of Vienna).[37] By the end of the 1870s, this attack on class interests became an attack on any special interests that detracted from the objective German nationality as well as from annexation with the German Empire. With Taaffe's formation of an administration inhospitable to the German minority, many Austrian Germans responded defensively with an extreme form of *völkisch,* pan-German nationalism. Followers of German nationalism, and especially the students among them, launched a campaign not only against Jews, but against Slavs, the church, and the political structure of the dynastic state. "Ohne Juda, Habsburg, Rome/Bauen wir den deutschen Dom"* was the haunting cry of its demagogic leader, Georg von Schönerer (1842-1921).

Dissatisfied with the liberal cause, which he promoted as a member of the Reichsrat after 1873, Schönerer helped to organize the *Deutscher Klub* within liberal circles, established brief contact with the Reformverein in the early 1880s, and, finally, formed an extraparliamentary German-nationalist following, the genesis of popular party politics in Austria. In 1885, he added to the *Linzer Programm* (1882), the nationalist manifesto, a twelfth point that established racial anti-Semitism as a persuasive ideological force. It demanded, as a measure of achieving economic and social reforms, "the removal of Jewish influence from all sections of public life."[38]

A strong influence on Schönerer and his student followers was the publication of a work by the Berlin Professor Eugen Karl Dühring (1833-1921). In *Die Judenfrage als Rassen- Sitten- und Kulturfrage (The Jewish Question as a Racial, Moral, and Cultural Question,* 1881), Dühring argued that it was a matter of "racial honor" to eliminate that "incomparably inferior race" from public office, business, and finance. At the same time, another German professor helped ignite contempt for Jews among the lower clergy and the lower middle class. Like Brunner and Vogelsang, August Rohling (1839-1931) claimed that the Talmud instructed Jews to commit ritual murder. The argument, which appeared in his book *Der Talmudjude (The Talmud Jew,* 1871), not only appealed to the discontented among the *Mittelstand,* but received judicial sanction in 1881. One member of the Reformverein, Franz Holubek, demanding the repeal of Jewish emancipation laws, successfully defended himself against the charge of libel, on the basis of Rohling's accusations.[39]

---

*Without anything Jewish, Habsburg, Rome
We are building the true German home*

By the end of the 1880s, members of the Reformverein and Catholic reformers united into a coalition of Christian Socialists. Vogelsang and Karl Lueger (1844-1910), who, like Schönerer, defected from the liberal cause, became dynamic leaders and effectively exploited popular suspicion of Jews in public life. The coalition's 1889 manifesto called for the elimination of Jews from civil services, the medical and legal professions, and many small businesses. The Christian Social Party, led by Lueger, entered Viennese politics in 1893, challenging the last bastion of political liberalism in the empire. On April 8, 1897, after two years of impressive gains in the city council, the Emperor Franz Josef reluctantly confirmed Lueger as mayor of Vienna. For the following 13 years, clerical, popular, and anti-Semitic party politics — the very antithesis of liberalism — ruled the city.[40]

If the anti-Semitic movement commanded considerable political and popular support, how deeply did it penetrate into the daily lives of the people? One contemporary observer noted that the movement in the decades before and after the turn of the century had some of the traits of Vienna's *Gemütlichkeit:* Jews were attacked only as a group, and usually in the manner of verbal abuse. The threat of violence to the individual did not exist.[41] Contempt for Jews took the form of derision or criticism in the theater, newspapers, and the political arena. At one parliamentary session in the late 1880s, there was a motion to discuss a matter concerning Jews, before discussion of the more general questions. The president of the Reichsrat rejected the motion, with the comment, "business before pleasure."[42] Even Lueger limited his anti-Semitism to the spoken word. For him, it was a device to attract the attention and support of the restless lower middle class. His denunciation of the Jewish capitalist rarely entered into the exercise of municipal reform. Indeed, he consulted Jewish businessmen to help effect his programs.[43] If abuse exceeded insult, it took the form of discrimination. There were efforts, many unsuccessful, to boycott businesses operated by Jews and to prevent Jews from entering the highest echelons of the civil service. Pressure on Jewish professors was intense. Seldom were Jews appointed to full professorships (in 1894, two of the 53 Jews teaching at the University of Vienna reached the highest rank).[44] Classes taught by Jewish professors were boycotted at the university. Efforts were made to limit the Jewish enrollment in gymnasia as well.

As the Viennese Jew and prolific novelist Stefan Zweig (1881-1942) observed late in his life, a judgment of the impact of this anti-Semitic movement on Viennese Jews is difficult for anyone familiar with the atrocities of national socialism. He warned that an acquaintance with the measures taken by the Nazis against Jews distorted, indeed made incomprehensible, the Vienna in which he grew up.[45] However, his attempt to defuse the emotional horror associated with the anti-Semitism, to put the nineteenth-century movement into proper perspective, resulted in a misrepresentation of the opposite sort. His description of the secure city environment reflected the desire to distinguish and separate, to contrast as much as possible, the forms anti-Semitism took in these two periods. "Not yet has every herd and mass feeling become so disgustingly power-ful in public life as today."[46]

For Viennese Jews of the nineteenth century, life was anything but secure. If only because the outbreak of anti-Semitism contrasted so sharply with the climate of unity during the decades of political liberalism, Jews were sensitive to the expressions of hostility, however mild in comparison with later develop-ments. Anti-Semitism made life uncomfortable for Jews. By the turn of the century, it completely demoralized them. Even in the 1870s, when the artisan movement augmented the anti-Semitism of the Catholic right, but still limited its attack to immigrant Jewry, assimilated Jews began to temper their antic-ipation of the new order of social integration. Jews already living in Vienna, or who had come from western parts of the empire (Bohemia or Moravia), began to feel the uncomfortable pressures of association, especially if they were living in or near the refuge quarters of the Leopoldstadt. From this point on, Jews resented the unassimilated *Ostjuden*. They were the loudest to approve of the cabaret artists who ridiculed this type, and the most embarrassed by the immi-grant's unfamiliar mien. "I will not deny that I am particularly sensitive to the faults of Jews," Schnitzler wrote in *The Road to the Open*, expressing the thought of many Jews. "If a Jew shows bad form in my presence, or behaves in a ridiculous manner, I have often felt so painful a sensation that I should like to sink into the earth."[47] With the emergence of racial anti-Semitism in the early 1880s, many assimilated Jews like Heinrich Friedjung (1851-1920) blamed immigrant Jews for their plight. A historian faithful to German liberalism, and from 1864 editor of the *Deutsche Wochenschrift*, Friedjung called for the assimilation of this "tenacious and alien part of the population."[48] Herzl, when still a student at the University of Vienna, condemned the "dull com-pulsion of the ghetto" and insisted that these foreign Jews intermarry and observe a common state religion.[49]

The seemingly inexhaustible immigration of Jews from the East after 1870 — by 1900, there were 146,926 Jews in Vienna, 8.7 percent of the city's popu-lation — and the correspondingly intensifying racial hostility forced western Jews to abandon such assimilationist proposals and to concentrate on distin-guishing themselves from East-European Jews. Disturbed by Dühring's anti-Semitic diatribe and by its popularity in the German nationalist movement at the university, Herzl stressed, in his diary (1882), the German author's failure to recognize the important difference between the *Ostjuden,* who, he felt, indeed lacked character, and assimilated Jewry, the "good" in Jewry. "But how could a race so devoid of gift and character [as Dühring insisted] have resisted for a millennium and a half the inhuman pressures of the surrounding world? How could it do this without possessing something good?" Dühring's indiscriminate slander, he added, was not dangerous, but was "ridiculous."[50] Many other Jews, like Spitzer, reacting to German anti-Semitic literature in Austria during the early 1880s, and specifically to Heinrich von Treitschke's denunciation of the "deluge" of "ambitious 'trouser-selling'[*hosenverkaufender*] youngsters" from the East, knew how right the Berlin professor was when he insisted that German Jews "feel German simply and rightly."[51]

Adherence to German liberalism provided assimilated Jewry not only a political and ideological position in Austrian society, but a way of averting the fate of East-European Jewry. Yet, rather than furthering the chances for assimilation, the German-Jewish insistence on German identity made assimilation even more difficult. In response to the initial stages of anti-Semitism, Jews reacted defensively. They defended a once-promising, but now-vulnerable, position, and they did so obstinately. In other words, by reaffirming their German-liberal loyalties, Jews insistently denied this mounting threat to assimilation. This rejection of anti-Semitic developments accelerated their isolation as anti-Semitism became an integral part of Austrian life.

At least until the late 1880s, Jews consistently refused to recognize the escalation of racism in political and social life. The anti-Semitic movement "will disappear," Herzl concluded in the diary passage on Dühring. "A new age will follow in which passionless and clear-headed humanity will look back upon our errors as the enlightened men of our time looked back upon the middle ages."[52] Contrary to the developments in German nationalism, many Jews believed that anti-Semitism was extraneous to the political movement's objectives. Two proponents of the movement in the early 1880s, Friedjung and Victor Adler (1852-1916), the founder of the Social Democratic Party in 1889, regarded Schönerer's early anti-Semitic sentiments as unfortunate and ideologically distractive.[53] In the widely disseminated publication *Berlin, Wien und der Anti-Semitismus* (1882), Isidor Singer (1859-1939) condemned Schönerer as well as Holubek for importing the *"Giftkraut"* of German anti-Semitism, and insisted that, in spite of its spread in Austria, the movement remained foreign to Austrian life.[54] Spitzer's treatment of anti-Semitism was a masterful stroke of deception as he applied preferred, but remote, perspectives to social commentary. For him, anti-Semitism was peripheral to social and political affairs. It was nothing more than a tactic which, once unmasked, would disappear. He criticized Schönerer's anti-Jewish agitation in parliament for obscuring the real problems of hospital, school, and street construction. Why haven't anti-Semites used the cholera epidemic in Salzburg for their political purposes? he mocked in 1886. His most effective weapon was the exposure of hypocrisy, the use, for example, of the same lack of restraint shown by the anti-Semitic press in its attack against "the unbridled press of the unconverted."[55]

The tendency to reject the severity of anti-Jewish hostility in politics and society, and to adhere to an image of the world gleaned from the good old days, contributed to the formation of what Claudio Magris called the "Habsburg myth." Magris detected in the literature and press of the bourgeoisie, and of the Jews among them, the determination to sustain the vitality of an era gone by, a longing, he claimed, that was tantamount to a flight from reality.[56] The appeal to bygone principles, and the insistence that anti-Semitism was not real, characterized the writings and sermons of Adolf Jellinek. Only during the last few years before his death in 1893 did he acknowledge the tenuousness of Jewish assimilation. Until then, he scolded the perpetrators of anti-Semitism for their inexcusable offenses against morality, humanity, and truth. Like Spitzer, Jellinek confirmed in deed the remoteness of his ideological perspective by confining his moral appeal to select and sympathetic audiences. Though Jellinek reacted in 1882 to Rohling's anti-Semitic calumny, he simply declared the "absolute untruth" of his allegations, refused to become involved in Rohling's ensuing attacks, and returned to the pulpit and to the pages of *Die Neue Zeit* to preach his position.[57]

In reference to this period, Schnitzler wrote in *The Road to the Open* that Jews suffered from "a mania for being hidden, a mania for being left alone, a mania for being safe."[58] This observation referred not only to the flight from reality, but to the anxiety this escape produced. The restlessness and, finally, the despair in the fugitive life of assimilated Jewry became especially apparent in the writings of those Viennese Jews who, in the 1890s, dominated the literary circle, *Jung-Wien*. Schnitzler and another Jew, Richard Beer-Hofmann (1866-1945), were among the circle's original four. Zweig and, by literary association, Herzl joined them at their meeting place, the Café Griensteidl, shortly after 1891 when the group first convened.[59] For the first time in decades, Jews acknowledged their social isolation. They could neither continue the self-deception nor share the memories or hopes of most other Jews who believed that the ideals of the Enlightenment were somehow still realizable. Rather, they renounced their assimilationist aspirations and examined the only free realm left to them, the inner life of the psyche. As Zweig recalled in his autobiography (1942), "We hungered for something that belonged to us alone, not to the world of our fathers [or] to the world around us."[60]

The themes of their literary, theatrical, and journalistic pieces were entirely apolitical and self-indulgent. Schnitzler portrayed his characters, especially the *süsses Mädel*, as frivolous and carefree in the quest for pleasure and happiness. Most typical of this genre was the sequence of ten erotic scenes, *Reigen* (1897-1900), which described life as a bacchanalian human chain binding all to the eternal instinctual element. The same aimless tone depicting middle-class idleness is found in Herzl's stories, sketches, and feuilletons written in the late 1880s, and in Beer-Hofmann's early literary attempts, especially in his first published works, *Das Kind* and *Camelias* (1893).[61]

As Schnitzler wrote in *The Road to the Open,* escape from reality failed to bring peace to assimilated Jews. As before, rejection of reality made life precarious. Only this time, because Jews in Jung-Wien dismissed not just the periphery of reality, but reality itself, life seemed even more disturbing, indeed maniacal. Carl Schorske noted that for the literati of the Jung-Wien circle, eros and mystery represented cosmic forces beyond human control. Their fascination with these forces reflected the experience of their isolation and the sensitivity to their insignificance. Disenchanted with German liberalism and deserted by German nationalism, Schnitzler "showed, like Freud, the inevitable cruelty to the self and to others which instinctual gratification involves." The destructive fatalism in *Reigen,* with its dizzying sexual merry-go-round, is found elsewhere in *The Road to the Open,* where social and political forces determine the life, inevitably frustrating, of the mostly Jewish dramatis personae. Beer-Hofmann's short stories portrayed the epicurean as lonely, drifting insecurely from one futile love affair to another. The aristocratic heroes in Herzl's writings expressed their isolation; the dreamers, their disillusionment and resignation before reality.[62]

By the time the circle formally broke up in 1897, any serious regard for assimilation appeared only as nostalgia or as wish fulfillment. Anti-Semitism did not disappear from Austrian life as Jews had hoped. It proved to be neither an extraneous nor a foreign phenomenon. Instead, it replaced liberalism as the legitimate will of the Viennese. Even the mildest Jewish estimation of Lueger conveyed the gravity and tension of this era. Zweig could not understand the reaction of Jews to Lueger's election as mayor. In contrast to the situation in Nazi Germany, Jews in Vienna "continued to live with the same rights and esteem as always." Yet, as remarkable as their reaction appeared to him, it remained vivid in his memory: they "trembled at the triumph of the anti-Semitic party."[63] Indeed, recognizing Lueger's inevitable victory, the *Neue Freie Presse* reported that liberals wore "a false nose [only] to conceal an anxious face. . . . Instead of the gay waltz, one hears only the cries of an excited bawling mob, and the shouts of police trying to disperse antagonists."[64]

During the final two decades of the empire, Jews lamented the vanishing prospects of social integration. Those who felt helpless in the shadow of ambient powers and could no longer wear a "false nose" expressed the distressing feeling of alienation. The bitter plaint of one Viennese businessman, who once invested so much hope in the peaceful coexistence of the empire's national aggregation, was typical. In 1916, he wrote how difficult it was to observe "the change in the social relations between Jews and Christians; I cannot even think of it without deep regret." Though he mourned the deepening abyss in politics and government, he was especially affected by everyday gestures and utterances. "The way people expressed themselves toward Jews had plainly changed. Even if there was absolutely no occasion for it, they would stare in an unfriendly way — everywhere, wherever they turned up. [Gentle] conversation . . . ceased all at once. There was an invisible distance between the tables where Christians sat and those where Jews sat. The genuine human need for social contact . . . was frustrated exactly by this revival of an atavistic, bestial feeling of race." For him, and for the many Jews he knew, this psychological repulsion was more irritating and painful than the physical ghettoization of Jews a century before, precisely because of the intervening period of hopeful assimilation.[65]

Schnitzler, too, resented the "unfortunate chasm" between Jew and non-Jew.[66] "Do you think there's a single Christian in the world, even taking the noblest, straightest and truest one you like, one single Christian who has not in some moment or other of spite, temper or rage, made, at any rate mentally, some contemptuous allusion to the Jewishness of even his best friend, his mistress or his wife, if they were Jews or of Jewish descent?"[67] This passage from *The Road to the Open* became the main theme in *Professor Bernhardi,* published five years later in 1912. The play examined conflict in contemporary Viennese society. On one level, there was ideological tension. Bernhardi had decided to prevent a priest from administering the last sacrament to his patient, to spare her from the realization that she was dying. The confrontation of medicine and the church deteriorated into furious social conflict. One character observed, "Only bad feeling could attempt to make anything like a *cause célèbre* out of a perfectly innocent incident, and, to speak quite plainly, . . . no one would have made the attempt, if Bernhardi had not happened to be a Jew."[68] Wishing only to practice medicine, Bernhardi suffered professional and political ostracism.

Whether Jews acknowledged the demise of the liberal tradition in Austria, or not, and whether they escaped political and social antagonism by looking within, to the past, or to the future, Jews shared with Zweig "the natural feeling of distance."[69] The former confidence in the *Rechtsstaat* had disappeared. For assimilated Jewry, who had relied on the promising liberal tradition or on the benevolence of government, the ideals now seemed inaccessible. "How dazed must be their consciousness of their existence," noted one character in *The Road to the Open.* They are caught in the dilemma "between the fear of appearing importunate and their bitter resentment at the demand that they must yield to an insolent majority, between the inner consciousness of being at home in the country where they lived and worked, and their indignation at finding themselves persecuted and insulted in that very place."[70]

SELF-DETERMINATION

At least in fin de siècle Vienna, assimilated Jews never recovered from the pain of social alienation. The reversals in the attitude toward Jews after 1880 made Jews who lived through this experience even more bitter. Yet, though disillusioned by anti-Semitic and antiliberal developments, many Jews were able to surmount the anxiety of their dislocation. Beginning in the early 1890s, a number of Jews began to accept the distance between Jews and non-Jews in a different light. Rather than bemoaning their isolation and the apparent collapse of Enlightenment ideals, they affirmed their own independent nationality. This break from the past was not complete, however. They abandoned their reliance on the capacity of moral persuasion or on German liberals to influence people's life, but not the liberal tradition itself. In fact, by adjusting to postliberal-era conditions in Austrian life, by asserting Jewish national pride, they not only restored their dignity as a people, but believed they could keep the Enlightenment ideals from disappearing with the liberal tradition in Austria.

Nor was the break from the past sudden for Jews living in the imperial capital. Jewish national resurgence had first emerged a decade earlier among those who had migrated from East Europe. While assimilated Jews dismissed Dühring's racial slander as ridiculous and peripheral to Austrian life, Jewish university students from the East organized, in the late months of 1882, the first Jewish national student association in Europe. This response, like others that were to follow, was only natural for migrant Jews. Their life in the pale of settlement had accustomed them to persecution. To them, anti-Semitism was commonplace and impossible to ignore. They were immune from the lingering hope that prolonged the emotional attachment to German liberalism among assimilated Jews. Moreover, having come from Jewish communities, East-European Jews had a mature national consciousness. In the eyes of German Jews, this appeal to positive pride and self-defense accentuated the alien presence of *Ostjuden* in Vienna. Their assertion of Jewish nationalism made assimilated Jews feel even more uncomfortable than they felt in the 1860s and 1870s. Even in the 1890s, when Jews from the West began to articulate their own Jewish pride, the two groups remained distinct. Though many German Jews now acknowledged the importance of independence, they desired, in the end, not autonomy, the goal of East-European Jews, but the social integration of Jews and non-Jews. Despite this dichotomy, the response of Jews from the East to anti-Semitism did anticipate and prepare the way for the positive response of German Jews in the 1890s. From the climate of renascent national-ism, to which the East-European Jews contributed, a number of influential German Jews developed a renewed sense of responsibility for their own fate as Jews and, as Jews, for the fate of Enlightenment ideals.

In addition to being the first of its kind in Europe, the national student association of the University of Vienna was the earliest organized Jewish response to anti-Semitism in Vienna. Called Kadimah, Hebrew for both "for-ward" and "eastward," the society was founded on March 23, 1883. One Jewish immigrant from an older generation, Perez Smolenskin (1842-85) had suggested the name and exerted an important influence on the society.[71] He had come to Vienna 15 years earlier from Odessa and established, shortly after arriving, the Hebrew monthly, *Ha-Shahar* (*The Dawn*), to express his nationalist views. "Let us be like all other people," he wrote in the foreword to the paper's first edition. "Let us, like them, be unashamed of our ancestry and be proud of our [Hebrew] language and the honor of our people." The appeal was directed to his East-European compatriots who suffered the hostile reception of the Viennese: "The day will come when the house of Israel will again acquire its independence."[72] Kadimah adopted this program. In the spring of 1883, the society posted its appeal around the university. Written by two of its leading members, Moritz Schnirer (1861-1941), the fraternity's president, who had emigrated from Bucharest three years earlier, and Nathan Birnbaum (1864-1937), the only one in the organization from Vienna, but still just one generation away from East Europe, the Hebrew and German document proclaimed the society's determination "to preserve and cherish the spiritual richness of the [Jewish] people." Like Smolenskin, the members condemned anti-Semitic persecution, "whose goal is the destruction of Judaism," and supported the independence of Jews, "the regeneration of the Jewish nation." It was not important how they would achieve independence — they advocated both autonomy in the Diaspora and Palestinian resettlement — as long as they could be sovereign. Unlike Smolenskin, they appealed to assimilated Jews. "In their effort [to destroy Judaism], our enemies are supported, only too willingly unfortunately, by those of our common heritage. . . . We can only defend ourselves against our enemies. This indifference, however, must be opposed."[73]

The confrontation between East and West was a two-way affair. The reaffirmation of Jewish national existence by the members of Kadimah was, at the same time, a challenge to the indifference of assimilated Jews to a heritage they could call their own. Reacting to anti-Semitism, and stimulated by renascent nationalism in the empire and among students, Jews in Kadimah thus struggled against Jewish as well as non-Jewish forces of negation.[74] Contrary to the method German Jews practiced to realize their emancipation, the students of Kadimah relied on their own determination to achieve freedom. In fact, they adhered closely to the compelling argument of the Russian Jew Leon Pinsker (1821-91), who wrote, the previous year, that the only path to freedom and respect was "*Autoemanzipation.*"[75] Sensitive not only to the national configuration of postliberal politics, they developed the style as well. "You must not be a slave, Jew — you stem from the Maccabees!" Birnbaum, the author of this statement, and influential within the society, promoted the image of the Maccabean struggle against the tyranny of Syrian rule in 167 B.C. as the example of Jewish regeneration. "The spirit which inspired Judah Maccabee to his unforgettable deeds has been revived," he exhorted on the occasion of the first Maccabean celebration of Kadimah, December 1883. "This spirit will create a free Israel, united in brotherhood."[76]

Kadimah's challenge to the West only exacerbated ill feeling between the two groups. German Jews regarded the challenge to their German-liberal loyalties as a threat not only to the prospects of assimilation, but also to their cherished liberal tradition. They resented the stress on independence since they believed it exposed Jews to an increasingly anti-Semitic populace and contributed to the conflict between nationalities. Jellinek would not listen to Pinsker when the latter came to Vienna. He rejected Birnbaum's nationalistic appeal when Birnbaum visited the rabbi in early 1883.[77] For different reasons, German Jews, like Jews from the East, had to contend with other Jews as well as with non-Jews. But within the circles of East-European Jews, Kadimah generated an enthusiastic response. Another rabbi, in Vienna from 1880, after studying at universities in Zurich and Munich, at Yeshivot in Hungary, and in Galicia, where he was born, expressed his support for the student fraternity, less than a week after its first plenary session in May 1883. By then, Joseph Samuel Bloch (1850-1923) was a familiar name in Vienna. In response to the acquittal of Franz Holubek, Bloch published a series of articles in a popular local newspaper, refuting the basis of his defense, Rohling's *Der Talmudjude.* Bloch accused

Rohling of misrepresenting the Talmud and, in subsequent articles, challenged the professor's integrity. The momentum of this counteroffensive resulted in the establishment of Bloch's own journal, the *Osterreichische Wochenschrift,* which Kadimah enthusiastically endorsed two months later, in December 1884, at its second Maccabean celebration.[78]

In this journal, and two years later, with the founding of the first Jewish civil-defense organization in Central Europe, the *Österreichische-israelitische Union,* Bloch was, for the following decade, a leading proponent of Jewish resurgence in Vienna. The union attacked anti-Semitism by defending not just the civil rights granted overall in the 1867 constitution, as assimilated Jews were doing, but specifically the civil rights of Jews. It also promoted pride in the heritage of the Jewish people by sponsoring lectures on Jewish scholarship and other educational programs.[79] In his effort at affirming the independent rights and the value of the Jewish people, Bloch, like Kadimah, attacked the apologetic strategy of emancipation that the assimilated Jews had followed. The Jew "will never give satisfaction no matter what he does," Bloch said in a speech before the Reichsrat in 1890 (Bloch represented a preponderantly Jewish district of East Galicia from 1883 to 1895). "If he spends too much, he is ostentatious, a spendthrift; if he spends too little, he is called stingy, a miser. If he keeps aloof from political life, he is lacking in public spirit; if he joins the government, you say, of course, the Jew is always on the side of the powers that be; if he joins the opposition, he is an element of dissatisfaction in political life."[80] This argument against assimilation was the focus of his editorial policy in the *Wochenschrift:* "National ostracism excludes Jews from its [non-Jewish] circles. . . . [This] cannot be ignored. . . . We cannot put on German-national or Czech airs without becoming a ridiculous caricature." He felt liberal ideals were just as illusory: "As soon as the people are permeated with the conviction that racial kinship is paramount, the bravest preacher of tolerance will not succeed in making the people accept [a] Jeiteles or [a] Kohn as their kindred."[81] He concluded that political sagacity as well as moral integrity dictated the policy of Jewish self-assertion.[82]

It was this protest against Jewish apologetics, and specifically against Friedjung's German liberal *Deutsche Wochenschrift,* that prompted the title of his journal. In his preference for an Austrian ideal, Bloch's vision differed from the Jewish national aspirations of Kadimah, as well as from Friedjung's assimilationist objectives. Bloch maintained that an honest federalistic structure, "the truly Austrian and Habsburg idea of state," would encourage "mutual toleration of confessions and peaceful coexistence of the races and peoples."[83] The same year Bloch founded his journal, Birnbaum, backed by Kadimah, began to edit his own. Borrowing Pinsker's concept of Jewish regeneration for the title, he concentrated on a policy of complete "*Selbst-Emanzipation*" vis-à-vis Bloch's notion of Austrian patriotism. Though he, too, had a small following, his particular brand of resurgent Jewish nationalism was familiar in Jewish circles until the mid-1890s. He called for Jewish national rebirth, offered ideas for the resettlement of Palestine, and, in 1892-93, proposed a Zionist convention — the term "Zionism" was his — of Jewish students from Vienna and Berlin. The pen name he adopted in the company of Kadimah in 1893, Mathias Acher, was a clear statement of his nationalist position. Mattathias, the leader of the Maccabean rebellion against foreign tyranny, and "Acher" ("another"), the rabbinic Hebrew designation for the prototypical apostate Jew, represented Birnbaum's commitment to a secular national struggle for Jewish independence.[84]

These various appeals to nationalism came to fruition at the turn of the century, several years after the first signs of the national surge among German Jews. Brief mention of this activity will indicate the extent to which East-European Jews attained independence before World War I. In response to the severe setbacks suffered by the liberals in the local and parliamentary election of 1897, Jews organized a populist movement to fill the dangerous political vacuum, as well as to oppose the increasing power and influence of conservative officials. The *Jüdischer Volksverein* (1897-1902) and its political successor, the *Jüdische Volkspartei*, were formed to establish a more effective platform for the protection of Jewish interests and for the realization of the Jewish nationhood (*Volksthum*). Besides combating political oppression, economic boycott, and social abuse, these organizations attempted to promote a "cultural Zionism," an independent administration of their own affairs, such as educational and financial matters, as well as a "Jewish realpolitik," a strategy of corroboration with other minority groups in the empire, such as the Czechs, to achieve constitutional reform favoring the principle of national self-sufficiency.[85] The party's newspaper, the *Jüdisches Volksblatt*, defended Jewish national sovereignty in the empire as the fulfillment of the dynasty's destiny: "Austria has not been a German state since 1866, even though many Germans still think so. . . . Austria is Austria, plain and simple: a polyglot state which has as its historical task the unification of all its diverse peoples . . . each proud of their national individuality, and the pledge to *national autonomy*, that is, to political and economic progress, as a testament to liberty, equality, and fraternity."[86] Birnbaum contributed to the development of this movement. In a series of articles written in 1905 for the *Volksblatt*, he expressed confidence in the realization of Jewish culture, including the Yiddish language, within the Austrian framework.[87]

Even as German Jews increasingly shifted their loyalties from German liberalism to Jewish nationalism, major differences between them and East-European Jews persisted. Like Kadimah and Bloch's *Wochenschrift*, the *Volksblatt* appealed in vain to western Jews. Repeating the earlier pleas, only now in the idiom of a political movement, the banner headline of the populist paper's first edition (February 18, 1899) exhorted, "Jews of Austria, organize yourselves!"[88] German Jews seeking independence resisted the plea for the same reason cosmopolitan or assimilated Jews did. As important as a collective response to anti-Semitism appeared to them, they could never accept as final the separation between Jews and non-Jews. They sympathized as little with the cultural Zionism of Jewish populism as they did with Bloch's ideal of preserving the religion and heritage of the Jewish people, or with Birnbaum's ideal of developing a Jewish national culture.[89] Contrary to East-European Jews, Jews of the West sustained the vision of social integration even when they accepted their social distance.

Beginning in 1889, German Jews gradually and, at first, reluctantly adjusted to the postliberal-era climate of national and class struggle. Many close to the affairs of the Jewish community acknowledged the importance of political involvement and decided, in that year, to replace the liberals, with Bloch's *Union* in the position of leadership, a position the *Union* controlled until 1936. No German Jew resisted Bloch's influence in the mid-1880s more than Jellinek. Jellinek opposed the government's proposal to appoint Bloch to a chair at the University of Vienna. For four years after Bloch organized the *Union* in 1886, Jellinek and the newspaper *Die Neue Zeit* refused to even recognize its existence. However, in 1890, three years before his death, Jellinek arrived at the conclusion that unity was important for the future of the Jewish people. After affirming the legitimacy of Bloch's endeavors, he endorsed his candidacy for the Reichsrat.[90]

The official acknowledgment of Bloch's position on Jewish independence and on self-defense marked the decisive change in the self-conception and the goal orientation of an increasing number of German Jews. For the first time in decades, Jews who aspired toward social integration believed that being Jewish was more important than being German. At the same time, the roundabout way in which Jellinek and others accepted Bloch foreshadowed both the circumscribed manner in which Jews similar to them would affirm their ethnic identities and the only partial rapprochement between West and East. German Jews did not care about religion or about cultural autonomy. Those who gravitated toward Jewish life did so because Jewish affirmation offered a stronger basis for self-assertion and for strength through unity than did identification with German liberalism.

One of the most dramatic manifestations of change in German-Jewish life was also among the earliest. In 1895-96, Herzl wrote the manifesto of political Zionism, *Der Judenstaat* (*The Jewish State*). As a movement, Zionism was the supreme affirmation of Jewish national pride. It extended the implications of resurgence further than had any other effort to this time. Yet, although an extreme appeal to independence, *The Jewish State* intoned the aspirations of a German Jew. Herzl did not abandon the liberal ideals of a rationally integrated social order. On the contrary, by adopting the postliberal tone of a national struggle, he discussed the ideals with renewed self-assurance. Moreover, Herzl's movement had an unprecedented impact on other German Jews. Even those who did not support Herzl's cause admired the tone of positive expression and solidarity. As an influential and, as Herzl noted in the subtitle to the manifesto, a "modern" response to conditions in Austria, Zionism provided a bridge for the liberal aspirations of German Jews before and after the 1890s.

Nowhere was this transition more apparent than and as sudden as in Herzl's own life. In 1893, the second year of his assignment as Paris correspondent to the *Neue Freie Presse,* and only two years before writing *The Jewish State,* upon his return to Vienna, Herzl offered a plan, for the immediate assimilation of Jews, that went far beyond his previous ideas of intermarriage and a common state religion. "Help us against anti-Semitism," he would say to the Pope, "and I in return will lead a great movement amongst Jews for voluntary and honorable conversion to Christianity." The rejection of his idea by the newspaper's editor only anticipated his later recognition of the plan's futility.[91]

Herzl completely reversed himself in *The Jewish State.* Instead of helplessness and despair, the document conveyed determination and exhilaration. Herzl no longer appealed to unsympathetic authorities, nor to the remote ideals of German liberalism. In fact, he stressed the complete exhaustion of German liberalism, condemning, as vehemently as did Kadimah or Bloch, those Jews who continued to believe in the return to a state of peaceful coexistence between Jews and non-Jews. "It is impossible to escape from this eternal circle [of mutual hatred]. 'No!' some soft-hearted visionaries will say: 'No, it is possible! Possibly by means of the ultimate perfection of humanity.' Is it necessary to point to the sentimental folly of this view?"[92] Realizing that the most difficult hurdle to "the promised land" would be the "narrow-minded, short-sighted members of our own race," Jews given over to patriotic zeal and to the assumption of universal brotherhood, he evoked the common misery of the Jews and proclaimed the Jewish people as "one people," noting that, once united, "we suddenly discover our strength." He argued that the Jewish state was not the vision of one man, but a historic necessity, a natural extension of the human condition. For, not only is it true that "might precedes right," but "antagonism is essential to man's greatest efforts."[93]

Herzl conceived of the promised land as the final fulfillment of a "long-sought object, . . . a free home!"[94] Yet, in spite of his recognition of anti-Semitism as an endemic phenomenon, and his desire for emancipation as well as for national sovereignty, neither populist Jews, nor the East-European Jews attracted to the nascent Zionist movement, were willing to accept Herzl's vision of the Jewish state.[95] Both within and without the Zionist movement, Jews from the East and West divided over objectives. Herzl desired the kind of freedom he and German Jews like him had sought for decades. In the chapter of *The Jewish State* discussing the details of the proposed Jewish state, Herzl described a culture that differed fundamentally from the ideal of cultural Zionism. He said that Hebrew would not be the national language since very few could converse in it. Thus, he said, "every man can preserve the language in which his thoughts are at home." Yiddish, too, and other "stunted jargons" would be left behind. Moreover, religion would be subordinated to the administration of the state. "Every man will be as free and undisturbed in his faith or his disbelief as he is in his nationality." The free Jewish state, promoting equality before the law, toleration for all, and "above and before all . . . our free thinkers who are continually making new conquests for humanity," promised, in short, the kind of life German Jews longed to attain. Herzl was interested in creating, not an environment for the development of Jewish culture, but rather, an environment for the development of a liberal culture that previously had been denied to Jews. He said, "We shall remain in the new country what we now are." In his diary, a few months later, he added, "All right, we shall move away; but over there too, we shall only be Austrians."[96]

As important as the ideals were to Herzl, his determination to unite Jews in a separate and distant land finally led many German Jews, including Schnitzler and Zweig, to dismiss the program. Offended by Herzl's attack against the common patriotic and ethical forms of assimilation, some Jews believed Zionism aggravated the tense relations between Jews and non-Jews. Herzl's newspaper refused to mention even the word "Zionism." In one of his most devastating criticisms of contemporary life, the Viennese satirist Karl Kraus (1874-1936) condemned Herzl's Zionism for introducing Jews to the hostile contest between nations.[97] Though Herzl's emigration scheme lost him German-Jewish supporters, it did not contradict the liberal ideals he and other Jews cherished. For Herzl, Jewish nationality was not the culmination of Jewish experience, as it was for East-European Jews. His emphasis on solidarity and movement, even his stress on might and on the separation of Jews from non-Jews, was only the means to the desired end of liberal culture. These powerful ideas comprised a new strategy for achieving the freedom and toleration he missed in Austria. Herzl believed it would have been preferable if "average humanity had become as charitably inclined as was Lessing when he wrote 'Nathan the Wise' "; if, that is, mankind could be educated to the poet's humanitarian principle of toleration, and, specifically, of respect for the Jew. "But its education would, even in the most favorable circumstances, occupy such a vast amount of time that we could, as already mentioned, remove our own difficulties by other means long before the process was accomplished." Since the "Enlightenment reached in reality only the choicest spirits," why endure hardships and privation, until the Enlightenment slowly penetrates average humanity, when "the world's spirit comes to our aid in another way"?[98]

Herzl felt closer to this "world spirit" than to the Jewish state. As he recalled, just after returning to Vienna, "In Paris, I was in the midst of politics — at least as an observer. I saw how the world is run. I stood amazed at the phenomenon of the crowd — for a long time without comprehending it." He was impressed by the honesty of French anarchists, who asserted their cause, as well as by the "political preparations" of French socialism and nationalism.[99] What they stood for was something else. In fact, he was disturbed by the French national response to the Dreyfus affair. But he was fascinated with the "curious excitement" of the day and with the aggressive, collective resolve of a political movement. Herzl adopted this mode of political expression to achieve his "long-sought object" and to escape, at long last, the eternal intolerance of the Jews.

Though German Jews rejected Herzl's emigration scheme, many were impressed by his efforts. Beer-Hofmann wrote to Herzl, within days after *The Jewish State* appeared in print: "Even more than the contents of the book, I was attracted to its implications. At last there comes again a man who does not carry his Judaism with resignation like a burden or a misfortune, but is proud to be a legal inheritor of an immemorial culture." He even proposed an idea for Zion's "initial institution" — a famous medical school that would attract students from "all Asia," though not from Europe (as the omission of it in his letter reveals).[100] Schnitzler, too, recognized Zionism as "a moral principle and a social movement," while Freud, writing to Herzl in 1902, expressed "the high esteem I — like so many others — have held many years [for] the poet and the fighter for the human rights of our people."[101] This selective praise of Herzl from German Jews who, like him, had previously advocated immediate assimilation, signals the vanguard arrival of German Jews to postliberal Austria. Rejecting the notion of separation, German Jews, who had now come of age, nevertheless sympathized with Herzl's postliberal emphasis on a positive national pride and movement. They realized the significance of Jewish initiative as a means of revitalizing humanitarian ideals.

While Herzl was still in Paris, German Jews at the University of Vienna formed a Jewish society, *Jüdische-akademische Lesehalle* (Jewish Academic Reading Room). It began in June 1894 as a place of refuge from the hostile, anti-Semitic university environment, but soon developed into an affirmative movement. The society endeavored to "raise Jewish consciousness" (*bezweckt die Hebung des jüdischen Bewusstseins*) and represented Jewish interests at the university. Up to a point, then, it shared with East-European Jews the concern for internal Jewish affairs. In fact, the group had Bloch's support. But it went beyond Bloch, for the student members were involved in a struggle "which Judaism waged not [only] for itself, but on behalf of all mankind."[102] So strong was the commitment to humanitarian ideals that in 1900, many student members established the popular *Lese- und Redehalle jüdischer Hochschüler* (Reading and Discourse Room of Jewish University Students), in a protest against a tendency within the Lesehalle toward an excessive concentration on strictly Jewish and Zionist matters. Like its predecessor, the Redehalle stressed Jewish pride; for this reason, it backed Zionism. But the group wished to direct this and other expressions of pride toward the original goal of the Lesehalle. Its members believed that the Jewish struggle was the struggle for the human rights of all mankind.[103]

The Redehalle sponsored many events expressing this humanitarian impulse. The first of a series of "Evenings with Young Jewish Authors," for example, concentrated on the theme of new definitions for modern ideas in literature that could transcend one-sided viewpoints, such as the racial perspective, and that stressed, instead, the importance of certain ideas for the common good of humanity. The keynote speaker remarked that this approach was a position Jews commonly took. He asked his audience to refrain from participating in the arena of partisan politics or that of social conflict and, instead, to explore what he called this important field of "Jewish art." One of those who participated in the event was Zweig.[104] He had just published his first book, a volume of poems, and a number of feuilletons. His autobiography revealed just how familiar he was with the concept of "Jewish art."[105] In reference to the turn of the century, he wrote, "The Viennese Jews had become artistically productive, although not in a specifically Jewish way; rather, through a miracle of understanding, they gave to what was Austrian, and Viennese, its most intensive expression. . . . [They] renewed the city's universal fame." Zweig believed the desire to "serve the glory of Vienna" was, above all, an expression of "their desire for assimilation." The longing to "attach themselves passionately to the culture of the world around them" was translated into a "love for Viennese art," for through art, "they felt entitled to full citzenship, and that they had actually become true Viennese." Indeed, the artistic effort at realizing the city's "spiritual supernationality" — that is, at harmonizing "all the national and lingual contrasts," and, thus, at achieving "a synthesis of all Western cultures" — was a desire assimilated Jews had cherished for decades. However, the desire, as Zweig expressed it, was no longer an expression of German loyalty or of isolated abstract principles. Rather, the timeless aspirations were given renewed plausibility through the miracle of Jewish understanding. Not as an artist only, nor as a German, but as a Jew, Zweig affirmed the spirit of cultural synthesis. His art was not, as he noted, "specifically Jewish." It was "Jewish art" as it was understood in German-Jewish student circles — a unique Jewish perspective into the mechanism of reconciliation.

The theme of reconciliation was not nearly as prominent in Schnitzler's writings as it was in Zweig's. Schnitzler's characters sought to establish order in their lives, but discovered the futility of this search and how much more natural chaos was.[106] Moral restraint or social commitment ultimately yielded to inner temptation or to the destructive social forces beyond their control. But while confusion and uncertainty prevailed, it would be misleading to conclude that Schnitzler could derive no meaning from the spiritual malaise he portrayed.[107] Magris and other literary historians have noted that about 1900, and especially in *The Road to the Open* and in *Professor Bernhardi,* Schnitzler developed into a more serious interpreter of social reality as he examined alternatives to the decadent weariness of life he described in his earlier writings.[108] Indeed, in contrast to Georg von Wergenthin, the composer-conductor who drifted into an unhappy love affair and longed for the carefree life, the character Heinrich Bermann searched for deeper understanding.

Schnitzler's concern for deeper understanding is apparent in *Professor Bernhardi* (1912). While serving his term in prison, the professor reflected upon the political and anti-Semitic reaction to his professional decision to keep the priest from seeing his dying patient. "The problem was no longer one of Austrian politics, or any kind of politics; all at once it seemed as though the broadest ethical issues were at stake; responsiblity and revelation, and finally the question of free will."[109] He recognized that the ideological motive, no matter how enlightened, was always artificial and had magnified innocent personal disagreements. The priest could not represent his case without defending the "holy cause." German nationalists exploiting the situation were also driven by their cause. When asked to join sympathizers in the fight against political anti-Semitism, Bernhardi refused: "I do not intend to let a skirmish with these people become my life-long work." Rather than joining the partisan struggle, which, as he observed, was "rising up from all sides," he preferred to do what he felt was best — to continue his professional work. Ending the play as he had begun, Schnitzler confirmed the moral principle which Bernhardi defended. Like the decision to bar the priest from the hospital, the decision to return to medicine was a matter of personal judgment based on what he felt was right and just.

Within the moral framework of these two works, Schnitzler paid close attention to the contemporary Jewish problems. The moral position which Bermann and Bernhardi exemplified was, at the same time, a refutation of the familiar process of assimilation. "There are Jews whom I really hate, hate as Jews," Bermann admitted. "Those are the people who act before others and often before themselves as though they did not belong to the rest [of Jewry] at all. [These are] the men who try to offer themselves to their enemies and despisers in the most cowardly and cringing fashion." As other characters observed, Jews who devoted themselves to German liberalism or to German nationalism were not only hurt by the reversals of these movement, but had forfeited their personal integrity.[110] Bermann and Bernhardi did not wish to escape the burden of their Jewishness. It was not even a burden for them. "I am not touchy any more about [anti-Semites]," Bermann remarked. They recognized that salvation came from within. The plight of the Jews was "a question which for the time being everyone has got to settle for himself." Salvation runs through "our own selves. . . . [It is] the courage to be what one naturally is."[111]

Unlike Schnitzler's concentration on the self in his writings of the preceding decade, this emphasis on the self was not an escape from reality. When Bernhardi rejected his superior, the minister of education, who pressed him to appoint a non-Jew to the staff so as to exculpate him from his action against the priest, he attempted not only to preserve his personal integrity, but to keep the world around him from disintegrating into an irreversible state of conflict. "What is essential here?" he asked the minister. "Don't you see it yourself? That the best man should be appointed to our section, the one to whom it will open out the possibility of rendering true service to humanity and science. That is something to strive for! That is the essential."[112] Berhnardi's profession, "to cure people,"[113] was more than the physician's ambition. He was, above all, the fighter for truth. Independent judgment was both ethical and the basis of a humane world. It was salvation for the individual and ultimately for the community of individuals.

Though Bermann and Bernhardi were exceptional characters in Schnitzler's literary oeuvre, they represented the synthesis of his two earlier concerns, the idea of the social whole and the inner life of the psyche in relation to instinctual and social forces. The two characters reflected Schnitzler's developed thinking as a Jew, for he assigned to them the roles of protagonists. They were proud Jews who boldly advocated "the essential" of reconciliation. Schnitzler gave them the responsibility of realizing the eternal ideals of the Enlightenment. "Do you know what [the coming together of people] will probably look like in the end?" asked Bermann. "That we, we Jews I mean, have been a kind of ferment in the brewing of humanity."[114] Like Herzl and Zweig, Schnitzler could revive the vision of social reconciliation only after shifting the locus of responsibility from a German to a Jewish movement. For him, Jewish initiative offered direct access to individual and universal redemption.

Though raised to a pitch of renewed purpose, the tone of Herzl's, Zweig's, and Schnitzler's appeal to reconciliation was not as expectant as it was in the 1860s. After all, Bernhardi reflected upon ethical issues in prison. Though he committed himself to science and to humanity, after returning from prison, he was told at the end of the play, "If we always did only the right thing . . . we should certainly land in jail."[115] As an iconoclast, Bernhardi served as a reminder that the return to the search for unity was accompanied this time by the sense of social distance Jews had felt for decades. Indeed, for all their concern for humanity, local Jewish students organized societies as a refuge from the anti-Semitic environment of the university and devoted themselves to the struggle for self-preservation. Zionism was perhaps the most emphatic statement of distance, for it was not only a movement which confronted society, but a movement away from the society in which Jews lived. Hesitation tempered the optimism of their renewed vision at the turn of the century. If Jews renewed their belief in social integration, they also were aware of the enormous social fissures which the ideas of the Enlightenment would have to span in order to build this decent home for humanity. It was a struggle without illusion.

German Jews who had come of age did so in one sense only. They adopted the nationalistic frame of mind, but they recognized how estranged from their society they really were. Their devotion to the traditional ideals, the habit of mind that prevailed in the 1860s, helped to sustain this feeling of social isolation. Even though they adapted to the postliberal climate of conflict and struggle, Jews continued to promote liberal ideals. Zweig desired to become not just Viennese, but "true Viennese," true to the city's "spiritual" unity, just as Schnitzler felt some Jewish writers were "more German" than many German writers.[116] Herzl believed Jews were strong enough "to form [not just another] state . . . [but] a model state"[117] — the model liberal state. Even though German Jews were proud and bold as Jews they adhered to the abstract, or more precisely, positivistic ideals of an earlier period. In this respect, their work resembled the sermons of Jellinek or the feuilletons of Spitzer.

While they still aspired toward distant goals, a number of German Jews discovered a more immediate way to achieve these goals than relying upon German liberalism. "No one ever thought of looking for the Promised Land where it actually is," Herzl wrote in 1895. "Yet it lies so near. This is where it is: within ourselves!"[118] The fusion of this belief in self-determination with the commitment to liberal ideals formed the basis of a new period in the German-Jewish search for the social whole. Jews saw it as their task to redeem or to purify liberal culture. Defiant of society and inspired by Jewish pride, they devoted themselves to constructing the basis of a more consonant world. "We shall live at last as free men on our own soil and die peacefully in our own homes," Herzl declared in *The Jewish State*. Just as important, "the world will be freed by our liberty, enriched by our wealth, magnified by our greatness. Whatever we attempt there to accomplish for our own welfare, will react powerfully and beneficially for the good of humanity."[119] Schnitzler referred to this Jewish sense of purpose as a "ferment in the brewing of humanity." Perhaps with the advantage of hindsight, Zweig understood the meaning of this self-imposed responsibility. Viennese Jews "felt that their being [truly] Austrian was a mission to the world."[120] It was a search for reconciliation that introduced the paradoxical element of Jewish superiority. No longer did some Jews feel merely compatible with progressive movements. They now believed they were the sole agents of progress. In the words of Solomon Liptzin, they affirmed "the desirability and even the necessity for the continued existence or the reconstitution of the Jews as a distinct people, tribe, or nation, but [saw] the primary justification for the survival of this unique group in its striving towards supranationalism, in its dedicating itself to the service of humanity at large."[121]

A JEWISH TASK

When Jacob Wassermann arrived in Vienna in 1898, he discovered an attitude among German Jews he had never encountered before: "One circumstance puzzled me before I had been long in Vienna. In Germany I had associated with Jews scarcely at all; only now and then did one appear in my circle, and no special stress was laid by either himself or others on the fact that he was Jewish. Here, however, it developed that all with whom I came into intellectual or friendly contact were Jews. And not only did others invariably emphasize this, but they emphasized it themselves."[122] The climate of nationalism in Vienna was indeed unusual in Europe before World War I. Even among Jews who had stressed the need for reconciliation, there developed a distinct national pride, with all the emotional, neo-Romantic trappings of the nationalistic sensibility.[123] To be sure, within the evolution of German-Jewish aspirations in Vienna, the feeling of national pride was not the medium of separation as it was for East-European Jews. On the contrary, Jewish nationalism in the form of redemptive zeal renewed the search for social reconciliation.

Jewish resurgence caught on in turn-of-the century Vienna. Not only did Jews who were uncomfortable with their isolation from non-Jewish society stress their distinction as Jews. Others who despised all forms of nationalism and even their own Jewishness recognized, in Jewish self-determination, the power of bringing about a supranational, supraethnic world. Self-assertion was a value that penetrated the work of even the most self-critical or "self-hating" Jews — the term Theodor Lessing used in his controversial study, *Der jüdische Selbsthass* (1930).[124]

To Karl Kraus and Otto Weininger (1880-1903), two subjects of Lessing's study, anti-Semitism was a welcome development. They believed it would be an effective purge of insidious Jewish influences in society. They used the terminology of the aggressors to condemn Jewish existence as rootless and lacking "character," and, therefore, as a "parasitic" impulse that sought satisfaction in hoarding money or in material possessions. Within a few years, they took steps to sever ties with the Jewish community.[125] However, their censure of Jewish life was more discreet than the ire of their anti-Semitic counterparts. It was more a protest against the transgression of morality than a desire to annihilate. Kraus made the point in 1913. He denied that his remarks against Jews represented a victory for "Ario-Germanentum." He noted, "We regard the tendency of such hatred of the Jews as something honorable when it strives to an origin [i.e., to urge them to recover their native morality], never to a goal [i.e., to obliterate them]." He expressed his sympathies with Judaism "up to the Exodus" and, since then, only with "the defenders of God and the avengers of an errant people."[126]

Weininger, too, distinguished his "low estimate of the Jew" from the anti-Semitic agitation for Jewish persecution. He believed that, though bereft of dignity and individuality, Jews possessed the "vague hope . . . that there must be something in Judaism for Judaism." In his immensely popular pseudoscientific study *Geschlecht und Charakter* (*Sex and Character*, 1904), Weininger developed a "racial anthropology" that divided the human constitution into amounts of "protoplasm," traits that determined the weaknesses or strengths of the individual. Judaism was one trait and, like femininity, a debilitating one. As a tendency of the mind, he believed it could inhabit anyone. In fact, Weininger believed that this trait dominated his own age. But he said it had "become actual in the most conspicuous fashion [only] among the Jews." The "vague hope" corresponded with the "germ of good," which he felt could be found in any person, and which indeed flourished among Jews before the birth of Christ. According to Weininger, Christ was "the only Jew to conquer Judaism." By overcoming this negative tendency, he "created Christianity, the strongest affirmation" of individuality and character, and abandoned to the other Jews the burden of Judaism. Like Kraus, Weininger searched for the original Jew who existed with positive, as well as with negative, possibilities.[127] In an article written before Lessing's seminal study, Hans Kohn defined the bitterness of these assimilated Jews not as self-criticism, but as criticism of only certain characteristics they believed were false. Despite their strong remarks about Judaism, they believed "that in each Jew there existed something else, an element of the 'sublime,' of the great primal substance of Judaism [*Urjudentums*]."[128]

This belief or self-conception was an integral part of Kraus's and Weininger's position as defenders of morality at the turn of the century. After attacking the position of Zionism in *Eine Krone für Zion* (*A Crown for Zion*, 1898), Kraus reaffirmed his "faith in the [Jewish] capacity to assimilate." He was convinced that Jews were "destined to fuse insolubly with their surrounding culture." This faith in a united society was the obverse of his broader polemic against the forces of social division, especially the multiple and often conflicting national and ideological claims to truth. He thus believed that there was no reason for fanning the fires of nationalism with the banner of Zion. Moreover, Jews would not only be a part of, but would "remain constantly a ferment" in, this process of unification.[129] Kraus had as little affinity with Schnitzler as he had with Herzl. But, even though the three approached the problems facing Jews in entirely different ways, Kraus's positive evaluation of the Jews in the process of reconciliation corresponded with Herzl's vision, and, indeed, with Schnitzler's very wording.[130]

Perhaps the most sophisticated expression of Jewish ethical responsibility is found in Weininger's work. He believed that Judaism was self-destructive, since he believed that Judaism was a trait that tended toward absolute negation. However, for Weininger, negation was the precondition for freedom. He posited that only from the "deepest abyss" could renewal arise. It required an act of "free will," the germ of good, "to surmount the nothingness" of Judaism, for "regeneration proceeds as a rebellion." According to this logic, it was no accident that Christianity evolved out of Judaism: "Christ was a Jew precisely that he might overcome the Judaism within him." The Jew possessed not only the capacity for inner renewal – indeed, the Jew's "war against himself" was essential – but the capacity for triumphing over what he felt was the most Jewish age in the history of mankind. He said, "There lies in Judaism the possibility of producing [another] Christ." For Weininger, this was the only metaphysical meaning of Judaism. Judaism was "the spring from which the founders of religion will come." He concluded, "The possibility of begetting Christs is the meaning of Judaism. . . . In the Jew there are the greatest possibilities."[131]

During the time he was writing *Sex and Character*, Weininger expressed the desire for converting to Christianity. He believed that such a conversion would fulfill more than a personal need. In a diary inscription (August 1903), Weininger wrote, "I believe that my gifts are such that in some way I can solve all problems. . . . I believe that I have deserved the name Messiah (Redeemer) because I have this nature." He felt that he possessed a vision for freeing mankind from the rootlessness and the "superficial anarchy" of his age, as well as for realizing "the reality in the whole, the totality of the universe and its infinite coherence." Moreover, he believed this as a Jew, for "from the new

Judaism the new Christianity may be pressing forth; mankind waits for the new founder of religion."[132]

What Zweig discerned in the perspective of his contemporary Jews, Weininger noted in their self-conception. Many German Jews regarded the redemptive mission as a messianic inspiration. They found a new way of affirming the vision of social reconciliation. Convinced of their power as Jews to effect reform, they often used religious metaphor to express the meaning of their life and work. Weininger believed that the redemptive religion represented "the will of man to become God." This notation of revelation – the deification of man through inner renewal – was particularly attractive to Rank.[133] Herzl invoked the deity to sanctify his mission. After remarking in his diary, while outlining *The Jewish State* (June 1895), that he was involved in solving the social question as well as the Jewish question, he added, "If it turns out to be true, what a gift of God to the Jews!" He did not mean the God of the pious. To him, God was nothing but a "dear old wonderful abbreviation," which stood for something tantamount to a "world spirit." But reference to providential wisdom served to elevate his cause. A few days later, he wrote that Zionism could be seen as God's chosen role for the Jews to play in the history of mankind.[134]

It was the "chosen people" motif that characterized Beer-Hofmann's new Judaism. The themes of loneliness and fatigue were still much in evidence in his work as late as 1900, when he wrote *Der Tod Georgs* (*The Death of George*). However, at the end of the novel, when the main character mourned the death of his friend, Beer-Hofmann expressed the decisive transformation: "Out of darkness and confusion emerged before him a new life. . . . He saw the life he had lived till now sink behind him. Only his destiny was real." It was a destiny he shared with those "whose blood flowed in him. . . . Their victories were God's victories, their defeats were God's judgement; they appointed themselves to witness his power – a people of redeemers."[135] A few years later, Beer-Hofmann planned an ambitious project, the biblical trilogy *Die Historie von König David* (*Story of King David*). The prologue, "Jaákobs Traum" ("Jacob's Dream"), which he started in 1909 and completed during the war, is regarded as his most mature work.[136] Like Schnitzler, Kraus, and Weininger, Beer-Hofmann criticized the materialism and greed of the current day: "The might that now expands among the nations will be ground / To dust! And like dust will blow away!" The Jewish dream of redemption ended this piece as it had ended the work of so many other Jews: God "has chosen my blood for a torch / Which blazes above the ways of all nations."[137]

In religious, political, and cultural circles, an influential minority of German Jews in Vienna frequently expressed their humanitarian views in terms of their renewed Jewish self-conception. Disagreements between the organized Jewish community and Herzl, between Herzl and Kraus, or between Kraus and Schnitzler, did not destroy their shared belief that Jews were responsible for the fate of humanity in the twentieth century. This feeling of responsibility not only renewed the German-Jewish vision of a universal order, but also inspired them toward seeking ways of overcoming the conflict and tension of their world.

For substantive and methodological reasons, the movement and the theory of psychoanalysis illuminate the emergence of self-assertion among German Jews, as well as the way this inner transformation impelled Jews toward restoring mankind to the ideal of universality. First of all, the movement was founded by a Jew and had attracted a predominantly Jewish following in Vienna before World War I. In fact, during the first four years, all the members of Freud's study circle — by 1906 there were 17 — were Jewish. Moreover, the direction of the movement was a humanitarian one. The early analysts studied a theory of human behavior and advocated the possiblities of genuine humanity. Finally, Freud and Rank were among those whom Wassermann portrayed as self-conscious Jews. Freud recalled that during the early stages of the development of psychoanalytic theory, he had a "clear consciousness of an inner identity" as a Jew.[138] Rank arrived at the conception of his new Judaism in the months before joining Freud's circle in 1906. Both analysts probed their Jewish self-conception as sensitively and, at times, as systematically, as they analyzed psychological states generally — an essential aid in our effort at elucidating the meaning and extent of their Jewish self-conception, as well as the way this self-conception entered into their work.

Besides being an impetus to their psychoanalytic endeavors, Freud's and Rank's Jewish self-assertion is significant as the outcomes of their long search for a vehicle that could bring them closer to reconciling hostile social differences. Herzl defined the meaning of Jewish assertiveness for German Jews, like Freud and Rank, who lived in the decades before and after 1900. Jews had found "another way" of pursuing the objective of social integration or wholeness. Without an appreciation of Freud's disappointment with assimilation, and of Rank's despair over his relations with authority, the feeling of momentous discovery that Jewish self-determination brought about is lost. Because of the previous period of disillusionment, and the recognition, at the turn of the century, that suddenly, by assuming responsibility for the welfare of mankind, human liberation was within reach, Freud and Rank renewed the search for the whole with unparalleled devotion and purpose. To them, their age was apocalyptic. Like Weininger and Beer-Hofmann, who aspired toward universal redemption, the two analysts were committed to the "Jewish struggle," or to the "Jewish task." The basis of the feeling that psychoanalysis was a Jewish mission of redemption is thus found in the early stages of assimilation, when Freud's and Rank's separate appeals to ulterior means of social or personal liberation had failed.

NOTES

1. Arthur Schnitzler, *The Road to the Open,* trans. Horace Samuel (New York: Alfred A. Knopf, 1923), 249. *Der Weg ins Freie* may be better translated as "The Way Out."

2. Reference in this chapter on the situation in Vienna is made to the Austro-Hungarian Empire and to its Austrian portion, since Vienna was both the imperial capital and the empire's center of culture. Implied in most of the references to Austria is its dominant German nationality; therefore, unless otherwise stated, Austria will mean German Austria.

3. Arthur Schnitzler, *My Youth in Vienna*, trans. Catherine Hutter (New York: Holt, Rinehart and Winston, Inc., 1970), 3. The autobiography was begun in 1915, but dated back to 1901 when Schnitzler started keeping a file of "miscellaneous autobiographical material."

4. See Sigmund Freud, *The Interpretation of Dreams*, trans. James Strachey (New York: Avon Books, 1967), 226.

5. Sigmund Mayer, *Die Wiener Juden: Kommerz, Kultur, Politik 1700-1900* (Vienna: R. Löwit Verlag, 1917), 309-35; Wolfgang Häusler, "Toleranz, Emanzipation und Antisemitismus des österreichische Judentum des bürgerlichen Zeitalters 1782-1918," in *Das österreichische Judentum: Voraussetzungen und Geschichte*, ed. Nicolaus Vielmetti (Vienna: Jugend und Volk, 1974), 103-4; Max Grunwald, *Vienna* (Philadelphia: The Jewish Publication Society of America, 1936), 285-311; Moriz Rosenmann, *Dr. Adolf Jellinek: Sein Leben und Schaffen Zugleich ein Beitrag zur Geschichte der israelitischen Kultusgemeinde Wien in der zweiten Hälfte des neunzehnten Jahrhunderts* (Vienna: Jos. Schlesinger Verlag, 1931), 170-73.

6. On this relationship, see Jacob Katz, "Die Entstehung der Judenassimilation in Deutschland und deren Ideologie," in *Emancipation and Assimilation Studies in Modern Jewish History*, ed. Jacob Katz (Westmead, England: Gregg International Publishers, 1972), 270. This is a reprint of Katz's doctoral dissertation (1934).

7. Mayer, 276-77, 320-22; Grunwald, 366-69; Georg Franz, *Liberalismus: Die deutschliberale Bewegung in der habsburgischen Monarchie* (Munich: Verlag Georg D. W. Callway, 1955), 422, 513; S. M. Dubnow, *Die neuste Geschichte des jüdischen Volkes*, vol. 2 (Berlin: Jüdischer Verlag, 1929), 380-81.

8. Grunwald, 370.

9. Rosenmann, 140.

10. See ibid., 101.

11. Arthur J. May, *The Hapsburg Monarchy 1867-1914* (New York: W. W. Norton and Co., 1968), 62-64; Dubnow, 379.

12. Franz, 186; see also, Hans Tietze, *Die Juden Wiens: Geschichte, Wirtschaft, Kultur* (Leipzig, Vienna: E. P. Tal, 1933), 197.

13. Max Grunwald, *Geschichte der Wiener Juden bis 1914 (Festschrift)* (Vienna: Selbstverlag der israelitischen Kultusgemeinde, 1926), 65.

14. Cited in Werner J. Cahnmann, "Adolf Fischhof and His Jewish Followers," *The Leo Baeck Institute Yearbook*, 4 (1959), 116.

15. Schnitzler, *My Youth*, 3.

16. Cited in Alexander Altmann, "The New Style of Preaching in Nineteenth-Century German Jewry," in *Studies in Nineteenth-Century Jewish Intellectual History*, ed. Alexander Altmann (Cambridge: Harvard University Press, 1964), 114-15; Rosenmann, 178n.

17. Cited in Peter G. J. Pulzer, *The Rise of Political Anti-Semitism in Germany and Austria* (New York: John Wiley and Sons, 1964), 148.

18. Richard Charmatz, *Österreichs innere Geschichte von 1848 bis 1895*, vol. 1 (Leipzig, Berlin: B. G. Tübner, 1918), 48-64; Albert Fuchs, *Geistige Strömungen in Österreich 1867-1918* (Vienna: Globus-Verlag, 1949), 5-12.

19. Katz, 270.

20. Cited in Walter B. Simon, "The Jewish Vote in Austria," *The Leo Baeck Institute Yearbook*, 16 (1971), 106, from Herzl's "Die Jagd in Böhmen" (1897).

21. Tietze, 223; Grunwald, *Vienna*, 398-99.

22. Cited in Cahnmann, 116.

23. Ibid.

24. Peter G. J. Pulzer, "The Austrian Liberals and the Jewish Question, 1867-1914," *Journal of Central European Affairs*, 23, 2 (1963), 131-42; Simon, 97-121; Fuchs, 7-8.

25. See Rudolf Obergruber, "Die Zeitschriften für jüdische Kulturinteressen im 19. Jahrhundert in Wien" (Doctoral diss., University of Vienna, 1941), esp., 78-79.

26. Daniel Spitzer, *Wiener Spaziergänge*, 7 vols (Vienna, Leipzig: Verlag von Julius Klinkhardt, 1879-1894). For a concise statement of his views, see vol. 7, 163. Moritz Benedikt, the first editor, and later a publisher, of the *Neue Freie Presse*, commented on the prevalence of Jews associated with his paper, in a letter addressed to Theodor Herzl, October 20, 1895: "Until now, we have been considered as a Jewish paper but have never admitted it." Theodor Herzl, *The Complete Diaries of Theodor Herzl*, vol. 1, ed. Raphael Patai; trans. Harry Zohn (New York: Herzl Press and Thomas Yoseloff, 1960), 246.

27. Schnitzler, *My Youth*, 77, 80.

28. Alex Bein, *Theodor Herzl: A Biography*, trans. Maurice Samuel (Philadelphia: The Jewish Publication Society of America, 1940), 25-27; on the *Akademische Lesehalle*, see P. M., "Die Kämpfe in den Lesevereinen," *Gedenkschrift: Die Lesevereine der deutschen Hochschüler an der Wiener Universität* (Vienna: Im Selbstverlage des Lese- und Redevereines des deutschen Hochschüler in Wien 'Germania,' 1912), 38-48.

29. Grunwald, *Vienna*, 398; see Rosenmann, 150.

30. Jacob Wassermann, *My Life as German and Jew*, trans. S. N. Brainin (New York: Coward-McCann, 1933), 188; Bein, 114. The rate of conversion increased precipitously after 1880. Tietze, 205. See Hermann Broch, *Hofmannsthal und seine Zeit: Eine Studie* (Munich: H. Piper, 1964), 103, for a discussion of *"Überkompensation"* in the assimilation process. *Überkompensation* referred to the effort of proving an assimilation as a fait accompli at every turn. Broch (1886-1951), a well-known Viennese novelist and essayist, converted to Roman Catholicism in 1908. Karl Kraus and Otto Weininger, discussed later in this chapter, also converted. Among prominent Viennese Jews who changed their names were Felix Salten (formerly Salzmann), Felix Dörmann (Biedermann), Peter Altenberg (Richard Engländer), and Egon Friedel (Friedmann). Conversion and name changing were concerns for Freud (Sigismund Freud) and for his close follower in the psychoanalytic movement, Otto Rank (Rosenfeld), as well.

31. Michael R. Marrus, *The Politics of Assimilation: A Study of the French Jewish Community at the Time of the Dreyfus Affair* (Oxford: Oxford University Press, 1971). See esp., 142-43, 162, 204-31.

32. Gershom Scholem, "Jews and Germans," in *On Jews and Judaism in Crisis: Selected Essays*, ed. Werner J. Dannhauser (New York: Schocken Books, 1976), 73-80; Jacob Toury, *Die politischen Orientierungen der Juden in Deutschland von Jena bis Weimar* (Bübingen: J. C. B. Mohr, 1966), 267-75; Peter Gay, "Encounter with Modernism: German Jews in Wilhelminian Culture," in *Freud, Jews and Other Germans: Masters and Victims in Modernist Culture* (New York: Oxford University Press, 1978), 93-168; Uriel Tal, *Christians and Jews in German Religion, Politics, and Ideology in the Second Reich, 1870-1914*, trans. Noah Jonathan Jacobs (Ithaca and London: Cornell University Press, 1975), 31-80; Katz, 269-70. Katz, like Scholem, grew up in the environment he described.

33. See Pulzer, 130-35; Tietze, 239.

34. Political anti-Semitism did in fact subside in the 1890s, but this does not mean that assimilation for Jews even then was stable and undisturbed, as Gay maintained in *Freud, Jews and Other Germans:* Their "love affair with German culture" (Gay, 114), never fully requited, concealed deeper anxieties that made them uncomfortably sensitive to their real differences from Germans. On this, see my article in *New German Critique*, 19 (Winter 1980), 151-65. The separation between Jews and Germans surfaced in Germany after World War I. See Eva G. Reichmann, "Der Bewusstseinswandel der deutschen Juden," in *Deutsches Judentum in Krieg und Revolution*, ed. Werner Mosse (Tübingen: J. C. B. Mohr, 1971).

35. On the East-European migration into Vienna and the growth of the anti-Semitic movement, see Mayer, 360-61, 368; Tietze, 203-12; Grunwald, *Vienna*, 402-7. Statistics on the migration are from Israel Jeiteles, *Die Kultusgemeinde der Israeliten in Wien mit Benützung des statistichen Volkszählungsapparates vom Jahre 1869* (Vienna: L. Rosner, 1873), 40; Arieh Tartakower, "Jewish Migratory Movements in Austria in Recent Generations," in *The Jews of Austria: Essays on Their Life, History, and Destruction*, ed. Josef Fraenkel (London: Vallentin, Mitchell and Co., 1970), 287-89; Hugo Gold, *Geschichte der Juden in Wien* (Tel-Aviv: Olamenu, 1966), 35. See also, Anson G. Rabinbach, "The Migration of Galician Jews to Vienna, 1857-1880," in *Austrian History Yearbook* 11 (1975), 44-54.

36. Dirk van Arkel, "Anti-Semitism in Austria," (Doctoral diss. Rijksuniversiteit, 1966), 50; Peter G. J. Pulzer, "The Development of Political Antisemitism in Austria," in *The Jews of Austria*, ed. Fraenkel, 431.

37. See Oscar Franz Scheuer, *Burschenschaft und Judenfrage: Der Rassen-antisemitismus in der deutschen Studentenschaft* (Berlin: Verlag Berlin-Wien, 1927), 46.

38. On Schönerer and his following, see Pulzer, *The Rise of Political Anti-Semitism*, 150-53; Arkel, 81-186; Fuchs, 176-86; Karl Eder, *Der Liberalismus in Altösterreich: Geisteshaltung, Politik und Kultur* (Vienna, Munich: Verlag Herold, 1955), 238-40.

39. On Dühring, see his *Die Judenfrage als Racen- Sitten- und Kulturfrage* (Karlsruhe, Leipzig: Reuther, 1881), 140; see also, Pulzer, *The Rise of Political Anti-Semitism*, 52-53, and Arkel, 25-26, 175. On Rohling, see Tietze, 243-45; Arkel, 14-21, 53; Rosenmann, 153-56.

40. On Lueger, see Robert A. Kann, "German Speaking Jewry During Austria-Hungary's Constitutional Era (1867-1918), *Jewish Social Studies*, 10 (July 1948), 245-49; Fuchs, 58-63; Arkel, 67-80; Pulzer, "The Development of Political Antisemitism," 432-34; Eder, 240-41.

41. Carl Furtmüller, "Alfred Adler: A Biographical Essay," in *Alfred Adler: Superiority and Social Interest, A Collection of Later Writings*, ed. Heinz L. and Rowena R. Ansbacher (Evanston, Ill.: Northwestern University Press, 1964), 330. Furtmüller was arguing that Adler (1870-1937), an important student of Freud's, and founder of the school of individual psychology, was not a victim of personal anti-Semitic hostility. The author, a member of Freud's early circle for two years, seceded, with Adler, from the psychoanalytic movement in 1911.

42. Grunwald, *Vienna*, 428.

43. See Pulzer, *The Rise of Political Anti-Semitism*, 202-5; Tietze, 254; Arkel, 191-93. Hannah Arendt commented that the era of Lueger was "actually a kind of golden era for the Jews," in idem. *The Origins of Totalitarianism* (New York: Harcourt, Brace and Co., 1951), 108n.

44. Eder, 225.

45. Stefan Zweig, *The World of Yesterday: An Autobiography* (New York: Viking Press, 1945), vii.

46. Ibid., 63.

47. Schnitzler, *The Road*, 153-54. See Grunwald, *Geschichte der Wiener Juden*, 71.

48. "Semitischer Antisemitismus," *Deutsche Wochenschrift* (1885), in Kann, 250n.

49. Bein, 35.

50. Ibid., 37-39.

51. See Spitzer, vol. 5, 241: January 28, 1881. Spitzer was referring to Heinrich von Treitschke's "Unsere Aussichten"; the essay was reprinted in *Deutsche Kämpfe: Neue Folge, Schriften zur Tagespolitik* (Leipzig: S. Hirzel Verlag, 1896).

52. Bein, 37-39.

53. See Pulzer, *The Rise of Political Anti-Semitism*, 152-54.

54. Isidor Singer, *Berlin, Wien und der Anti-Semitismus* (Vienna: D. Löwy, 1882), esp. 8-9.

55. Spitzer, vol. 6, 44-47: October 15, 1882; vol. 7, 39: September 26, 1886; vol. 7, 244-45: March 24, 1889.

56. Claudio Magris, *Der habsburgische Mythos in der österreichischen Literatur*, translated from the Italian by Madeleine von Pasztory (Salzburg: Otto Müller Verlag, 1966), esp., 167-238.

57. Rosenmann, 151-61. See Joseph Samuel Bloch, *My Reminiscences*, vol. 1, trans. A. R. Smith (Vienna and Berlin: R. Löwit, 1923), 63-65.

58. Schnitzler, *The Road*, 250.

59. Herzl edited many pieces written by members of Jung-Wien for the *Neue Freie Presse*. See Harry Zohn, "Three Austrian Jews in German Literature: Schnitzler, Zweig, Herzl," in *The Jews of Austria,* ed. Fraenkel, 78. For a good discussion of the Jung-Wien circle, see Eduard Castle, "Jung-Österreich und Jung-Wien: Die neue Generation um Hermann Bahr," and Alfred Zohner, Carola Seligmann, and Eduard Castle, "Jung-Österreich und Jung-Wien: 'Café Griensteidl,' " in *Deutsche-Österreich Literaturgeschichte: Ein Handbuch zur Geschichte der deutsche Dichtung in Österreich-Ungarn von 1890 bis 1918,* ed. Eduard Castle (Vienna: Verlag Carl Fromme, 1937), vol. 4, 1649-1702, 1715-36.

60. Zweig, 43.

61. For an excellent summary of Schnitzler's works, see Friedrich Kainz, "Jung-Österreich und Jung-Wien: Arthur Schnitzler und Karl Schönherr," *Deutsch-Österreich Literaturgeschichte,* ed. Castle. See also, Magris, 202-14. On Herzl, see Bein, 46-55. On Beer-Hofmann, see Zohner, 1730-31.

62. For a concise statement of Carl Schorske's views on this period, 1880-1900, see his "The Transformation of the Garden: Ideal and Society in Austrian Literature," *American Historical Review,* 72 (July 1967), 1302-14. For his views on Schnitzler, see his "Politics and the Psyche in fin de siècle Vienna: Schnitzler and Hofmannsthal," *American Historical Review,* 66 (July 1961), 930-40. On Herzl, see his "Politics in a New Key: An Austrian Triptych [Schönerer, Lueger, Herzl]," *Journal of Modern History,* 39 (December 1967), 367-69. These articles can also be found in his *Fin-de-siècle Vienna: Politics and Culture* (New York: Alfred A. Knopf, 1980). Schorske's articles from the 1960s and 1970s have had a profound impact on European historians, compelling their reinterpretation of the most important work coming out of Habsburg Vienna. Indeed, his method of revealing the layers of historical experience below the surface of this work has stimulated my own thinking. However, by attributing solely to the political transformations in Vienna the force which propelled the creativity of Schnitzler, Herzl, Freud, and others, he overshadows the existence of other cultural forces, such as changes in Jewish life.

Also on Schnitzler, see Hans Kohn, *Karl Kraus, Arthur Schnitzler, Otto Weininger: Aus dem jüdischen Wien der Jahrhundertwende* (Tübingen: J. C. B. Mohr, 1962), 17-24. On Herzl, see also Bein, 46-58. On Beer-Hofmann, see Solomon Liptzin, *Richard Beer-Hofmann* (New York: Bloch Publishing Co., 1936); idem., "Richard Beer-Hofmann: A Biographical Essay," in *Jacob's Dream,* by Richard Beer-Hofmann (New York: Johannespresse, 1946), 1-26; and idem., "Richard Beer-Hofmann," *The Jews of Austria,* ed. Fraenkel, 213-19.

63. Zweig, 63. The texture of tension and remorse in the Jewish response to anti-Semitism came out even more clearly in some of the conversations I had in Vienna in January 1975, with Jews who had lived during this period. For example, one businessman, Benno Mautner (1892-   ), who experienced the anti-Semitism of his peers, and especially of his teachers, while attending gymnasium, vividly conveyed the pain of social ostracism.

64. *Neue Freie Presse,* March 2, 1897, cited in Schorske, "Politics and the Psyche," 932.

65. Mayer, 469-70. In a pamphlet entitled *Die soziale Frage in Wien* (1870), Mayer (1831-?1920) encouraged the leaders of the liberal government to reaffirm liberal principles by extending the franchise beyond the German middle class. See his *Ein jüdischer Kaufmann 1831-1911: Lebenserinnerungen* (Leipzig: Verlag von Duncker und Humblot, 1911), 227, 236.

66. Arthur Schnitzler, *Professor Bernhardi: Comedy in Five Acts*, trans. Hetty Landstone (New York: Simon and Schuster, 1928), 127.

67. Schnitzler, *The Road*, 250.

68. Schnitzler, *Professor Bernhardi*, 43.

69. Zweig, 22; see Magris, 15-16.

70. Schnitzler, *The Road*, 111.

71. Gold, 38; Cahnmann, 131; Nahum Sokolow, *History of Zionism 1600-1918* (London: Longmans, Green and Co., 1919), vol. 1, 197-98; Werner J. Cahnmann, "The Fighting Kadimah," *Chicago Jewish Forum*, 17 (Fall 1958), 25. See Häusler, 128. Smolenskin was elected an honorary member of Kadimah, at its first plenary session in May 1883.

72. Gold, 37.

73. Gold, 38.

74. See Cahnmann, "Adolf Fischhof," 131, and Erika Weinzerl, "Die Stellung der Juden in Österreich seit dem Staatsgrundgesetz von 1867," *Zeitschrift für die Geschichte der Juden*, 5, 2/3 (1968), 90-91. Cf. David Vital, *The Origins of Zionism* (London: Oxford University Press, 1975), 222-23.

75. Cahnmann, "The Fighting Kadimah," 25; see Tietze, 247. Pinsker published " 'Autoemanzipation' Mahnruf an seine Stammegenossen von einem russischen Juden" in 1882. Like Smolenskin, he was recognized as an honorary member of Kadimah in May 1883.

76. Cahnmann, "The Fighting Kadimah," 26.

77. Rosenmann, 215.

78. J. S. Bloch, *My Reminiscences*, 61-76, 81-84; see also Arkel, 14-27, and Tietze, 244. The journal's first issue was on October 15, 1884; on Kadimah's reception, see Cahnmann, "Adolf Fischhof," 131n.

79. J. S. Bloch, *My Reminiscences*, 188-94.

80. Joseph S. Bloch, *Israel and the Nations*, trans. Leon Kellner (Berlin, Vienna: Benjamin Herz, 1927), xiii-xiv.

81. J. S. Bloch, *My Reminiscences*, 158-59. The passages appeared in an article entitled "Der nationale Zwist und die Juden in Österreich" (1886), the title of a pamphlet Bloch published the same year.

82. A good representation of Bloch's views is found in his *Der nationale Zwist* (Vienna: Gottlieb, 1886), a compilation of several articles taken from the *Österreichische Wochenschrift*. See, e.g., January 30, 1885, 55-62 for one plea for steadfast Jewish allegiance.

83. J. S. Bloch, *Der nationale Zwist*, 43.

84. Bein, 180-81; Cahnmann, "Adolf Fischhof," 132-33; Josef Fraenkel, "Mathias Acher's Fight for the 'Crown of Zion,' " *Jewish Social Studies*, 16 (April 1954), 115-16.

85. See *Jüdisches Volksblatt*, March 23, 1900.

86. *Jüdisches Volksblatt*, April 13, 1900.

87. See Cahnmann, "Adolf Fischhof," 133-34.

88. *Jüdisches Volksblatt*, February 18, 1899, 1.

89. See Nathan Birnbaum, *Die nationale Wiedergeburt des jüdischen Volkes in seinem Lande, als Mittel zur Lösung der Judenfrage. Ein Appell an die Guten und Edlen aller Nationen* (Vienna: J. Dux, 1893), chap. 1. See also, Cahnmann, "Adolf Fischhof," 132-33.

90. Rosenmann, 169, 177; Bloch, *My Reminiscences*, 155-56, 160-61, 200-1; Tietze, 246-48.

91. Bein, 94-96.

92. Theodor Herzl, *The Jewish State: An Attempt at a Modern Solution of the Jewish Question*, rev. ed., trans. Jacob Alkow (New York: American Zionist Emergency Council, 1964), 76, 91-92, 153.

93. Ibid., 76, 153.

94. Ibid., 133.

95. J. S. Bloch often disputed Herzl's notion of the secular Jewish state. See Chaim Bloch, "Theodor Herzl and Joseph S. Bloch: An Unknown Chapter of Zionist History Based on Verbal Statements and Written Notes," in *Herzl Year Book*, 1 (1958), 154-64. Chaim Bloch, no relation to J. S., settled in Vienna after World War I and became active in Jewish affairs.

96. Herzl, *The Jewish State*, 133, 145-47; idem, *The Complete Diaries*, 247: October 20, 1895. Cf. Schorske, "Politics in a New Key," 365-86.

97. Karl Kraus, *Eine Krone für Zion* (Vienna: Verlag von Moriz Frisch, 1898). In *The Road to the Open*, Schnitzler wrote, in reference to Zionism, "I don't think for a minute that migrations like that into the open should be gone in for in parties. . . . It was only the home, not the fatherland which had any real significance" (252, 109). Zweig maintained that he "only approached [Zionism] curiously for Herzl's sake," since Herzl was the first to recognize publicly his youthful literary merits. Zweig, 105-9.

98. Herzl, *The Jewish State*, 74-75, 77.

99. Herzl, *The Complete Diaries*, 5; Bein, 112.

100. Cited by Bein, 186-87, and by Herzl, *The Complete Diaries*, 318: April 9, 1896.

101. Schnitzler, *The Road*, 110; Ernst Simon, "Sigmund Freud, the Jew," in *The Leo Baeck Institute Yearbook*, 2 (1957), 274.

102. *Jahresbericht der Jüdisch-akademischen Lesehalle in Wien, über das Vereinsjahr 1897* (Vienna: Verlag der Jüdisch-akademischen Lesehalle, 1897), 3-4, 14-15; *Statuten der Jüdisch-akademischen Lesehalle in Wien* (Vienna: Bergmann, 1896).

103. *Jahres-Bericht der Lese- und Redehalle jüdischer Hochschüler in Wien, über das Vereinsjahr 1904* (Vienna: Verlag der Lese- und Redehalle jüdischer Hochschüler, 1905), 50-53; *über das Vereinsjahr 1906/1907* (1907), 1, 28; *Jüdisches Volksblatt*, October 19, 1900, 4-5, and March 1, 1901, 5.

104. The event was reported in the *Jüdisches Volksblatt*, January 31, 1902, 2; February 7, 1902, 4, 6.

105. Zweig, 20-24.

106. See Hans Kohn, "Eros and Sorrow: Notes on the Life and Work of Arthur Schnitzler and Otto Weininger," in *The Leo Baeck Institute Yearbook*, 6 (1961), 156-62.

107. This was Schorske's conclusion: Schnitzler "could not create a new faith." Schorske, "Politics and the Psyche," 940.

108. Magris, 338, n. 99; Kainz, 1755.

109. Schnitzler, *Professor Bernhardi*, 132-34, 158.

110. Schnitzler, *The Road*, 78, 154, 280. See, e.g., 187, for Schnitzler's mercilessly critical characterization of the assimilant Jew.

111. Schnitzler, *The Road*, 99, 252; see Schnitzler, *Professor Bernhardi*, 132-33.

112. Schnitzler, *Professor Bernhardi*, 71. The parallel between Schnitzler and Freud is striking. In 1897, Freud maintained that the minister of education in Vienna rejected his appointment to a full professorship on the basis of "denominational considerations." Freud, *The Interpretation of Dreams*, 170.

113. Schnitzler, *Professor Bernhardi*, 134.

114. Schnitzler, *The Road*, 251.

115. Schnitzler, *Professor Bernhardi*, 160.

116. See Zohn, 173.

117. Herzl, *The Jewish State*, 92.

118. Herzl, *The Complete Diaries*, vol. 1, 105: June 16, 1895.

119. Herzl, *The Jewish State*, 157. While writing the outline of this appeal, Herzl noted, in his diaries, that the ideas he was formulating should be a treasure "of all mankind, not merely the Jews." Moments later, he added, "Today the thought arises in me that I may be solving much more than the Jewish Question. Namely, *tout bonnement*, the social question!" Herzl, *The Complete Diaries*, 94, 96: June 12, 1895.

120. Zweig, 23.

121. Solomon Liptzin, *Germany's Stepchildren* (Philadelphia: The Jewish Publication Society of America, 1944), 270.

122. Wassermann, 187.

123. As Hans Kohn remarked, "One cannot speak of Vienna at the turn of the century, and the position of the Jews there, without stressing that they all were influenced and afflicted by national and racial thinking, for this kind of thinking prevailed at the time in Central Europe and especially in Vienna." *Aus dem jüdischen Wien*, 69.

124. Theodor Lessing, *Der jüdische Selbsthass* (Berlin: Zionistischer Bücher-Bund, 1930).

125. Kraus, *Eine Krone für Zion*; Otto Weininger, *Sex and Character* (London: William Heinemann, 1906), 302-30.

126. Karl Kraus, "Er ist doch e Jud," in *Untergang der Welt durch schwarze Magie,* vol. 8 of *Werke von Karl Kraus,* ed. Heinrich Fischer (Munich: Kösel-Verlag, 1960), 331-38. Cf. the poem "Gebet an die Sonne von Gibeon," in *Worte in Verse,* vol. 7, ibid., 109-14, in which Kraus discussed the Jewish worship of false gods. Kraus's view of Jewish existence, and Weininger's, which follows, are important for correcting common misconceptions about Jewish dependence on German culture about 1900. Though many borrowed from Germans an anti-Jewish rhetoric and, at times, a national consciousness, Jews rarely, if ever, felt what Germans felt when expressing Jewish hostility or national superiority. In light of Kraus's sympathetic reprimand of his Jewish contemporaries, it is untenable and misleading to magnify the self-reproach of Jews into "Jewish anti-Semitism." See Lessing, and Gay, 189-230, for a discussion of the limited dependence of Jews on German culture.

127. Weininger, 302-3, 327-28.

128. Hans Kohn, "Das kulturelle Problem des modernen Westjuden," *Der Jude,* 5 (August/September 1920), 288n. Kohn referred only to Weininger, though the remark applies to Kraus as well. Search for the *Urjudentum,* moreover, describes a parallel interest among Jewish theologians, about 1900, in determining the "essence of Judaism." The interest was in part a response to contemporary developments in liberal Christian theology, and in part a reflection of long-term developments in Reform Judaism. Rank searched for a positive, nontheological essence in his Jewish heritage.

129. Kraus, *Eine Krone für Zion*, 23-24.

130. Fifteen years later, Kraus welcomed Jewish nationalism as a means of escape from the "pseudonymous culture" that surrounded and suffocated the Jewish people. See Karl Kraus, "Pro Domo et Mundo," in *Beim Wort Genommen,* vol. 3 of *Werke von Karl Kraus,* ed. Heinrich Fischer (Munich: Kösel-Verlag, 1955), 38.

131. Weininger, 312, 326-29.

132. David Abrahamson, *The Mind and Death of a Genius* (New York: Columbia University Press, 1946), 97; Weininger, 330; idem., *Über die letzten Dinge,* ed. Moriz Rappaport (Vienna, Leipzig: Wilhelm Braumüller, 1912), 65. This last volume, a collection of essays, discourses, and aphorisms, was first published in 1904, shortly after Weininger's death.

133. Ibid., 140-41.

134. Herzl, *The Complete Diaries,* 96: June 12, 1895; 101: June 14, 1895.

135. Richard Beer-Hofmann, *Der Tod Georgs,* in *Gesammelte Werke,* ed. Otto Kallir (Frankfurt a/M: S. Fischer Verlag, 1963), 616, 621-22.

136. See Martin Buber, "Geleitwort," in ibid., 5-12.

137. Beer-Hofmann, "Jaákobs Traum," in *Gesammelte Werke,* 77, 83.

138. Sigmund Freud, *Letters of Sigmund Freud,* ed. Ernst L. Freud; trans. Tania and James Stern (London: The Hogarth Press, 1961), 367: May 6, 1926.

2

FREUD AND
THE PSYCHOLOGY OF MOVEMENT

Early in the morning, on September 14, 1883, three of Freud's medical colleagues came into his room at Vienna's General Hospital to announce the shocking suicide of his friend Nathan Weiss. "We just could not believe it," he wrote his fiancée, two days later. "It was too difficult to conceive of a man who combined in himself more restlessness and zest for life than we had seen in anyone else, as dead and silent. Even now, though I have just heard the thud of the earth on his coffin, I cannot get used to the thought."[1] Although he did not want to spoil the monthly anniversary of the day they became engaged (June 17, 1882), he could not conceal from Martha Bernays (1861-1951) the deep agony caused by the loss of his companion. Having duly apologized, Freud proceeded to write a 3,500-word analysis of Weiss's suicide. It is one of the earliest, and among the most searching, analyses Freud ever wrote.

More than just an expression of grief, the letter allowed Freud to examine some disturbing questions: "Why did he do it?" "What drove him to it?" Why, he wondered, would someone with such an "extraordinary appetite for life" wish to hang himself? The letter appeared at a time of reassessment in Freud's life. While still training as a medical intern, Freud began to reexamine the relationship between the individual and authority, as well as the reactions of the individual to authority — concerns which were to occupy him for the remainder of his life. Perplexed by the apparent contradiction between Weiss's zest for life and his desire to kill himself, Freud wondered if his friend's drive for success and for acceptance was ultimately self-destructive. Incipient doubt about the value of such ambition (which he later termed a compulsive neurosis) and about the demands of society dominated his thoughts. In short, by the questions it raised and by the deeper understanding it achieved, the letter illustrates Freud's growing disaffection with the drive to satisfy worldly expectations. His reflections on Weiss revealed something even more specific about this shift in stress from social demands to individual need. Referring to Weiss as a Jew, Freud indicated a sensitivity to the problems of Jewish assimilation as well.

Just as he later attributed significance to the role of the father in neurogenesis, Freud's first step in the analysis of Weiss was a discussion of Weiss's father. The latter was a vain and endlessly demanding man, and, according to Freud, this aroused in Nathan an "incessant restlessness," as well as a "one-sided" preoccupation with success. Freud noted that Weiss indeed had few friends, was selfish, and was exceedingly ruthless. Despite "his inborn good nature," he could not enjoy "human and natural things." Even in his one serious excursion into romance, Weiss "believed that he could force love as he had forced all his other successes." Freud remarked that Weiss's compulsive drive allowed no room for sentiment or affection: "Influenced perhaps by the happiness of lovers around him, he tried and tried and allowed no time to let it come his way." Weiss's rejection by the girl in the affair only drove him to final despair: "He sacrificed everything recklessly with the single object of not having to face the world as a failure. . . . A false shame prevented him from letting the world know that he had been rejected."

Weiss's self-destructive drive for success in the affair bothered Freud even as his friend courted the girl. He warned him "to give her time and not press her too much." Unable to persuade Weiss, Freud tried to understand him by discussing the situation with his closest friend, Josef Breuer (1842-1925). Freud was impressed by Breuer's insight. He noted that Weiss's behavior reminded Breuer "of the story of the old Jew, who asks his son: 'My son, what do you want to be?' And the son answers: 'Vitriol, the stuff that eats its way through everything.' " With this Jewish reference, Freud appreciated more completely Weiss's compulsive behavior. He believed it was an appropriate description of the fatal drive for worldly acceptance. To Freud, the father-son relationship immediately and unmistakably provoked Weiss's inner conflict between external demands and his internal good nature. The conflict took on more meaning when Freud realized that Weiss's drive was the incessant drive of the Jew who, at his father's bidding, endeavored to please the world.

The criticism of assimilation in this letter was modified by the implicit suggestion that, had Weiss been true to his own good nature, rather than to the false standards of his world, he would have been spared the fate of inner turmoil. Indeed, though by implication only, this letter represents one of Freud's earliest acknowledgments of the value of Jewish self-assertion. However, compared with his later letters affirming his Jewish pride, his Weiss letter is more firmly rooted in the past, for Freud had not yet completely overcome his inclination to assimilate. Having grown up in the tolerant atmosphere of political liberalism in the 1860s and 1870s, Freud, like other contemporary German Jews, tried to maintain congenial relations with non-Jews even when racial anti-Semitism intensified at the beginning of the following decade. Just after describing the shame Weiss felt before the judgment of the world as "false," Freud expressed to Martha the same Jewish fear of social rejection. He could not endure the embarrassment he felt at the funeral when Weiss's family and friends bitterly blamed the girl's family for the suicide: "We were all petrified with horror and shame in the presence of the Christians who were among us. It seemed as though we had given them reason to believe that we worship the God of Revenge, not the God of Love." More than a reflection on Weiss, the letter, written just after this personal experience of shame, was a self-reflection on the social pressures Freud himself felt. The letter is evidence of the intensity of Freud's Jewish assimilation during the liberal era in Austria, as well as of his first doubts about assimilation in the early 1880s.

GODLESS, BUT ETHICAL – AND GERMAN

Freud's childhood home was typical of Jewish families in liberal Austria adjusting to the prevailing influences of secular life. Having come from the Jewish pale of East Galicia, his parents were familiar with Jewish law and customs – Jacob (1815-96), with nascent Chasidism, and Amalia (née Nathonssohn, 1835-1930), with Orthodox Judaism.[2] While these backgrounds must have directly affected the education of their children, the westward migrations of the Freud and Nathonssohn families, both by 1848, and Jacob's exposure to the influences of the cosmopolitan traditions of the Haskalah in his travels as a merchant, mitigated any rigid or comprehensive adherence to Jewish ritual.[3] As Sigmund Freud noted, already a decade before coming to Moravia to establish a business there, his father "had been estranged from his native [Chasidic] environment."[4] Amalia Nathonssohn tended to leave Jewish orthodoxy behind her as well. Assimilating to the cosmopolitan culture of Vienna, the family spoke German and ignored such observances as kashrut and the Sabbath. What religion remained in the home was an observance of the major Jewish holidays – the High Holy days, Passover, and Purim – and Jacob's adept reading of the Talmud (probably in Hebrew), as well as his Hebrew recitation of the Passover service.[5]

The latter point is noteworthy because Jacob Freud was Sigmund's first and exclusive teacher until he entered gymnasium in 1865.[6] Through his father, Freud took an early and immediate interest in the Bible.[7] At gymnasium, Freud's interest in Judaism continued to grow, largely because of the influence of his instructor in Jewish religion, Samuel Hammerschlag (?-1904). As Freud recalled in the obituary he wrote for his instructor, Hammerschlag "was one of the personalities who possess the gift of leaving ineradicable impressions on the development of their pupils."[8] Freud took courses from Hammerschlag at least during his last two years of gymnasium (1871-73), and possibly as early as 1865, when he entered school.[9] He praised Hammerschlag for his inspired teaching and warm rapport with students: "From the material of Jewish history, he was able to find means of tapping the sources of enthusiasm hidden in the hearts of young people." In a special pamphlet issued in 1869, as director of the school of religion of the Viennese Jewish community, Hammerschlag expressed a strong interest in inciting "the sensitive mind and feelings of youth." He argued that, just as the descriptions of the heroic age of classical antiquity have excited the imagination of youth, so too "the image of [biblical] heroism represents the spiritual and moral deed and consequently provides an occasion for inflaming and inciting [students] to the accomplishments of truly great men."[10]

Freud recalled, with appreciation, Hammerschlag's use of the sources of classical antiquity as models of instruction, as well as his effort at educating students "toward the love of the humanities." He believed his instructor's emphasis on the humanities reflected "the ideal of humanism of our German classical period which governed him." Indeed, Hammerschlag was sensitive to the liberal currents of the constitutional era. Like his contemporary, Adolf Jellinek, he tried to show how Judaism contributed to the ideals of modern society.[11] He believed that the Old Testament, "the Jewish point of view," was "the root and origin of the theory of the free, autonomous personality and the innate rights of man." The Old Testament was an inspiration for the modern day as well, he said, for "even in our own progressive time, [human rights have] not been fully realized." According to Hammerschlag, humanitarian ideals were central to Jewish teaching: "It was one of our prophets who first fashioned the ideas of a moral world order for the exercise of power." Moreover, the laws are "infused with such selfless love and most tender regard for the fellow man." Like Jellinek, Hammerschlag tried to show how Judaism realized "recent endeavors towards progress and the ideas of humanity." He argued that the particular features of Judaism, "the unique, spirited characteristics that ethnic origin, language, or religion have bestowed upon a particular group," were meaningless if they did not refer to the universal truths of mankind. "The cultivation of [the group's] own bias and strengths [is only the] . . . means to achieve in its own way the ultimate goal common to all — that is, the highest form of cultural and spiritual understanding. . . . The specific capacities and spiritual possessions with which nature or the course of history endowed each individual group of mankind — whether its character is national or religious — are at the same time means to fulfill through their development and perfection its part of the obligation in the common work of the whole. Attention to the whole is the highest task of the group."[12]

In recalling his instructor's accomplishments, Freud neglected to mention the attention Hammerschlag paid to the unique characteristics of Judaism. The stress Hammerschlag placed on the Hebrew language, for example, little affected this student.[13] Instead, Freud was grateful for his instructor's ability to present the material of Jewish history in such a way as to inspire his students "beyond the limitations of [narrow] nationalism and dogma."

In the years following his studies with Hammerschlag, Freud adhered to the ethical view of the Bible, as well as to the humanistic conception of religion. He expressed this discreet religious appreciation in a letter sent to Martha in 1882.[14] When he was visiting his fiancée at her home near Hamburg, early in the summer of that year, Freud had met an old Jewish engraver, whom he grew to like. He had the same first name as Freud's fated friend Weiss, but to Freud, that "jovial old gentleman" reminded him more of another Nathan, the title character in the play *Nathan the Wise,* by the German dramatist Lessing. Freud borrowed from the play a passage to introduce his engraver-friend to Martha: "The Jew is called Nathan (a strange Jew – h'm!). Continue worthy Nathan. . . ." The discussion between Freud and the engraver touched on several topics about Jewish law, and was characterized by the attempts the old Jew made "to explain and support the scriptures." Freud would not be convinced. "The Holy Scriptures' claim to truth and obedience could not be supported" by any method, he felt. But Freud was impressed with the way the gentleman approached the Bible: "Traits of Nathan the Wise now began to appear in what he said." Freud learned that the old engraver had adopted this approach from that of his master, Isaac Bernays, once the chief rabbi of Hamburg and – unknown to the engraver – paternal grandfather of Freud's fiancée. As Freud commented, in his letter to Martha, this method of teaching was inspired by "great imagination and humaneness. . . ." He continued:

> If someone just refused to believe anything – well, then there was nothing to be done about him; but if someone demanded a reason for this or that which was looked upon as absurd, then he would step outside the law and justify it for the unbeliever from there. . . . Religion was no longer treated as a rigid dogma; it became an object of reflection for the satisfaction of cultivated artistic taste and of intensified logical efforts, and the teacher of Hamburg recommended it finally not because it happened to exist and had been declared holy, but because he was pleased by the deeper meaning which he found in it or which he projected into it.

Like his admiration for Hammerschlag, Freud's interest in this method of teaching shows the influence of liberalism on his grasp of Judaism. He found Jewish teaching inspiring when "traits of Nathan the Wise began to appear," that is, when Judaism supported or enhanced Enlightenment ideals. The religion appealed to Freud when it taught the love of humanity or fostered unity and freedom among fellow men. Similarly, the Bible inspired Freud as an aesthetic or rational document. In the course of his life, Freud freely used biblical images and passages, as is evident in *The Interpretation of Dreams* and in many of his letters, where he unwittingly integrated some passages into his stream of thought.[15]

However, Freud's Judaism was more liberal than the Judaism of his teachers. Though his father and Hammerschlag responded to the attractive atmosphere of toleration, both tended to remain faithful to the tradition and ritual of Judaism, as well as to the Hebrew language. To Freud, observance of the ancient customs interfered with a direct and complete affirmation of liberal ideals. By the end of his first year in medical school (1874), he was hopelessly skeptical of the authority or "dogma" of scripture, and had repudiated the metaphysical as well as the ritualistic dimensions of religion. Writing to his friend Eduard Silberstein (1857-1925) in 1874, he disagreed with some who felt "that everything considered immoral according to the letter of the bourgeois and Mosaic law is also unpoetic." On the contrary, "it is quite possible that poetry, supported by the force of passion, could idealize and lend an aspect of beauty to things 'immoral,' or rather those which society deems unpermissible." As he renounced the prescribed codes of Jewish religion, he rejected the equally insupportable notion of a divinity. He admitted that as an "empirically-minded man of medicine," he was "godless."[16] He preferred to "gain insight into the age-old dossiers of nature, perhaps even eavesdrop on her eternal processes," as a natural scientist, rather than rely on the "workings of divine power," which were, at any rate, "inscrutable."[17]

Freud refused to observe the Jewish holidays that his father held sacred. In an unpublished letter written to his friend Silberstein in September 1874, just weeks before declaring to him his skepticism about the existence of God, Freud conveyed his remoteness from Jewish ritual observance by blithely mocking it: "Religion is often unjustly accused" of being "too metaphysical" and not accessible enough to the senses. He believed it is "intimately related to the senses," and especially to the stomach. The Passover meal, for example, "causes constipation." Yom Kippur is such a "dreary day," not because of "God's wrath," but because of the plum preserves which are unpleasant to eat. He knew when the day was "drawing nigh," by the presence of a goose and two fish in his home. And he concluded:

> Our festivals have outlived our dogma, like the funeral meal has outlived the dead. . . . [When] we children of the world [eat], we no longer think, like the pious, that we have done a good deed; rather, we are simply conscious of having a good dish.[18]

Writing to a friend four days after Purim in 1873, he vividly described a lady from his neighborhood who "drilled" him and others as actors and actresses for the traditional festive theater performance, thus "forcing" them to earn the holiday meal, "well-known to be not among the worst."[19]

During these adolescent years, that is, between the ages of 13 and 18, Freud took steps toward abandoning the Jewish culture of his home life as well as the traditions and customs of religion. The rejection of all traces of traditional Judaism makes clear Freud's desire to surrender his Jewish heritage to the dominant liberal ideals of human freedom and social rationality. Just before the start of his final year at gymnasium (September 1872), Freud visited his birthplace and stayed with friends of his parents, the Fluss family. It was the first time he had visited Freiberg since his family moved in 1859, when Freud was three. Though a "sentimental" trip for Freud,[20] the visit made one uncomfortable aspect of his life quite vivid: Like the Leopoldstadt, where he lived, the region of Moravia in which Freiberg is located contained many unassimilated, provincial Jews. On the journey home, he met one such family. As he wrote to his new friend Emil Fluss, he found their company "unpalatable" and was irritated by the father:

> Now this Jew talked the same way as I had heard thousands of others talk before, even in Freiberg. His face seemed familiar — he was typical. So was the boy with whom he discussed religion. He was cut from the cloth from which fate makes swindlers when the time is ripe: cunning, mendacious, kept by his adoring relatives in the belief that he is a great talent, but unprincipled and without character. I have enough of this rabble.[21]

The language Freud used was extreme, and more emotional than his cynical pokes at ritual observance or religious piety. He had to resort to a stronger means of protest because of his proximity to provincial Jewry. Not only did he live in the Viennese district to which thousands of Jews from East Europe had migrated, but, as the trip brought to mind, Freud himself — the son of Galician parents — had East-European roots. His expression of contempt for the unassimilated indicated a strong desire to break away from this heritage.

The direction of his assimilation became apparent a few years earlier when, in 1869 or 1870, he decided to change his first name on the records of his gymnasium.[22] At this time, Freud formally adopted the name "Sigmund," a German variation of the name "Sigismund," given to him by his father. Jacob named his son after the sixteenth-century Polish monarch, whom he admired for his policy of toleration toward Jews.[23] The decision to change the name was in part a reaction to the increase in anti-Semitic sentiment at the end of the 1860s, for the name "Sigismund" gained currency as a favorite term of abuse in anti-Semitic jokes.[24] By replacing his given name with a Germanic-sounding name, Freud severed this important link with his Jewish background to identify more closely with the progressive German-liberal culture.

The intensity of Freud's desire to be assimilated at this time is illustrated by his efforts at introducing some of his Jewish classmates to German culture. In the higher classes, Freud met, and soon drew close to, a boy three years his senior, who had left his home in Moravia to attend school in Vienna. In 1870, Wilhelm Knöpfmacher (1853-1937) enrolled at Freud's gymnasium. As is known from the current scholarship, Knöpfmacher worked closely with Freud on the Matura (gymnasium-leaving exam) and remained in contact with him, at least until 1878. He came from Nikolsburg, a small town distinguished by its autonomous Jewish community. In a "Purimstück" written just two years before coming to Vienna, Knöpfmacher had defended traditional Judaism and the idiomatic "alt-Nikolsburger-Jüdisch-Deutsch" against new forms of religious life and the more respectable Hochdeutsch. As Knöpfmacher recalled to a friend, years later, Freud disliked these habits he had brought to Vienna. In his gradual surrender of this traditional past, in favor of the spiritual persuasions of the literary and social life of Vienna, he regarded Freud as an early and essential influence.[25]

To Freud, Jewish traditions were conspicuously anachronistic in an era of democratic reform. At times, his enthusiasm for the German advancement overwhelmed even the appreciation he had for humanistic Judaism. In response to a sad letter from Fluss in the summer of 1873, Freud complained, why couldn't they be "journeymen imbued with Christian-German fervor," instead of sentimental, "prosaic" Jews who find it difficult to leave their commonly esteemed Freiberg.[26] A few months later, upon entering the medical school at the University of Vienna, Freud took a step in this direction when he decided to join the radical German student society, the *Leseverein der deutschen Studenten Wiens*. His affiliation with the organization lasted until 1878, when it was dissolved by the government.

From its start in 1871, the society regarded itself as the representative of German interests at the university.[27] It advocated a political and economic alliance between Germany and Austria-Hungary. This meant an endorsement of German policies that extended the franchise and guaranteed civil liberties. In the course of the decade, and especially after the economic crash of May 1873, which confirmed for many the complete bankruptcy of the laissez faire order, the organization became more militant, and its appeal even more radical. During the following five years, which coincided with Freud's affiliation, the Leseverein denounced laissez faire social policy as competitive, materialistic, and divisive. At the same time, the society affirmed a return to nature. It strived to recover the elemental, emotional, and passionate qualities of life, as well as the organic and collective impulses of social existence. Concisely stated, the society advocated the "common national interest" over "personal and specific interests."[28]

Several of Freud's letters dating from this period, which indicated the direction of his political interests, show that his views corresponded with the ideas of the German-nationalist movement. Like the society, Freud examined the alternatives to the laissez faire order, declaring in a letter to Silberstein, in March 1875, his sympathy with the vision that sought to "improve institutions, such as education, the distribution of goods, the modes of 'struggle for existence,' and so forth." But Freud remained in the background of active political reform, for, while he explained that he was "not against socialist tendencies," he doubted the practicality of the socialist alternative. Freud also appeared sympathetic with the society's search for a less restrictive, more natural basis for social existence. As he wrote Silberstein, within a week of his letter on socialism, by going "through passion," man can "lose himself in wild sentiments, even . . . free himself from the restraint imposed by morality."[29]

Embracing the ideals of equality, humanity, and individual freedom, Freud's assimilation was positive and hopeful. Moreover, in the Leseverein, he found a forum for his germinating ideas. A fellow member of the radical German student society, Solomon Ehrmann (1854-1926), offered another perspective of the assimilation of German Jews during this period of progress and optimism. Ehrmann was a student at the medical school, where he and Freud became friends in the fall of 1874.[30] He noted, "We abandoned the altars upon which our fathers served and offered ourselves — in common with our fellow man of a different confession — to what was allegedly new, because we were told that now a new ideal, the ideal of humanity, the fraternization of mankind, was to be worshiped." Though he rejected religious worship for the new ideal of brotherhood and social equality, Ehrmann did not abandon Judaism altogether. While advocating the superiority of the collective whole, he adhered to the humanism in Jewish teaching. He believed the Jews always have supported humanitarian ideals.[31] Like Ehrmann, Freud accepted Judaism only in its most modern, ethical form. Humanistic Judaism complemented German liberalism, engendering the belief in the peaceful coexistence between Jews and other religious or national groups. Like his contemporary German Jews, Freud had "cheerful hopes" for social integration.[32]

ENCOUNTER WITH ANTI-SEMITISM

With the emergence of the anti-Semitic movement in Vienna, the assimilation of Freud and other Jews could never be done with entire confidence. They were anxiously aware of how its development theatened and dampened the prospects of peaceful social coexistence. Though the movement did not become systematic and widespread — indeed racial — until the 1880s, forms of economic and political discrimination against the most conspicuous pariah segment of Viennese Jewry had gained momentum at the end of the 1860s. Attacks against Hungarian and Galician Jews had the effect of disturbing the relations between Germans and German Jews as well. Living until 1882 in the Leopoldstadt, where almost all *Ostjuden* settled, Freud was particularly exposed to the sudden rise of anti-Jewish sentiment. At the Sperl Gymnasium, which opened in 1864 to absorb the growing population, Freud experienced more directly the influx of Jews. During his first four years (1865-69), the number of Jews attending the school increased from 68 to 227, jumping from 44 to 63 percent of the school's total enrollment. By the time Freud graduated in 1873, 300 Jews made up nearly three-fourths (73 percent) of the school's enrollment.[33] Thus, Freud had the occasion to observe the precipitous reaction against Jews: "In the higher classes I began to understand for the first time what it meant to belong to an alien race, and anti-Semitic feelings among the other boys warned me that I must take up a definite position."[34]

Freud's association with Jews from the East, Jews who disrupted Jewish/ non-Jewish relations and threatened to subvert the assimilation of German Jews, no doubt contributed to his vehement contempt for provincial Jewry. Indeed, one reason he dropped the name "Sigismund" was to sever his connection with the victims of cultural anti-Semitism. While still a student at gymnasium, then, Freud broke away from his East-European heritage in part to avert any association with an "alien race."

When Freud enrolled at the medical school of the University of Vienna in the fall of 1873, he found tensions between Jews and non-Jews there as well. In progressive student circles, only the Jew of German origin was acceptable. Already in 1867, the emphatically German-nationalist Burschenschaft Olympia discriminated against East-European Jews. As a contemporary member perceived the situation, the student club began to doubt the German quality of Jews.[35] Anti-Semitism against Jews from Hungary and Galicia was especially pronounced at the medical school. The reason for this was the increased demand for the limited number of positions at the school, and the subsequent intensification of the competitive atmosphere. Many students argued that Jews from the hinterland came to Vienna with far less preparation than Germans had to pursue the same medical education.[36] Moreover, Jews appeared predatory in the pursuit of their education. Indeed, they held a disproportionate number of positions at the medical school – 38.6 percent of the total student enrollment in 1880.[37] Though German Jews who attended the university at the beginning of the 1870s were regarded, according to one observer, "as perfect equal[s] . . . and were valued as friends" – even in the staunchest pro-German nationalist student societies[38] – Jewish students from the East and the West felt the pressure of proving their allegiance to the German national culture. Freud felt this pressure the moment he became a student: "When, in 1873, I first joined the University, I experienced some appreciable disappointments. Above all, I found that I was expected to feel myself inferior and an alien because I was a Jew."[39]

The pressure of disgrace by association with East-European Jews was aggravated by Freud's sensitivity to his personal image. According to Heinrich Braun (1854-1927), his closest friend at gymnasium, and later a prominent socialist politician, Freud was deeply self-conscious, and unsure of himself, and especially sensitive to social rejection.[40] The insight illuminates the emotional intensity behind Freud's bitterness and embarrassment over provincial Jews, and behind the endeavor to separate himself and at least one companion from them. This aggressive escape from the unpopular, indeed alienating, image of East-European Jewry as well as the deeper pain of rejection and exclusion reveals just how strong Freud's early assimilationist hopes were, hopes which had found expression in his sympathy for humanistic Judaism and German nationalism.

Freud's sensitivity to social rejection is one explanation for his vulnerability to the anti-Semitic movement. The other basic reason for it was his firm liberal commitment to social integration. Anti-Semitism frustrated both his need to belong and his desire for social reform. This desire for reform was not merely a by-product of his adolescent search for acceptance. Freud's hope for social coexistence satisfied separate and equally intense needs. In his letters to Fluss, the independent intensity of his ideological beliefs is clearly perceptible. These letters show that Freud enjoyed Fluss's esteem. He never had to prove himself to his close, trustworthy friend. Thus, Freud's protest against the indecent character of East-European Jews was not motivated by the desire to convince his friend that he, unlike them, was decent. Provincial customs and ritualistic behavior were, like political privilege, social stratification, and special economic interests, anathema to Freud's universalist sensibility. Combined with the psychological longing to belong, his ideological attachment to liberal ideals built up in him a strong desire to assimilate, which broke down that much more painfully when he experienced anti-Semitic hostilities.

Although German Jews escaped the discriminatory effects of cultural anti-Semitism in the early 1870s, tolerance of German Jews was severely eroded near the end of Freud's affiliation with the student society. In 1875, a crisis erupted in response to a seven-page passage that Theodor Billroth (1829-94), an eminent Viennese medical professor and surgeon, published as part of a lengthy examination of medical education at German universities.[41] In this passage, Billroth — a member of the teaching faculty in Vienna since 1867 — openly challenged the legitimacy of accepting Jews from Hungary and Galicia at the Viennese Medical School. Arguing against the policy of open admission for citizens of the state, and thus arguing from a position of reasonableness, Billroth explained that these impoverished Jews were "for the most part lacking the talent for the natural sciences, and . . . absolutely unsuitable to become physicians." This was true because the immigrant Jew never had an exposure to a good preparatory education or to a stimulating culture. Nor, he argued, would the Jew be able to overcome this cultural and educational limitation. Once he came to Vienna, the struggle for subsistence would deprive him of the time to study and would make it difficult for him to become a part of the general culture. He claimed that this situation threatened the high standards of the Vienna Medical School, since backward, ignorant, starving students could only become backward, ignorant, starving physicians.[42]

Billroth's suggestion that a numerus clausus be imposed on Jews from the eastern part of the empire probably marked the first time anyone proposed a definitive and institutionalized solution to the Jewish-immigrant problem. The cogency of his argument alone mobilized the discontented among the student body. But it was his elaborate footnote to this argument that generated deeper, more emotional feelings. He explained that his views of the relevant problems were based on personal feelings and observations, as well as on reasoned thought: "I do not wish to be connected with the fashionable abuses against

Jews which now appear so popular, and thus will not restrain myself from a discussion of my experiences in relation to this issue [of open admission]." Billroth acknowledged that there were many Jews who had achieved the highest professional success, "for the important men among the Jews are for the most part visionaries, idealists, humanists." Yet it was a different situation when those without talent aspired toward the same goals. He said, "To begin a [medical] career with insufficient means and with unfounded optimism as well as with unrealistic confidence in luck and raw energy is a specifically Jewish characteristic." As a supporting member of the Leseverein, Billroth relied heavily on nationalistic rhetoric to bring his thoughts on "the Jews in the German universities" to a close:

> It is often forgotten that the Jews are a well-defined nation and that a Jew — just as little as a Persian, Frenchman, New Zealander or African — can never become a German. Whatever is meant by Jewish German, it is only coincidental that they are speaking German, only coincidental that they are educated in Germany. . . . They lose their [Jewish] national tradition just as little as the Germans lose their German manner no matter where they live. . . . It is thus neither expected nor desirable that the Jews ever become German-nationalists or participate in the national struggles like the Germans themselves. Above all, they cannot possibly be sensitive to the accumulated influence of medieval romanticism, upon which our German sensibilities — more than we want to admit — are based; for, the Jews, have no occasion to ponder with special delight the German middle ages. . . . It is certainly clear to me that, in spite of all reflection and individual sympathy, I deeply feel the cleavage between pure German and pure Jewish blood.[43]

Under different circumstances, an argument against the policy of open admission would not have had to go beyond the problems of insufficient academic preparation and financial support; but, because circumstances had already defined the problems in cultural terms, Billroth directed his argument against the culturally deprived immigrant Jews.

The argument indeed shifted the focus of public concern from the cultural problems of the immigrant to a Jewish problem. Whatever genuine concern Billroth might have had for the plight of immigrant Jews,[44] and however carefully he attempted in the text to isolate Galician and Hungarian Jews as the source of the problem, his broad nationalistic claim that Jews were distinct from Germans, and thus incapable of becoming German, unleashed a racially anti-Semitic response. On the tenth of December, 1875, just days after the release of Billroth's book, racial slurs, taken directly from the book, and the resounding cry "Juden hinaus!" could be heard throughout the medical school. In his class that day, there ensued a clash between Jews demonstrating against Billroth and the German-nationalist counterdemonstrators. Jewish demonstrators were eventually overpowered and thrown out of the class. For a week thereafter, clashes continued in other classes of the medical school and on the pages of the press.[45]

Though Billroth later regretted the "racial hatred" his statement generated,[46] the damage was already done. The mounting indignation among students against Jewish "intruders" from the East had spread quickly into indiscriminate attacks against Jews as a people. This placed German Jews like Freud and other Jewish members of the Leseverein in a most perilous position. Never before had the German quality of Western Jews been so openly and widely challenged. Indeed, Jews whose backgrounds were not clearly German, if they were to escape anti-Semitic attacks, were now faced with an even greater task of proving their German allegiance.

The response that Victor Adler (1852-1918) issued in regard to the Billroth affair illustrates the inner conflict of German Jews who were active in the German-nationalist movement. Shortly after the anti-Semitic response reached its crescendo, Adler prepared a statement defending his German identity. As a member and leader of the Leseverein, he probably delivered it to the society. He agreed with Billroth that Jews had not participated in German life for centuries. But he believed this situation was changing. Already, two generations of Jews had been under the influence of German culture. Unlike their ancestors, they were quite familiar with the national traditions. Refuting Billroth's conclusion that Jews could not fight German-nationalist struggles, Adler stressed that the recent Jewish involvement in the German-nationalist movement had brought Jews closer to the German nation. He said the blood shed in this effort "forms a bond which ties the next generation of Jews even closer to the German nation." Germans could thus expect a growing German-Jewish alliance. They should even desire it, for the Jews "are an important factor in the cultural development of the [German] nation."[47]

Adler endeavored to reaffirm the differences between Jewish immigrants from the East, whose culture had been distinct from German culture for centuries, and Western Jews, who had lived at least under the influence of German culture for some two generations. Once he made the distinction, he went about proving his loyalty to German nationalism. The situation called for nothing less. His appeal reflected the general response of the Leseverein and of its many Jewish members to the demonstrations and counterdemonstrations incited by Billroth's book. The executive committee, on which Adler sat, published a resolution disapproving the Jewish agitation against Billroth. Moreover, the society's membership overwhelmingly decided to publish its support of Billroth — an unqualified statement of praise for his struggle on behalf of German nationalism.[48]

The indications that Freud took a position similar to Adler's are strong. They shared an uncomfortable association with East-European Jewry, since they both lived in the Leopoldstadt ghetto and had parents who had come from traditional Jewish environments. Moreover, living in the district settled by immigrant Jews, and attending medical school at the university, they both were exposed to the centers of friction between Jews and non-Jews. As Jews, they felt inferior. In 1870, just two years before Freud mourned the absence of "German-Christian fervor" in his "prosaic" Jewish existence, Adler wrote, in reference to a budding romance, "We understood each other at first sight! Imagine! I, a poor, stuttering, ugly Jew, awkward and clumsy; she — beautiful, gifted, cultured. How do I attract her?" Both Freud and Adler celebrated the ideals of assimilation. In 1867, Adler expressed his belief in the complete equality of Jews and non-Jews. He believed the distinction itself was arbitrary and meaningless. Meeting at the Leseverein, they remained members of the German-nationalist society through and beyond the Billroth affair.[49]

In the mid-1870s German Jews responded the way they responded, earlier in the decade, to the threat of anti-Semitism. They censured Jews from the East, supported the voices of German nationalism, and held on to their beliefs in the possibilities of social integration. But unlike the earlier response to the strictly cultural character of anti-Semitism, the German-Jewish response to the specter of racial anti-Semitism was more searching, and betrayed a mixture of urgency and uncertainty. Adler's solicitous justification of his German identity would have been unnecessary a few years earlier. Even at the end of his appeal, he could not be certain whether he had effectively proved himself German: "I don't know whether my personal relation to this question is not obscured by the fact that I am myself a Jew."[50] The German Jews in the Leseverein generally responded quickly — in fact, only hours after the clash between Jews and Germans erupted in Billroth's class — by condemning Jewish intruders in the name of German nationalism. The day after, the *Neue Freie Presse,* the leading Viennese liberal newspaper, which had many German-Jewish writers on its staff, printed a "solution" to the tensions between Germans and Jews by referring to the example students had set in the past: "In the most serious moments, the student body as a whole has stood together regardless of whether this student or that was a Christian, a Jew, or a heathen."[51] But was there not, behind the immediacy of the German-Jewish response in the Leseverein, a sense of the possible escalation of anti-Jewish hostility? And was not this same tone of uncertainty over the future coexistence of Jews and Germans implied in the newspaper's appeal to the past, that is, to the renewal of demonstrated student unity, in the face of a uniquely disruptive situation?

Racial anti-Semitism, before it developed into an infectious and unyielding movement a few years later, had pushed to the extreme the German Jews' effort at justifying their identity and worth as Germans. Moreover, the racial movement made it difficult for German Jews to establish their independence from the unassimilated migrant Jews living in Vienna. It was thus the gradual crystallization of the movement, during the years just before and after 1880, that completely frustrated, for many, the feeling of German loyalty, as well as the effort at proving their German worth. Though the immediate wave of anti-Semitic rancor generated by Billroth receded, the emotional and ideological foundations of racial hatred had taken root. The increasing migration of Jews from the East certainly aggravated German student intolerance. But the immediate popularity of the term "anti-Semitism" — introduced in the German-nationalist societies in 1878-79 — indicates that it was the Jew, more than the immigrant, who was the object of intense and growing discrimination. At this time, the Burschenschaft *Libertas* became the first to exclude Jews from its membership. By 1883, very few Jews indeed were affiliated with the German-nationalist movement. The *Verein der deutschen Studenten* (Society of German Students), for example, had no Jews among its members. In this period, members of the *Deutsch-österreichischer Leseverein, Germania,* and other German-nationalist societies endeavored to keep Jews out or to place pressure on Jews already in their organizations. When they met resistance from Jewish members or from members sympathetic to Jews, they organized *Kneipen,* i.e., strictly German social meetings, and German cross-society cartels. Among these groups, German students considered Jews as unworthy of the honor associated with dueling and thus would not recognize Jews as worthy dueling opponents. These de facto German organizations and their shared rejection of Jews became the basis of many subsequent efforts at ostracizing Jews from life inside and outside the university. These attempts culminated in the formation of the aggressive *Waidhofer Verband,* which declared in 1896 that all Jews were, once and for all, incapable of giving satisfaction. When Erich Schmidt (1853-1913), the professor of German language and literature, came from Strassburg to Vienna in the early 1880s, he was dismayed to find that students were driven just as much by anti-Semitic agitation as people were in Germany.[52]

It was in this atmosphere that Freud completed his medical education. The Leseverein, to which he had belonged, was dissolved by the government, for political reasons, in December 1878 when German-nationalist students began to regard German Jews as their enemies. Though it is thus impossible to determine the degree of his German allegiance after 1878, there is no evidence that Freud was affiliated with other German organizations. He did not, for example, join the *Akademische Lesehalle,* the society that absorbed most of the German students from the Leseverein.[53] It is likely that Freud experienced the same feelings of disappointment he felt when he first entered medical school, only much more deeply. For the discrimination he felt then was considerably less severe and not, at any rate, given significant support by the German-nationalist movement for which he had such high hopes.

The years just before and during his internship at the General Hospital were years when Freud went through deep personal change. Upon his graduation from medical school, Freud's twofold pride as a German and a Jew had vanished. Racial anti-Semitism produced the feeling of dislocation. As he expressed in his Weiss letter (September 1883), Freud felt uncomfortable about being a Jew. He responded with "horror and shame" to the way the Jews who attended Weiss's funeral conducted themselves in front of Christian observers. At the same time, Freud felt bitter about being German. In the mid-1920s, he recalled, "I considered myself German intellectually until I noticed the growth of anti-Semitic prejudice in Germany and German Austria. Since that time, I considered myself no longer a German." Indeed, when the subject of German nationalism came up in the 1880s and later in his life, Freud felt uneasy and wanted to "suppress" the "frightening" feelings stirring inside him. Nor under the circumstances could Freud sustain any longer his cheerful hopes for social integration. These hopes for "love extended to all mankind" had become "illusions" due to his "sobering" experiences as a Jew in Vienna.[54]

KOLLER, BREUER, AND THE SOCIETY OF PHYSICIANS

The deterioration of life in Vienna, due to the anti-Semitic movement, was a disillusionment par excellence for Freud. Perhaps as painful for him as the loss of self-pride, and of confidence in the capacity of liberal values to fashion moral behavior, was the disappearance of an active forum for the exchange and dissemination of progressive views. Freud could no longer associate his deepest humanitarian beliefs with the increasingly divisive and hostile German-nationalist movement. The Weiss letter is an indication of the anguish Freud must have felt with the loss of such a forum. The reference to his consultation with Breuer about the causes of Weiss's suicide, and the fact that the letter itself was an exhaustive communication of the reasons for the tragic event, describe a man who needed support for the development of his views.

The irony of the impact of incipient racial anti-Semitism on Freud, and on German Jews like him, was the influence it had on their discovery of a new basis of emotional and ideological support. Though the movement frustrated the aspirations Jews associated with German nationalism, it stimulated, at the same time, a positive Jewish response — the feelings of self-defense, pride, and courage, as well as the mutual recognition among Jews of shared beliefs and of strength through unity.

Like the initial response of other German Jews, Freud's early reaction to anti-Semitism was actually a mixture of disappointment and the determination to defend himself as a Jew. Both shame and an appreciation for self-assertion appeared in the Weiss letter. Three months later, in December 1883, a personal experience accelerated the change in Freud's Jewish sensibility. While on a train ride to Leipzig, where he would meet his half-brother Emanuel (1833-1914), coming from England, Freud inadvertently disturbed other passengers by opening a window. Suddenly "the whole situation took on a different color," he wrote Martha, just after its occurrence. Their demands to have him shut the window had lapsed into deliberate abuse: "There came a shout from the background: 'He's a dirty Jew!' . . . My first opponent [who had asked him to shut the window] also turned anti-Semitic and declared: 'We Christians consider other people; you'd better think less of your precious self,' etc." He went on:

Even a year ago I would have been speechless with agitation; but now I am different; I was not in the least frightened of that mob, asked the one to keep to himself his empty phrase which inspired no respect in me, and the other to step up and take what was coming to him. . . . I was glad I refrained from joining in the abuse, something one must always leave to the others.[55]

Freud remarked that the experience was unpleasant at the time. Even later in his life, when he fully affirmed his Jewish pride, Freud reacted to anti-Semitism with similarly unpleasant feelings. Yet, already in this letter, a more positive response to anti-Semitism emerged. In fact, he regarded the experience as "pleasant in retrospect . . . : I do think I held my own quite well, and used the means at my disposal courageously; in any case I didn't fall to their level."[56] In significant contrast to the Weiss letter, in which he expressed embarrassment over the behavior of Jews in the presence of Christians, as well as concern for maintaining peaceful, even if fragile, Jewish/non-Jewish relations, Freud stressed his independence and self-confidence as a Jew, in spite of the judgment of those passengers with whom he traveled. He felt neither the pain of inferiority nor that of social alienation that he had associated a few years earlier with being an outsider, for the judgments of the passengers were nothing, anyway, but "empty phrases which inspired no respect" in him. Indeed, as an outsider, he felt superior to them: He would not diminish his dignity, which he was defending, by exchanging abuses with them.

The General Hospital, where Freud lived and worked until August 1885, was not immune from the effects of anti-Semitism. More than one Jew complained of the hardship he had to endure there at the time, and of the restraints placed on him in his pursuit of scientific activity.[57] Freud himself was aware of this hostile atmosphere, but it was when he sympathized with his friend Carl Koller (1858-1944) that he affirmed his own growing positive Jewish pride in response to "the general bitterness" of the anti-Semitic atmosphere. In September 1884, Koller had gained considerable respect for proposing the anesthetic use of cocaine in local ophthalmic surgery. Even though Freud was disappointed that the medical community gave Koller the credit for the discovery, when, in July of that year, he had published the preliminary results of his own pioneering research on cocaine, a few months later, he fully supported another of Koller's victories. This episode began with an argument between Koller and a surgeon over a technical matter. Suddenly, the latter called Koller a *Saujud* (Jewish swine). "We would have reacted just as Koller did, by hitting the man in the face," Freud reported to Martha. Unlike German students at the university who were by now refusing to honor Jews as worthy opponents, the surgeon was obliged to challenge Koller to a duel, since they were both reserve officers.[58] Like the incident he encountered on his journey to Leipzig, the episode upset Freud deeply, but the results were indeed most gratifying. Freud rejoiced when he learned of Koller's triumph: "We are all delighted; a proud day for us. We are going to give Koller a present as a lasting reminder of his victory."[59]

Though Freud went through important change in a few short years, it was not until the mid-1880s that his Jewish pride matured beyond self-defense. He expressed renewed appreciation of his Jewish heritage in a letter to Martha, from Paris, where he had been studying with the well-known neurologist Jean-Martin Charcot (1825-93), during the winter of 1885-86. As Freud remarked, the letter was full of "silly confessions" about himself — his fear of some people, "inaccessibility to and gruffness with strangers," and how these weaknesses would disappear "to the extent to which I grow stronger and more independent."[60] Then he was reminded of what his close friend Josef Breuer had told him recently:

> He told me he had discovered that hidden under the surface of timidity there lay in me an extremely daring and fearless human being. I had always thought so, but never dared tell anyone. I have often felt as though I inherited all the defiance and all the passions with which our ancestors defended their Temple and could gladly sacrifice my life for one great moment in history.

The passage reflects a much closer Jewish identification than had his previous expressions of self-defense. His feeling of dignity as well as his sense of justice were not simply the bases of renewed Jewish pride, but were now the results of the prototypical experience of the Jewish people. His identity as a Jew was no longer an anti-Semitic reflex, but now a deeper and more pervasive resource that had informed his growing strength and resoluteness. Asked one evening, at Charcot's home, to comment on the political tension between the French and German states, Freud promptly replied, "I am a Jew, adhering neither to Germany nor to Austria."

Freud's difficult and, at first, hesitant shift from German to Jewish allegiance had crystallized by the mid-1880s. Though he remained sensitive to anti-Semitism and continued to suppress German feelings, he decisively dismissed assimilation, regarding it as both futile and personally destructive. The shift of allegiance not only defined a new source of pride, but gradually made it possible for Freud to give renewed expression to his feelings of justice and dignity. Jewish pride filled the vacuum created by his disillusionment with the German-nationalist movement, by strengthening and giving direction to his convictions. In reaction to the anti-Semitic abuses he received on the train ride to Leipzig, Freud defended himself as a Jew, a response which helped in restoring his feelings of self-confidence and courage. During the Koller episode, two years later (1885), Freud discovered sources of strength in Jewish unity as well as in Jewish pride. He relegated his professional jealousy of Koller in favor of their common defense against anti-Jewish abuse. The culmination of these developments appeared in his 1886 letter from Paris. In this letter, he attributed to his Jewish heritage the passion for preserving a worthwhile cause. In short, over the three-year period 1883-86, Freud acquired a Jewish sensibility that renewed the sense of dedication and purpose — indeed, the feeling of a movement — that he had associated with German nationalism a decade earlier.

Josef Breuer was the most important single influence in shaping Freud's growing pride in his Jewish heritage as well as his sense of Jewish unity. Between 1883 and 1886, Breuer was Freud's best and most trustworthy friend. Freud often solicited his advice on personal, professional, and financial consider-ations,[61] as well as on Jewish matters, as is evident in the Weiss letter and in the letter from Paris. It was more than a relationship of occasional counsel, however. Freud depended on the elder Breuer like a son. Writing to Breuer in 1884, he admitted to being "jealous of your opinion, even a nuance of your opinion."[62]

Freud indeed depended on a man who was strongly critical of the self-doubts and moral weaknesses of his Jewish contemporaries. Once, in 1894, Breuer felt so enraged with the way Jewish students were reacting to anti-Semitism that he wrote a letter of protest to Kadimah, the Jewish fraternity. "Our epidermis has almost become too sensitive," he wrote. "I would wish that we Jews had a consciousness of our own value, [which would make us] quiet and half indifferent to the judgement of the others, rather than this unwavering, easily insulted, hyper-sensitive *point d'honneur*. Be that as it may, that *point d'honneur* is certainly a product of the 'Assimilation.' "[63] Breuer frequently offered Freud the same advice. He persuaded Freud to interpret Weiss's restless energy as a self-destructive impulse — the Jewish drive for worldly acceptance motivated by self-shame — rather than merely as a zest for life. Similarly, when Freud rebelled in 1886 against the prospects of an orthodox Jewish marriage ceremony, by threatening to convert, it was Breuer who discouraged him.[64]

Moreover, Breuer strongly believed in the importance of Jewish unity for developing ancestral pride in each individual Jew. Since the 1870s, Breuer had been active in the local charitable Jewish burial society, *Chevra-Kadischa* (Holy Fellowship). He joined the century-old society in 1873, the same year Freud joined the German-nationalist Leseverein.[65] The society, to which he belonged probably until his death in 1925,[66] was, beyond a religious organization, a social meeting place that emphasized the value of fraternity among Jews. On the date of Breuer's induction, one member of the executive committee introduced the new members to the society's ideal: "Intimacy and brotherhood are very deep and inalienable elements of the Jewish heritage; intimacy and brotherhood are also the bases of Chevra-Kadischa."[67] At least on one occasion, Breuer persuaded Freud to value mutual trust and support among Jews. In January 1884, Freud received a sum of money from Samuel Hammerschlag, to assist him while he trained at the General Hospital. "At first I felt very ashamed," Freud said. He felt that the need to borrow money was a mark of personal failure. "But later when I saw Breuer and he agreed [with Hammerschlag that Freud should (should welcome the offer) acknowledge the charitable gesture], I accepted the idea of being indebted to good men and those of our faith with-out the feeling of personal obligation."[68] In the context of the close relationship between Breuer and Freud — Breuer recalled how "intimate" it was[69] — his effort to encourage in Freud the feeling of Jewish interdependence as well as of Jewish independence would have exercised considerable influence on Freud.[70]

Freud's expression of debt to those of his faith was an acknowledgment of past influences as well as a prophecy of later developments. In Hammerschlag and Breuer, he found moral support, which, on the one hand, diminished the feelings of self-doubt and helplessness and, on the other, contrasted with the bitterness he felt at the General Hospital. Interpreting and, in part, shaping the role of Judaism in modern society, Hammerschlag had elevated the meaning of Judaism that Freud's father had first instilled in him. Through the 1870s, when Jews commonly regarded assimilation as a positive and peaceful development, Freud could retain connections with the humanistic traditions of his religion, for they complemented his moral and social visions and thus confirmed, for him, the basic moral agreement among men.

The development of racial anti-Semitism generally, and especially within the German-nationalist movement, made painfully clear to Freud, and to other German Jews, the illusory character, or at least the remoteness, of their visions of social integration. Freud mourned the escalation of anti-Semitism in a deeply personal way, for, like the immigrant Jews from East Europe, he was the victim of vicious and degrading abuse. After a certain period of bewilderment and disorientation, Freud began to regard such abuse differently. Rather than seeing it as an unfortunate intrusion into otherwise stable social relations, and therefore as something to avoid, Freud regarded anti-Semitism as a serious affront to his dignity, and therefore as something to oppose. He also discovered and contributed to a developing Jewish subculture. Freud once remarked that as long as discrimination against Jews persisted, they had "no choice but to band together."[71] This feeling of Jewish unity surfaced in Freud's response to the Koller episode. At the same time, he felt "deep-seated sympathy" for Hammerschlag,[72] suggesting a sense of camaraderie with him as well.

Freud's friendship with Breuer also matured into an intimate relationship at the time that anti-Semitism grew more and more threatening. But Breuer was more than a friend to Freud. He was a father figure who nurtured the fullness of Freud's Jewish pride. The change in Freud's Jewish self-conception became apparent in the letters he sent to his fiancée during the early 1880s. In the earlier letters, Freud suggested that the source of his Jewish pride was the triumph over the abuses of anti-Semitism. As he became more certain of the trust and fellowship of other Jews — something Breuer also encouraged in his friend — Freud could regard his rich Jewish heritage as the source of his personal triumphs. In three years, Freud's Jewish consciousness developed from an anxious and erratic self-defense to an all-embracing sensibility inspiring deep passions.

Though Freud gained strong feelings of Jewish pride and allegiance, he remained firmly opposed to religious dogma. Disturbed with his fiancée's Jewish orthodoxy, Freud flatly told her, early in their engagement, that he was determined to make "a heathen" of her. He was annoyed, for example, with her fast on Yom Kippur: "My Martha's health shall not suffer by yielding to a crazy piety." When Martha wrote Freud in secrecy on the Sabbath day, the day of the week when writing was forbidden, he called her "weak" for not standing up to her pious mother. As hard as he tried to dissuade his fiancée from observing these "foolish superstitions," the force of tradition prevailed. Freud became anxious when their wedding day (September 14, 1886) approached: He knew there would be an orthodox religious ceremony. After pondering a conversion to the Protestant confession, he finally surrendered, and made the bridegroom's declaration in Hebrew — with the assistance of Martha's orthodox uncle.[73] It was a Pyrrhic victory for the defenders of tradition, however, for Freud was the more resolute in establishing a nonreligious home. Martin Freud, his oldest son (1889-1967), recalled that "we were brought up without any traces of . . . or instruction in Jewish ritual." To the best of his memory, none of the children ever attended synagogue.[74]

Freud's disparagement of religion, as being the domain of "foolish superstitions," indicates that even as he abandoned the anticipation of full assimilation, he remained attached to the secular ideals of the Enlightenment. When Freud wrote to Martha about his courageous encounter with his anti-Semitic opponents on the train ride to Leipzig, he took pleasure in the preservation of his dignity, because ultimately he felt that he had indeed preserved his freedom and had remained equal to his rivals. Even though he was threatened on the one hand by persistent religious practices and, on the other, by anti-Semitic developments, liberal values continued to be emotionally central in Freud's life. They enhanced the feeling of Jewish pride, just as Jewish pride gave him a focus for expressing these values.

Though Freud's Jewish consciousness strengthened his commitment to liberal values in the early 1880s, it would be over a decade before this new source of strength would restore the confident and positive resolve of his commitment to these values, which he had expressed in the 1870s. As for most German Jews, the 1880s were years of profound disillusionment and moral outrage for Freud. In contrast to his active pursuit of the ideal of universality, which characterized his assimilation in the 1870s and his dedication to psychoanalysis in the late 1890s, deep inner reassessment and quiet gestation characterized this period of Freud's life. Thus, the effort at preserving his sense of justice proved to be an exercise of inner freedom only. As it came into prominence during the 1880s, Freud's Jewishness was limited to this private realm.

Freud's Jewishness in the 1880s contrasted with his earlier and later expressions of Jewish pride in other ways. As an outgrowth of self-preservation, his Jewish consciousness contained elements of hostility aimed directly at his anti-Semitic aggressors. The defiant assertion of his independence as a Jew, as well as his sense of superiority to the maniacal hostility of an intolerant society, sealed his disillusionment with the realization of liberal ideals, and isolated him even more than did his self-defensive posture. Consistent with his characteristic sense of dignity and justice, his assertion of pride conspired with the anti-Semitic movement in subverting the achievement of his former hopes. His relation to the prestigious Viennese *Gesellschaft der Ärzte* (Society of Physicians) illustrates the tendency within his Jewish self-consciousness to foster the conditions of mutual hostility.

On October 15 and on November 26, 1886, Freud presented, to the medical society, his impressions of Charcot's investigations into male hysteria and hypnotism. Many Viennese physicians, including his mentor Theodor Meynert (1833-92), regarded the latter as pure charlatanry and the former as contrary to the then-common belief that hysteria afflicted only women. His decision to communicate Charcot's discovery was considered an audacious challenge to the established, internationally respected body.[75] The response to his communication was mixed. Freud, however, felt rejected. He felt his first presentation was badly received, and noted that although he received applause after presenting the second paper, in collaboration with his colleague Leopold Königstein (1850-1924), "the impression that the high authorities had rejected my innovations remained unshaken. . . . I found myself forced into the opposition." In this account, written in 1925, he reported that soon thereafter, he was restrained from research and academic pursuits. "I . . . ceased to attend the learned societies. It is a whole generation since I have visited the *Gesellschaft der Ärzte*."[76]

On the surface, it is perplexing why Freud's reaction was so bitter. It could not have been a result of his having high expectations. Nor did the authorities reject him out of hand. One eminent medical journal regarded his second paper as "very interesting."[77] Upon closer examination, however, it was his image of the society that was said to aggravate his response to the moderate reception. As Freud said, the society was authoritarian and had the ignoble power of personal and academic restraint. From a letter Freud wrote in 1888 to Wilhelm Fliess (1858-1928), his friend and the Berlin physician, it is clear Freud had another reason to be unhappy with the society:

> There was a terrific row at the Medical Society yesterday. They wanted to force us to subscribe to a new weekly which is intended to represent the pure, elevated and Christian views of certain dignitaries who have long since forgotten what work is like. They will naturally carry their proposal through; I feel very inclined to resign.[78]

Already opposed to the despotic use of authority, Freud felt contemptuously superior to the non-Jews in the society. This attitude separated him even more from his opponents and made it that much more difficult to forgive and to resume scientific dialogue. In effect, Freud did resign from the society after delivering his two papers in 1886. He never gave a paper to the society again and, though he continued to pay dues, he did so primarily to retain the privilege of using one of Europe's best medical libraries.[79]

Throughout the 1880s, Freud had a low estimation of non-Jews and expressed the desire to remain separate from, indeed above, them. "Gentiles [are] learning and practising the usual things and [are] not striving after discoveries and delving too deep," he wrote to Martha in 1883.[80] It was probably in the same vein that Freud decided to begin his medical practice on Easter Sunday, April 25, 1886. Just after returning from Paris, Freud announced his intention to begin work on the day when the rest of Catholic Vienna, observing the holiday, would be idle.[81] Whatever feeling for a movement he might have had during the 1880s, it was hostile and abrasive. To be sure, the oppositional attitude had been a prominent feature of Freud's personality before the outbreak of anti-Semitism — in his attack on capitalism, and generally in his affiliation with the German-nationalist movement. But unlike his confrontation in the 1880s, the earlier struggle against the abuses of authority was directed toward an active reaffirmation of humanitarian ideals.

In view of his development of psychoanalysis at the turn of the century, Freud's feelings of Jewish pride, independence, and superiority appear in a different light. Instead of destroying, or even seriously weakening, the prospect of social reconciliation, Freud's Jewish consciousness in the 1880s laid the foundation for his positive psychoanalytic movement. By strengthening his liberal convictions, and by inspiring the feelings of dedication as well as the sense of solidarity, Freud's Jewish pride sowed the seeds of renewed determination that eventually reoriented him toward building the basis of a stable universal order. Disappointed with the German nationalist movement, Freud discovered that he could overcome the feeling of betrayal or desertion through Jewish affirmation and, as a consequence of inner renewal, recover from the agony of lost hope. Providing a new basis for confidence, Freud's Jewish self-assertion became less abrasive, and more of an inspiration. Jewish self-dignity not only helped in preserving his personal freedom, but preserved human freedom as an ideal. Jewish pride became less a self-protective device than a source of inner resolve. The feeling of Jewish superiority no longer fostered condescension, but encouraged the belief in a personal mission aimed at reconciling hostile social differences. Jewish unity, once a necessary means of common defense, provided the assurance of mutual support and collective purpose.

The next chapter will demonstrate the maturity of Freud's Jewish consciousness of strength, solidarity, and a movement as he formed the theory and the movement of psychoanalysis. Freud's concurrent interests in the Jewish society B'nai B'rith and in psychoanalysis point to the interpenetration between his Jewish consciousness and his professional commitment. Indeed, as it became the central component of his lifelong rebellion, his Jewishness helped in structuring his development of the psychoanalytic movement.

NOTES

1. Letter from Sigmund Freud to Martha Bernays, September 16, 1883, in *The Letters of Sigmund Freud 1873-1939*, ed. Ernst L. Freud; trans. Tania and James Stern (London: The Hogarth Press, 1961), 73-80 (henceforth cited as *Letters*).

2. See *Letters*, 394: to A. A. Roback, February 20, 1930; and Martin Freud, "Who Was Freud? " *The Jews of Austria: Essays on Their Life, History, and Destruction* (London: Vallentin, Mitchell, 1967), 201. Freud's mother was born in Brody. She spent a part of her childhood in Odessa, in southern Russia. Martin Freud, 201. Freud's father was born in Tysmienica, 90 miles south of Brody. A. F. Bernays, "My Brother, Sigmund Freud," *The American Mercury*, 51 (November 1940), 424-25.

3. In 1844, Jacob became the business partner of his maternal grandfather, of Freiberg, and shortly thereafter moved there to join him. Bernays, 424-25. Ernest Jones, Freud's biographer, acquaintance, and colleague, recalled how vivid Amalia's memories were of the 1848 revolution in Vienna. Ernest Jones, *The Life and Work of Sigmund Freud*, vol. 1 (New York: Basic Books, 1953), 3. Jacob and Amalia were married in Vienna in 1855. On Jacob Freud and the Haskalah, see Josef Sajner, "Sigmund Freuds Beziehungen zu seinem Geburtsort Freiberg (Príbor) und zu Mähren," *Clio Medica*, 3 (1968), 169.

4. *Letters*, 394: to A. A. Roback, February 20, 1930.

5. Martin Freud, *Glory Reflected: Sigmund Freud – Man and Father* (London: Angus and Robertson, 1957), 11; Henry F. Ellenberger, *The Discovery of the Unconscious: The History and Evolution of Dynamic Psychiatry* (New York: Basic Books, 1970), 426; Jones, vol. 3 (1957), 375; Judith Bernays Heller, "Freud's Mother and Father," *Commentary*, 21 (May 1956), 419; Reuben M. Rainey, "Freud As Student of Religion: Perspectives on the Background and Development of His Thought" (Doctoral diss., Columbia University, 1971), 40-41 (material from unpublished letter from Freud to Silberstein, September 18, 1874); S. Freud, "Some Early Unpublished Letters," trans. Ilse Schier, *International Journal of Psychoanalysis*, 50, no. 4 (1969), 423: to Emil Fluss, March 17, 1873; Heller, 419.

6. A. F. Bernays, 336. Sources conflict about Freud's elementary education (Volksschule). Jones (vol. 1, 18) followed Bernays, but misinterpreted her account. Renée Gicklhorn, who had done the most original research into Freud's education, believed Freud did attend Volksschule, but it is not clear how she arrived at this conclusion. The impression one gains from her account is that she assumed Freud must have attended such a school because most children at that time did. Gicklhorn, "Eine Episode aus S. Freuds Mittelschulzeit," *Unsere Heimat*, 36 (1965), 18. But Bernays, Freud's younger sister by two years, is most convincing: "Normally children in Old Austria attended a primary school . . . before entering high school [gymnasium]. But Sigmund never went to such a school. My father taught him privately until he entered high school [1865]."

7. See S. Freud, *The Interpretation of Dreams*, trans. James Strachey (New York: Avon Books, 1967), 622. The edition which Jacob and Sigmund Freud had read together was the Reform Jewish *Philippson Bible* (*Die israelitische Bibel*, ed. Ludwig Philippson), a version of the Old Testament with parallel columns in German and Hebrew. It first appeared in 1839-54 (2d ed., 1858). See Willy Aron, "Notes on Sigmund Freud's Ancestry and Jewish Contacts," *YIVO Annals of Jewish Social Science*, 57, no. 11 (1957), 289.

8. This and other quotes are from the obituary in Sigmund Freud, *The Standard Edition of the Complete Psychological Works of Sigmund Freud*, trans. and ed. James Strachey (London: The Hogarth Press, 1953), vol. 9, 255-56 (hereafter cited as *SE*, followed by the volume number and page[s]).

9. In a personal communication to Reuben Rainey, Anna Freud noted that to the best of her knowledge, Freud studied with Hammerschlag from 1870 to 1873 at the gymnasium. Rainey, 64n. When Freud went to school, religious education was compulsory in Austria; see Samuel Hammerschlag, "Das Program der israelit. Religionsschule in Wien,"

in *Bericht der Religionsschule der israelitischen Cultusgemeinde in Wien über die Schuljahre 1868 und 1869* (Vienna: Im Selbstverlage der israel. Cultusgemeinde, 1869), 15. According to a list of instructors at the Sperl Gymnasium, Hammerschlag was the instructor in Jewish religion for the years 1871-73. *Festschrift des k.k.Erzherzog Rainer-Real-Gymnasiums im II. Gemeinde-Bezirke in Wien/Früher: Leopoldstädter kommunal-Real-u. Obergymnasium: Aus Anlass seines fünfzig Jahre andauernden Bestehens* (Vienna: Verlag der Anstalt, 1914), 174. In his last year at gymnasium, Freud received highest marks in religion. Gicklhorn, 24. Rainey argued that Freud "probably" studied with Hammerschlag at the school of religion of the Jewish community, from the beginning of his gymnasium education. See Rainey, 63-64.

10. Hammerschlag, 27, 28. See also, 1-3. Hammerschlag served as director of the school from 1857 to 1873. His predecessor was Leopold Breuer (1791-1872), the father of Freud's close friend of the 1880s.

11. Jellinek is discussed in Chapter 1.

12. Hammerschlag, 11-12, 27-28.

13. Hammerschlag, 11. See *Letters,* 394: to A. A. Roback, February 20, 1930.

14. *Letters,* 35-40: July 23, 1882.

15. See John E. Gedo and Ernest Wolf, "Die Ichthyosaurusbriefe," *Psyche* (Stuttgart), 24 (October 1970), 790-91.

16. Heinz Stanescu, "Young Freud's Letters to his Rumanian friend, Silberstein," trans. J. Meron, *Israel Annals of Psychiatry and Related Disciplines,* 9 (December 1971), 201: August 22, 1874; 199-200: November 8, 1874.

17. S. Freud, "Some Early Unpublished Letters of Freud," 424: to Fluss, May 1, 1873; and 422: to Fluss, February 7, 1873.

18. Cited and translated in Rainey, 40-41; letter dated September 18, 1874.

19. S. Freud, "Some Early Unpublished Letters," 423: to Fluss, March 17, 1873.

20. Ibid., 419: to Martha Bernays, October 28, 1883.

21. S. Freud, "Some Early Unpublished Letters," 420: to Fluss, September 18, 1872. I have translated "Gesindel" as "rabble," instead of "lot."

22. *Jahresbericht des Leopoldstädter Communal-Real-und Obergymnasiums in Wien* (Vienna: Verlag des Leopoldstädter Real- und Obersgymnasiums, 1866-73).

23. Earl A. Grollman, *Judaism in Sigmund Freud's World* (New York: Bloch Publishing Co., 1965), 47.

24. See Friedrich Heer, "Freud, the Viennese Jew," *Freud, the Man, His World, His Influence,* ed. Jonathan Miller (Boston: Little, Brown, 1972), 6. Heer was born and rasied in Vienna after World War I.

25. Arnold Ascher, "Ehren-Vizegrosspräsident Dr. Wilhelm Knopfmacher – 80 Jahre," *B'nai B'rith Mitteilungen für Österreich,* 33 (June 1933), 219-20.

26. S. Freud, "Some Early Unpublished Letters," 426: to Fluss, June 16, 1873.

27. The society has already been carefully and thoroughly studied by William J. McGrath. The material which follows is taken largely from his work. See *Dionysian Art and Populist Politics in Austria* (New Haven and London: Yale University Press, 1974), 33-82. Also worth consulting on the subject are his earlier articles, especially the pioneering essay "Student Radicalism in Vienna," in *Journal of Contemporary History,* 2 (March 1967), 183-201. Freud's membership is documented in the membership lists of the society, *Jahresbericht des Lesevereines der deutschen Studenten Wiens, über das Vereinsjahr, 1873-1874* to *1877-1878* (Vienna: Selbstverlag des Lesevereines der deutschen Studenten Wiens, 1873-78) (the report for the year 1875-76 is missing from the collection in the Österreichische Nationalbibliothek), and in Freud, *The Interpretation of Dreams,* 246.

28. *Jahresbericht des Lesevereines der deutschen Studenten Wiens, über das Vereinsjahr 1874-1875,* 4.

29. Stanescu, 204: to Silberstein, March 7, 1875; 202: to Silberstein, February 27, 1875.

30. *Jahresbericht des Lesevereines der deutschen Studenten Wiens, über das Vereins-jahr 1874-1875*, 23; Solomon Ehrmann, "Meine persönlichen Beziehungen zu Sigmund Freud," in "Festsitzung der 'Wien' anlässlich des 70. Geburtstages Br. Univ. Prof. Doktor Sigmund Freud," *B'nai B'rith Mitteilungen für Österreich*, 26 (May 1926), 132-34.

31. Solomon Ehrmann, "Über die Function des Judenthums innerhalb der Mensch-heit und der B'nai B'rith innerhalb des Judenthums," *Vierteljahrsbericht für die Mitglieder des österr. israel. Humanitätsvereins 'B'nai B'rith,'* 4 (January 1902), 101. Idem, "Was Wir Wollen," in ibid., 1 (October 1897), 3, 6.

32. S. Freud, *The Interpretation of Dreams*, 225-26.

33. *Jahresbericht des Leopoldstädter Communal-Real-und Obergymnasium in Wien:* 1866, 29; 1889, 86; 1873, xlvii.

34. S. Freud, *The Interpretation of Dreams*, 229.

35. Paul Molisch, *Politische Geschichte der deutschen Hochschulen in Österreich von 1848 bis 1918* (Vienna and Leipzig: Wilhelm Braumüller, 1939), 120. Molisch derived his information from an untitled essay that existed in the club's archives.

36. See August Fournier, *Erinnerungen* (Munich: Drei Masken Verlag, 1923), 74-75.

37. Peter G. J. Pulzer, *The Rise of Political Anti-Semitism in Germany and Austria* (New York: John Wiley and Sons, 1964), 13.

38. Fournier, 74-75.

39. *SE* 20, 9. The passage continues: "I refused absolutely to do the first of these things. I have never been able to see why I should feel ashamed of my descent or, as people were beginning to say, of my 'race.' I put up, without much regret, with my non-acceptance into the community." These concluding sentences differ in one important respect from the opening sentence of the quote cited in the text: They express a reaction to, rather than his experience of, disappointment. Indeed, Freud did refuse to feel inferior to his Jewish enemies, and was proud of being outside an intolerant community. But this pride developed after the outbreak of racial anti-Semitism in the 1880s. The change from shame to pride – lost here in Freud's account – is the primary subject of concern in the remainder of this chapter.

40. Julie Braun-Vogelstein, cited in untitled interview by Kurt Eissler, executive secretary of the Sigmund Freud Archives, New York, January 5, 1954 (MS., The Julie Braun-Vogelstein Nachlass [New York], 1954), 3-5, 22-3; Braun-Vogelstein, "Besprechung am 23. Februar 1959, 8.30 p.m. zwischen Dr. [Kurt] Eissler und Frau Julie Braun-Vogel-stein" (Ms., The Julie Braun-Vogelstein Nachlass, 1959), 3-4. In a letter written to Braun sometime between 1867 and 1869, Freud complained, "Why must I bear this burden of ugliness" – a remark Braun felt was entirely groundless but consistent with Freud's sense of insecurity. Significantly, Freud responded with self-assurance when, among the upper classes, he gained the trust of his schoolmates as head boy. Braun-Vogelstein, interview, 3; see *Letters*, 215: to Martha Bernays, February 2, 1886.

41. Theodor Billroth, *Über das Lehren und Lernen der medizinischen Wissenschaften an den Universitäten der deutschen Nation nebst allgemeine Bemerkungen über Universi-täten: Ein culturhistorische Studie* (Vienna: Carl Gerolds Sohn, 1876). The book was actually released in mid-December 1875, with the 1876 postdate. The relevant passage appeared on pages 148-54, with the most invective remarks appearing in a footnote, pages 152-54. Billroth came from Zurich and Berlin to teach at the Vienna Medical School in 1867.

42. Ibid., 148-52.

43. Ibid., 152-54n.

44. In a sequel, Billroth emphasized his concern for students who suffered from financial and educational disadvantages: "I . . . wanted to keep them from misery and distress." Billroth, *Prof. Dr. Billroths Antwort auf die Adresse des Lesevereines der deutschen Studenten Wiens* (Vienna: Carl Gerolds Sohn, 1875), 9-10. Years later, Billroth expressed sympathy for the persecuted Jew. In 1883, he wrote to a friend about the problems

Jews have had in securing professional appointments: "But that crooked nose! Sad that the nose today determines the filling of chairs at German universities." Letter dated July 3, 1883, cited in Pulzer, *The Rise of Political Anti-Semitism*, 252. He was one of the few professors at the university active in the *Verein zur Abwehr des Antisemitismus* (Society to Combat Anti-Semitism) during the 1890s. Molisch, 135.

45. *Neue Freie Presse*, December 11, 1875, 6; *Deutsche Zeitung*, December 10, 1875, 2; *Illustriertes Wiener Extrablatt*, December 11, 1875, 3; Karl Beurle, *Beiträge zur Geschichte der deutschen Studentenschaft Wiens* (Vienna: Lesk u. Schwidernoch, 1893), 34.

46. Billroth, *Prof. Dr. Th. Billroths Antwort*, 8.

47. Julius Braunthal, *Victor und Friedrich Adler: Zwei Generationen Arbeiterbewegung* (Vienna: Verlag der Wiener Volksbuchhandlung, 1965), 17-19.

48. Ibid., 17; *Deutsche Zeitung*, December 14, 1875, 6; December 13, 1875, 4; "Adresse des Lesevereins der deutschen Studenten Wiens an der Professor Dr. Th. Billroth (überreicht am 15. Dezember 1875)," in Billroth, *Prof. Dr. Th. Billroths Antwort*, 5-7.

49. Material on Adler's youth and Jewish identity is in Braunthal, 13-21. Adler's father was raised on the Galician frontier, his mother in Nikolsburg. Born in Prague, Adler moved to Vienna in 1856, attended the Catholic Schottengymnasium, from 1859 to 1867 (an indication of the family's early retreat from Judaism), and earned his medical degree from the Vienna Medical School. He expressed his self-punishing complaint in 1870 (ibid., 21). Adler's membership in the Leseverein is documented in the society's membership lists, *Jahresbericht des Lesevereines der deutschen Studenten Wiens, über das Vereinsjahr 1871-1872* to *1877-1878*. (Besides the report for the year 1875-76, the report for 1872-73 is missing from the collection in the Österreichische Nationalbibliothek.)

50. Braunthal, 19.

51. *Neue Freie Presse*, December 11, 1875, 6.

52. Beurle, 53-55; Molisch, 121-31; *Gedenkschrift: Die Lesevereine der deutschen Hochschüler an der Wiener Universität* (Vienna: Im Selbstverlage des Lese- und Redevereines des deutschen Hochschüler in Wien 'Germania,' 1912), 42; Oscar Scheuer, *Die geschichtliche Entwicklung des deutschen Studententums in Österreich mit besonderer Berücksichtigung der Universität Wien von ihrer Gründung bis zur Gegenwart* (Vienna, Leipzig: Verlag von Ed. Beyers Nachf., 1910), 280-97; Schmidt's remark in *Deutsche Zeitung*, October 30, 1881, 6. Scheuer noted that Austrian Burschenschaften were far more radical than their counterparts in Germany. Idem., *Burschenschaft und Judenfrage: Der Rassen-antisemitismus in der deutschen Studentenschaft* (Berlin: Verlag Berlin-Wien, 1927), 45, 61.

53. *Gedenkschrift*, 33; *Jahresbericht der Akademischen Lesehalle in Wien, über das neunte Vereinsjahr* (Vienna: Selbstverlag der Akademischen Lesehalle, 1879), 4-5. Freud's name does not appear among the members of the Lesehalle for the years 1878-80.

54. George S. Viereck, *Glimpses of the Great* (London: Duckworth, 1930), 30; *Letters*, 216, 346, 367: letters to Martha, February 2, 1886; to the B'nai B'rith, May 6, 1926; and to Romain Rolland, March 4, 1923.

55. *Letters*, 92-94: December 16, 1883.

56. *Letters*, 92-93.

57. See Ehrmann, "Meine persönlichen Beziehungen zu Sigmund Freud," 133.

58. See Molisch, 132.

59. *Letters*, 143-44: to Martha, January 6, 1885.

60. *Letters*, 212-16: February 2, 1886.

61. See Martin Freud, *Glory Reflected*, 22; Jones, vol. 1, 187.

62. *Letters*, 130: June 23, 1884.

63. Ellenberger, 424. Ellenberger obtained the letter from one of Breuer's daughters-in-law.

64. Jones, vol. 1, 183.

65. Breuer was inducted on March 9, 1873. His name is listed with those of other new members in a Festschrift commemorating the occasion: *Zur Erinnerung an die General-Versammlung des Vereines für fromme und wohlthätige Werke: Chewra-Kadischa am 10. Adar 5633 (9. März 1873)* (Vienna: Im Selbstverlage des Vereines, 1873), 50.

66. *Rechenschafts-Bericht des im Jahre 1764 organizierten Vereines für fromme und wohlthätige Werke Chewra Kadischa, uber die Verwaltungsjahre 1892, 1893, 1894* (Vienna: Im Selbstverlage des Vereines, 1895), 54.

67. Sigmund Hirschler, "Toast auf die neueingetretenen Mitglieder" in *Zur Erinnerung an die General-Versammlung des Vereines*, 30-31.

68. *Letters*, 101-2: to Martha, January 10, 1884.

69. Breuer to Auguste Forel, November 21, 1907, cited in P. F. Cranefield, "Josef Breuer's Evaluation of His Contribution to Psychoanalysis," *International Journal of Psychoanalysis*, 39, pt. 5 (1958), 318-20.

70. There are other indications of Jewish intimacy in the Freud-Breuer relationship. Though their friendship is commonly dated from the late 1870s, when they both conducted research at Brücke's Institute of Physiology (see Jones, vol. 1, 223), their relationship may have had earlier roots. Breuer's father, Leopold, a respected instructor in religion and an author of several books on Jewish education, was both a colleague and a friend of Hammerschlag at the Jewish school of religion in Vienna, until his death in 1872. Hammerschlag, 1; see Jones, vol. 1, 223. Josef Breuer, too, felt close to Hammerschlag. He used "Hammerschlag" for the middle name of his second child, born in 1870. Jones, vol. 1, 223. Freud may have met Josef Breuer through Hammerschlag, for Hammerschlag was not only Freud's instructor in religion until 1873, but a personal friend. *Letters*, 102-3: to Martha, January 10, 1884; Jones, vol. 1, 163. If Freud had visited his religious instructor at Hammerschlag's home in the early or mid-1870s as he did in the 1880s, the chances that he met Breuer this way increase, as the Breuer and Hammerschlag families lived in the same apartment building. Jones, vol. 1, 223.

Though Breuer had a profound religious sensibility and a reverence for God (see Robert A. Kann, ed., *Marie von Ebner-Eschenbach-Dr. Josef Breuer: Ein Briefwechsel, 1889-1916* [Vienna: Bergland Verlag, 1969], 122-23: Breuer to Marie von Ebner-Eschenbach, May 18, 1912), which Freud could never accept, he shared with Freud the German Jew's discreet appreciation of the humanistic aspect of Judaism. Like Adolf Jellinek and Hammerschlag, the Chevra-Kadischa insisted that Judaism was neither "superficial" nor observant of religious "formalities." Judaism possessed "an inner, spiritual, moral, and ethical nature," and was infused with "genuine humanity." Hirschler, 31-32. Breuer intoned the same sentiments in his autobiography, written in 1923, two years before his death. He condemned the "intellectual servitude" of Jewish ghetto life and praised the "intellectual energy" of West-European Jews, who aimed "to become a part of the literature, poetry, and philosophy of the German people . . . in a congenial atmosphere of joint endeavor." Josef Breuer, "Curriculum Vitae" (MS., Archiv der Akademie der Wissenschaft in Wien, 1923), 10-11. For both Breuer and Freud, Judaism was essentially ethical as well as humane. As such, Judaism was beyond the reproach of the critics of provincial Jewry. Its dignity preserved, Judaism offered to them a resourceful heritage and a community of the faithful.

71. Joseph Wortis, *Fragments of an Analysis with Freud* (Indianapolis: Bobbs-Merrill, 1963), 144. He made the comment in an interview with Wortis in 1935.

72. *Letters*, 103: January 10, 1884.

73. Jones, vol. 1, 116-17, 123, 167; Aron, 292.

74. M. Freud, *Glory Reflected*, 11, 14; "Who Was Freud?," 203.

75. See Sigmund Freud, *The Origins of Psycho-Analysis: Letters to Wilhelm Fliess, Drafts and Notes: 1887-1902*, ed. Marie Bonaparte, Anna Freud, Ernst Kris; trans. Eric Mosbacher and James Strachey (New York: Basic Books, 1954), 20n (note by the editors).

76. *SE* 20, 15-16; see Jones, vol. 1, 228-32.

77. Jones, vol. 1, 231.

78. S. Freud, *The Origins of Psycho-Analysis*, 55: to Fliess, February 4, 1888.

79. K. Sablik, "Sigmund Freud und die Gesellschaft der Ärzte in Wien," *Wiener klinische Wochenschrift,* 80 (February 9, 1968), 107-9. In the "Desideraten Buch" of the Gesellschaft der Ärzte, an open book available to members for expressing almost anything, Freud complained in 1894 about the inadequacy of the library at the Physiological Institute. A copy of the complaint is in the Freud Gesellschaft, Vienna.

80. *Letters,* 69: to Martha, September 4, 1883.

81. Siegfried and Suzanne Cassirer Bernfeld, "Freud's First Year in Practice, 1886-1887," *Bulletin of the Menninger Clinic,* 16 (March 1952), 37; Jones, vol. 1, 143.

3

THE PREFIGURING OF THE
PSYCHOANALYTIC MOVEMENT:
FREUD AND THE B'NAI B'RITH

FORGING A JEWISH BOND

At the end of January, or in early February 1897, Hermann Nothnagel (1841-1905), the respected professor of internal medicine, and Freud's friend on the faculty at the medical school, told Freud that he was going to propose him for a professorship. It had been over 12 years since Freud's appointment as Privat-dozent, the lowest faculty appointment — comparable to an instructorship, but without a stipend or privileges to attend faculty meetings; despite its low rank, Freud had been gratified by the appointment in September 1885. The title had improved his prospects for securing a medical practice, and was the necessary first step for university advancement, a goal Freud had already desired for years. "A professorship [is] a rank which in our society turns its holder into a demi-god to his patients," Freud wrote later, adding emphatically, "One must look somewhere for one's salvation and the salvation I chose was the title of professor." Despite the proposal for promotion, neither Freud nor Nothnagel was sanguine about its going through. Said Freud: "I at once warned myself not to attach any expectations to the event. During the last few years the ministry [of education, the final arbiter for such appointments] had disregarded recommendations of that sort.... I therefore determined to meet the future with resignation." Nothnagel himself warned Freud of the dim prospects: "You know the further difficulties"; the proposal "may do no more than put you on the *tapis.*" Freud and Nothnagel were aware of the problem behind the case. Freud believed that any delay in promotion was due to "denominational considerations." Nothnagel had long recognized the mounting pressures among students and faculty, as well as in government circles, to limit the number of Jews at the university.[1]

A month later, Freud was visited by a Jewish friend who also had been a candidate for a professorship for a considerable period of time. Just after talking with the minister of education, the visitor — it was probably Leopold Königstein, one of Freud's closest Viennese friends at this time, and a candidate for promotion since 1881[2] — confirmed Freud's deepest suspicions that anti-Semitic sentiment was indeed delaying their promotions. "It was not news to me, though it was bound to strengthen my feeling of resignation," Freud lamented.[3] In the summer, and for the following four years, the ministry rejected Freud, thus heightening his sensitivity to the injustices of anti-Semitism and recalling the despondency of his earlier reaction to the first waves of racial anti-Semitism in the 1880s. There was cause for an even deeper sense of despair. In April 1897, the Emperor Franz Josef confirmed Karl Lueger as mayor of Vienna, after overturning his election to office four times since 1895. As the leader of the Christian Socialists, Lueger had campaigned successfully on an anti-Semitic platform, claiming that big business was in the hands of Jews. When the emperor overturned the second election in 1895, Freud lit a cigar "for joy at Lueger's non-confirmation in office." With the emperor's capitulation, two years later, to the pressure of Rome (Pope Leo XIII), Jews everywhere were convinced that anti-Semitic intolerance would be an institution in Vienna. Freud contrasted this "dreary present to the cheerful hopes of the days of the Bürger ministry [1867-79]." He added nostalgically, "There had even been some Jews among [the ministers]."[4]

In the early months of 1897, there occurred a series of dreams that expressed a strong wish, "a longing to visit Rome."[5] Freud's discussion of the dreams now became a record of his reaction to academic and political anti-Semitism, for he noted that the dreams were stimulated by "the increasing importance of the effects of the anti-Semitic movement upon our emotional life." Freud noted that he first expressed the desire to reach Rome as a schoolboy's identity with the Carthaginian general Hannibal. Sympathizing with the Carthaginians in the Punic Wars, Freud regarded Hannibal as "the favorite hero of my later school days." To Freud, Hannibal represented something more than a great military leader: "To my youthful mind Hannibal . . . the semitic general . . . and Rome symbolized the conflict between the tenacity of Jewry and the organization of the Catholic church." In an apparent reflection upon the papal persuasions in current Viennese politics, he added that the Catholic church in Rome meant to him, even then, "the effects of the anti-Semitic movement." Frustrated by the dreary daytime reality of academic and political anti-Semitism, Freud internalized this "perseverance and single-mindedness" of Hannibal's Roman siege. In the dream that, at last, took him to Rome, he recognized the influence of a Jewish anecdote that communicated this prototype of Jewish tenacity. It concerned a Jew who, despite poverty and external restraint, was determined to reach his destination. "To Karlsbad," he told an inquiring acquaintance "if my constitution can stand it."

At the end of this dream, an additional dimension of his inner rebellion against the social and political barriers of anti-Semitism emerged. He "noticed a Herr Zucker (whom I knew slightly) and determined to ask him the way to the city." The Hannibalian conquest could not be achieved without assistance. Freud recognized, from another Jewish anecdote, how important the element of Jewish solidarity was in his psychological rebellion against anti-Semitism. He noted the connection between his dream relation to Herr Zucker and the story of a confused Jew, alone and lost in a strange city, who received the kind of reassurance that only a fellow Jew could offer.[6]

Freud felt that the fulfillment of his wish to reach Rome was "at the moment . . . little favored by destiny. . . . For a long time to come, no doubt, I shall have to continue to satisfy that longing [only] in my dreams."[7] Indeed, Freud rejected the university for inhibiting his freedom. Similar to his reaction to the "Christian views" of the Society of Physicians a decade earlier, Freud considered resigning from the university in January 1897, and, at any rate, discontinued teaching, beginning in July 1898, for ten consecutive terms, until October 1903.[8] Moreover, after the disappointing reception that the members of the Society of Psychiatry and Neurology gave to a paper he presented in 1896, Freud gave only one paper to a professional society until 1904.[9] However, his rejection of the university and the professional societies did not keep him from searching for justice and satisfaction outside his dreams.

His work in psychoanalysis represented in part this search. Two years earlier, beginning with the "Project for a Scientific Psychology" (1895), Freud proceeded to shift the focus of his work from the domain of psychopathology, which included hysteria and child paralysis, to a "metapsychology" comprehending "normal" behavior. Increasingly, from this point on, Freud was engaged in a theoretical and philosophical reconstruction of human behavior. Exploring the psychic foundations of dreams, he proclaimed that the unconscious not only disturbed behavior but "must be assumed to be the general basis of psychical life . . . in normal as well as in pathological life." Freud indicated the direction of his interests on December 5, 1897: "Every now and then ideas whirl through my head which promise to explain everything, and to connect the normal and the pathological. Psychoanalysis provided Freud with a basis for reinterpreting human behavior, for making sense out of the chaos and divisiveness of his social environment, and for determining the common basis of all human life. The discovery of a uniform structure of the psyche yielded such work as "The Psychical Mechanism of Forgetfulness" (1898), "Screen Memories" (1899), *The Interpretation of Dreams* (1899-1900), and *The Psychopathology of Everyday Life* (1901). Moreover, during this period, he collected material for his book *Jokes and Their Relation to the Unconscious* (1905).[10]

Freud could not sustain his revolutionary investigations alone. As he dreamt of Herr Zucker, he cultivated the friendship and professional association of

Wilhelm Fliess. In fact, in a letter to Fliess dated January 3, 1897, Freud addressed him as he had addressed Herr Zucker in his nocturnal search for his destination: "We shall not be shipwrecked. Instead of the passage we are seeking, we may find oceans, to be fully explored by those who come after us; but, if we are not prematurely capsized, if our constitutions can stand it, we shall make it. *Nous y arriverons.* Give me another ten years and I shall finish the neuroses and the new psychology."[11] As Ernst Kris observed, after the death of Freud's father in October 1896, Freud looked to Fliess as a transference figure as well as an audience for his scientific interests.[12] Though the psychological character of this relationship bound Freud closely to Fliess, it also created fluctuations in Freud's feelings about his analyst-friend. Freud's active self-analysis of his relations with his father in the summer of 1897 intensified these disturbances during the subsequent months and years.

Freud joined the Viennese lodge of the International Order of the B'nai B'rith on September 29, 1897. As he expressed to B'nai B'rith members, years later, his hostile professional reception and general sense of isolation "aroused in me the longing for a circle of excellent men with high ideals who would accept me in friendship despite my temerity. Your lodge was described to me as a place where I could find such men." In both of his extant letters to the lodge, called *Wien* (Vienna), Freud stressed the need for relieving the burden of ostracism. "I felt as though outlawed, shunned by all," he wrote in 1926. Nine years later, he added, "I soon became one of you, enjoyed your sympathy, and almost never neglected to go to the place, surrounded by extreme hostility, where I was certain to find friends." Freud longed not just for friends, but, by joining the B'nai B'rith, for Jewish friends. His reference to the "extreme hostility" suggests one reason for this: He had sought refuge specifically from anti-Semitic ostracism.[13]

This affiliation with an isolated Jewish society brought to the surface the feelings of mutual support he had experienced with Carl Koller, and those of "secret sympathy" he had felt with Breuer and Hammerschlag a decade earlier, when he first faced anti-Semitism. It met the need for Jewish companionship, which his weekly taroc entertainment with Leopold Königstein, with his family pediatrician, Oscar Rie (1863-1931), and with other Jews, fulfilled in part, and which his Wednesday-evening meetings, to discuss psychoanalysis with Jewish colleagues, would meet five years later. "I can hardly remember a non-Jewish person among the many guests at our home," recalled Martin Freud in reference to the household at the turn of the century.[14] Freud joined the B'nai B'rith at the beginning of the society's fifth term, the first possible moment after he recognized the pervasiveness of anti-Semitism in Viennese politics and academic life. Indeed, in response to the public support of Lueger, and to the discrimination, earlier in the year, against Jews in the ministry of education, he dreamt of joining such an association, as he identified strongly with the Semitic figure Hannibal and sought the aid and encouragement of another Jew in the midst of an alien environment.[15]

Much of the appeal of the society during these years was precisely this form of protection and mutual support. Its exclusively Jewish membership provided, for many, a refuge from the disgrace and abuses of anti-Semitism. This was true for Wilhelm Knöfpmacher (1853-1937), the first member Freud met in the fall of 1897, and an old friend from the days of Freud's secondary and university education. "Without anti-Semitism," Knöpfmacher claimed, "we would never have formed this union in the first place."[16] Another classmate of Freud's, Solomon Ehrmann (1854-1926), intoned the same sentiment: "Indeed, if anti-Semitism did not exist, we would never have been in the situation to become B'nai B'rith. Above all, it forcefully demonstrated to us the necessity of joining other like-minded men, since we suddenly and innocently lost our support from, and intercourse with, equal and like-minded fellow citizens of other confessions." Ehrmann's claim that "the B'nai B'rith has a function as long as anti-Semitism continues to exist" was mirrored later by Freud when he said that Jews must "band together" as long as there was an anti-Semitic movement.[17]

The significance of the B'nai B'rith for Freud went beyond consolation. Had he merely been a participating member, the society might have been nothing more to him than a retreat from social and professional hostility – a circle of friends. But, as in the Karlsbad dream and in his association with Fliess, his association with Jews in the society became an integral part of the search for his destination, the "new psychology" of psychoanalysis. Only a month after his November letter of complaint to Fliess, Freud presented the first of two lectures to the B'nai B'rith, on the results of his work on dream interpretation. The occasion marked one of his earliest efforts at communicating his burgeoning views on dreams. Only Fliess and another Jewish society (*Jüdische akademische Lesehalle*), which he had addressed once in 1896 and again the following year, had heard his views on the subject before. The response of the B'nai B'rith, and Freud's reaction to its reception, launched a new, triangular relationship among the Jewish society, Freud, and psychoanalysis. One member acclaimed the "principles of self-contained theory" presented by Freud and the "ingenious [*geistvollen*] interpretation." Another vividly recalled the impact Freud made on the brotherhood. "From beginning to end, everyone present listened with rapt attention to Freud's words. He made the results of his recent studies clear to us not only in the cogency of his ideas but in his overall lucidity." Still another commended his "masterful art of delivery," remarking that his talk on dreams before the brotherhood made for "one of the most enjoyable evenings. The audience expressed their gratitude and approval with unrestrained applause."[18]

Freud was jubilant about the lecture's enthusiastic reception, and proclaimed, "I shall continue it next Tuesday."[19] Indeed, he continued to address the Jewish society many times after presenting the material on dreams. At the time he published the article on forgetfulness, Freud lectured to the B'nai B'rith on the same subject. Again he succeeded in provoking his attentive audience, which in turn inspired subsequent lectures given to the society. The following year (1900), he delivered two papers, "The Psychic Life of the Child" and "Chance and Superstition."[20] Here was an audience that had greeted, debated, and discussed Freud's theoretical construction of psychoanalytic psychology, often before he published the results. Having abandoned the academic circles for the time being, Freud filled, through the B'nai B'rith, the professional as well as the social vacuum in his life. The Jewish society became an active intellectual forum for his metapsychological views during the productive five-year period 1897-1902, and, in this respect, was a precursor of the movement of psychoanalysis (Freud convened the first study session in October 1902). As Freud later said to the brotherhood, "At a time when no one in Europe would listen to me and I had no pupils in Vienna, you offered me your sympathetic attention. You were my first audience."[21] Moreover, like Fliess, the society exceeded the effectiveness of his reading public by encouraging his thinking, on the theory of dreams and parapraxis.

Besides pursuing his social and professional life within the B'nai B'rith, Freud contributed to the development of the B'nai B'rith itself. He attended almost every meeting for a decade after he joined and frequently spoke at the festive evening meals of the brotherhood.[22] He also enlisted at least three members — two long-time friends, Königstein and Rie,[23] and Eduard Hitschmann (1871-1958). Freud approached the latter two as part of his responsibility as a member of the B'nai B'rith search committee to form a second Viennese lodge (1901-3).[24] Moreover, he was instrumental in establishing the foundation for the new lodge by participating in its planning stages and by recruiting Rie, in the spring of 1901, as its first member. Within the older lodge, Wien, Freud was a member of the judicial committee and chairman of the cultural committee. The latter committee was responsible for creating a vigorous intellectual atmosphere by maintaining a library, providing lectures, promoting publications, and holding discussions and debates. In 1901, Freud introduced a discussion on a topic current in the brotherhood, "Goals and Purposes of the B'nai B'rith Societies." The next year, Freud initiated a discussion on "The Role of the Woman in Our [B'nai B'rith] Union."[25]

Freud's considerable efforts at promoting the B'nai B'rith suggest the significance of the society as a forum for articulating his Jewish identity. By regarding the brotherhood as his only audience for his scientific investigations prior to the organization of his own study group, the society assumes an additional significance as a complement to the theory and the movement of psychoanalysis. Indeed, an examination of the purposes of the B'nai B'rith Wien provides an unusual opportunity for appreciating the relationship between Freud's Jewish consciousness and his work in psychoanalysis. The relationship, of course, was strong: The B'nai B'rith was a prefiguration of the psychoanalytic movement not only as an early study circle, but as a vehicle for attracting a following. The three members Freud recruited for the second lodge took an interest in his psychoanalytic endeavors. Hitschmann was one of the most active and prolific members of Freud's circle; and Rie, even before joining the circle

— in fact, at the time that Freud introduced him to the B'nai B'rith, served as an adviser for the publication of data on the Dora case.[26] Moreover, an assessment of the Jewish society illuminates the dynamic interrelationship between Freud's Jewish sensibility and psychoanalysis, by identifying "the truth of what we commonly believe."[27]

THE B'NAI B'RITH IN VIENNA

The *Israelitische Humanitäts-Verein "Wien" B'nai B'rith* was founded in Vienna on October 13, 1895, as the 449th member lodge of the international order. The day was chosen to commemorate the date the order was founded in New York City 52 years earlier. It was then that a group of German-Jewish immigrants, under the leadership of Heinrich Jonas (Henry Jones), formed an alliance and called themselves *Bundes-Brüder,* brothers of the union. Only later did they adopt the name "B'nai B'rith" (Sons of the Covenant) as a Hebrew designation, not because of its literal translation, but because the name, approximating the German appellation, retained the German initials. Often, just the initials were used in referring to the alliance as an incorporation of both German and Jewish allegiance. The original German name suggests that from the beginning, the organization stressed the value of unity and fellowship, rather than the religion of Judaism. In the American context, members of the B'nai B'rith endeavored to orient other Jewish immigrants to the new culture as well, and thus recognized, as their task, the elevation of living standards for those who suffered from impoverishment and ignorance. In Europe, the impetus for the founding of the B'nai B'rith was the spread of anti-Semitism, which threatened the material and moral fabric of the lives of Jews who were already settled. Unlike in America, the first lodge, established in Berlin in 1882, had a limited appeal at the beginning. Only a small fraction of the lower-middle-class segment of Jewry who experienced, more directly, the effects of anti-Semitism joined. Jews in the professions and in the intelligentsia expressed little interest. With the escalation of anti-Semitism in Germany and Austria, more and more Jews from all social strata began to recognize the importance of a Jewish union. The first B'nai B'rith in the Austro-Hungarian Empire was in Bielitz, Lower Silesia. After it opened in 1889, other lodges opened in quick succession: in Pilsen (Bohemia) and in Cracow (Galicia) in 1892, and during the following two years, in Prague, Reichenberg, and Karlsbad, all in Bohemia.[28]

An interest in the B'nai B'rith in Vienna crystallized in the winter of 1894 when 12 members, affiliated with one lodge or another, but without a place to meet, formed an ad hoc association. In the spring of that year, these members made an effort at formally establishing a B'nai B'rith society. According to protocol, the responsibility for founding a new society belonged ultimately to a parent society. The senior society inducted members on a provisional basis, as the genesis of the new society. This procedure began in Vienna with the induction of ten local Jewish residents into the lodge located in Prague. This core group, which included some from the ad hoc association, evolved into a search committee, led by an industrious figure, Edmund Kohn (1863-1929). By profession, Kohn was a gynecologist. He trained in general medicine at the medical school in Prague, where he received his degree in 1885, and afterward at the General Hospital in Vienna, where he worked with Nothnagel, among others. In 1895, Kohn approached Freud to persuade him to become a member. His respect for Freud was a steadfast admiration which lasted for the remainder of his life, and which Freud reciprocated.[29] Kohn believed Freud was a worthy candidate to fulfill the ideals of the B'nai B'rith as they were expressed in the preamble to the society's statutes; that is, to perform

> the mission of uniting Israelites in the work of promoting their highest interests and those of humanity; of developing and elevating the mental and moral character of the people of our faith; of inculcating the purest principles of philanthropy, honor and patriotism; of supporting science and art; alleviating the wants of the poor and needy; visiting and attending the sick; coming to the rescue of victims of persecution; providing for, protecting, and assisting the widow and orphan on the broadest principles of humanity.

Though Freud did not accept the invitation at this time, he regarded Kohn as the one person who enticed him into the B'nai B'rith.[30]

Kohn and other members of the search committee had little trouble attracting other candidates. Their efforts were significantly enhanced when the president of the Austrian district of the B'nai B'rith in Prague came to Vienna in March 1895 to describe the purpose of the society. Greeted by a full house, the speaker explained that anti-Semitism was a basic reason for the consolidation of Jews into an organized union: "The individual who is not capable of withstanding the influences of the day by himself finds strength in the community with others." Just as important as unity was the notion of discovering the value of Jewish identity: "In the circle of our union, he [the brother] learns to respect Judaism in a historical framework, he understands the value of our religious ideas and arrives at the conviction that Judaism is tantamount to true humanity and that its teaching lays the ground for the moral development of mankind." It was the amalgam of both aspects, the reaction to anti-Semitism and a renewed inner conviction, that characterized the purpose, indeed the mission, of the B'nai B'rith as

> a phalanx of intelligent and educated Jews with high principles, an ethical society based upon and within the scope of Judaism, an eloquent and energetic protest — despite the many problems — against the remonstrances directed toward Judaism. . . . Our task is now upon your shoulders, Gentlemen! The currents of hostility and rage which are a burden for us all have been concentrated in Vienna for years.

Austrian Jewry now expects from Vienna your assistance, alliance and leadership.

Several observers present remarked about the immediate impression this appeal made upon the audience. During the following weeks, more than 20 Jews, including Knöpfmacher and Ehrmann, indicated their desire to join the parent society. This raised the Vienna membership to nearly 50, a number deemed sufficient for the installation of the B'nai B'rith Wien.[31]

Upon the induction of members into the society in the years that followed, Kohn frequently expressed the message used to attract membership candidates. He asserted that the B'nai B'rith stimulated the best of Judaism and of humanity by encouraging in each brother, and for its common mission, the highest moral and ethical precepts.[32] When Freud joined the society in 1897, he claimed that the "humanitarian" interests of the B'nai B'rith strongly appealed to him. He acknowledged that these principles and the intimate atmosphere had "meant much to me and [had] done much for me."[33] To appreciate the character of his Jewish consciousness, and its influence on his work, it would be instructive to examine what "humanitarian" meant to the brotherhood; why the Jewish society adopted this essentially universal ideal as part of its name and as one of its centers of gravity; and how the ideal propelled the society both internally, as a consolidating agent, and externally, as an object of its mission. The society's manifesto is an appropriate place to begin, not only because of its ideological and representative nature, but also because it connects with Freud. The manifesto, entitled "Was Wir Wollen" ("What We Want"), came out in the first issue of the society's *Quarterly Report.* It thus appeared during Freud's first term as a member, indicating the direction of Wien when Freud joined in the fall of 1897. Moreover, the article was written by the journal's editor and Wien's president at that time, Ehrmann, a close friend of Freud's since the beginning of their student days at the University of Vienna, as well as Freud's personal and professional counterpart in their prior affiliation with the *Leseverein der deutschen Studenten Wiens,* in their work at the same medical laboratories; and in their prolonged anticipation of academic promotion, which, making them sensitive to anti-Semitism, stimulated their return to Judaism through the B'nai B'rith.[34]

Ehrmann established the scope of the society in the manifesto's first paragraph:

> Formed out of an inner urgency, the Humanitarian Societies of B'nai B'rith embark courageously and consciously upon their difficult and as yet unfulfilled tasks: to work on "elevating the mental and moral character of the people of our faith," to arouse and perfect the inherent virtues of our people [*Stammes*], to eliminate as far as is humanly possible the defective influences which seize every nation, and thus to work on behalf of mankind. For good reasons we therefore bear the sublime word humanity in our name.

Ehrmann preferred to discuss the importance of perfecting the Jewish nation within the broader historical and social framework. He said that the founding and the existence of the B'nai B'rith belonged to a rich, humanitarian tradition. The ideal of humanity was first cogently expressed by the Greeks, revived in the Renaissance, and, finally, fully realized in the Enlightenment. Ehrmann said these periods, interrupted by Byzantine, medieval, and modern, post-Enlightenment influences, all promoted, in an increasingly democratic way, the ideals of "brotherhood among men," "the old Jewish and Christian doctrine of love for one's neighbor," and "equal and innate rights." The Enlightenment, which emancipated Jews from the ghetto, produced "the protagonists of genuine humanity as we mean it." In their appeal for universal brotherhood and equality, Rousseau, Voltaire, and Lessing were thus the moral ancestors of modern Jewish existence. As Ehrmann's survey implied, hand in hand with the moral legacy was the united struggle to overcome forces antagonistic to these ideals. He believed that the parallel development of a new middle-class elite and the propagation of "scientific" doctrines, such as racial anti-Semitism, or the distortion of others, such as the evolutionary doctrine of survival, had eclipsed the practical realization of humanitarian ideals. Thus, the task of the B'nai B'rith was both substantive and strategic: "We want always to preserve this legacy of our ancestors. . . . This requires a systematic, resolute, and persistent effort at strengthening the proven ideals and a continuous, spiritual rapport between those who have fraternized for the common struggle."[35]

The five-page document firmly rooted the B'nai B'rith in the tradition of the Enlightenment and reflected the humanistic tradition of Jewish religion. It also suggested the importance of Jewish unity. But Ehrmann left unresolved the relationship of the B'nai B'rith with the rest of society. Why should the B'nai B'rith remain a strictly Jewish union if its ideals were nonsectarian and, in fact, the antithesis of social division? It seems contradictory that a manifesto affirming the "national" unity of the Jews would warn "never to separate our freedom from the freedom of our fellow man." Also confusing were the references to the Jewish people in terms of human rights or of the common struggle, and not, with the sole exception of the first paragraph, in terms reflecting the plight of Jews. Even in his discussion of the twofold task of the B'nai B'rith, Ehrmann neglected these more specific problems. This sectarian-nonsectarian distinction surfaces in Ehrmann's view of the society's place in the surrounding world. On the one hand, he affirmed the isolation of the B'nai B'rith not only from a hostile environment, but even from those who were persecuted and/or sympathetic with the ideals of brotherhood and equality. On the other hand, by expressing the desire "to strengthen the proven ideals" in a spirit of fraternal rapport, he conveyed the society's discomfort with its isolation.

Ehrmann left unresolved this relationship between the internal needs of the Jewish society and its humanitarian principles because it was not resolved among the brothers he represented. In fact, it was the one question that threatened to divide the brotherhood during these early years of its existence.

Every brother agreed that the ideals were worth fighting for. Moreover, there was a consensus on the need, indeed on the urgency, for a union of Jews. But how the universal ideals and the concern for mankind were to be reconciled with the desire for a self-contained Jewish community and with the concern for the problems facing the Jews was a hotly debated issue. "A true fever gripped almost every brother," Kohn reported.[36] The debate, ignited on the first day (September 29, 1897) of the society's fifth term, when Ehrmann announced the time for Wien to shift its concern from internal organization to the broader social arena outside the organization, and sustained more or less passionately throughout the following years, was coterminous with Freud's active affiliation. From the moment he joined the brotherhood, to his own contribution to the question of the goals and purposes of Wien in the fall of 1901, and beyond, Freud was exposed to the fundamental question of his own Jewish identity — the relationship between Jewish attachment and a commitment to humanitarian ideals.

Even among Freud's closest friends, different positions were taken on this difficult question. Kohn was a leading exponent of a program designed to benefit the Jewish community. Elected president for Wien's first two terms, Kohn had been responsible for fashioning the brotherhood into a binding structure. Indeed, at the first meeting of business after the installation of Wien in the fall of 1895, Kohn stressed that for Jews, happiness and strength could be found only among fellow Jews. Warning that any attempt to assimilate to Viennese culture only provoked further hostility, he appealed for the revitalization of the Jewish home and for greater reliance on the Jewish family.[37] Kohn believed that the atmosphere of intense political and economic conflict made unity a necessary condition of Jewish life. Indeed, he argued that the current spirit of national renascence, the tension between artisans and the forces of industrialization, the unionization of the working class, and anti-Semitism itself forced Jews to unite themselves as a movement for survival:

> We need this strength — the times in which we live demand it. What do we see all around us? Unity among each nation, unity for every kind of trade to maintain its existence, unity for the proletariat. . . . We see international congresses for the protection of the worker, for the protection against epidemics. What we do not see is the unity of the Jews for the protection against an international poisoning of the heart and soul, against the defamation of their religion [e.g., ritual murder]. Neither do we see Jewish unity for the protection against assaults on their business, their possessions, even on their life. From "Do not buy from Jews" to murder and indiscriminate killing is only a step.[38]

Kohn encouraged comradeship among the brothers of the B'nai B'rith on two fronts. He took steps to ensure a spirit of fellowship within the society, and initiated or supported charitable programs for the economic assistance of Jewish immigrants in Vienna and of East-European Jews who had decided to remain in the pale.

These two programs, Jewish fellowship and Jewish welfare, became integral features of the society. In an address given on the tenth anniversary of Wien, Kohn described how the atmosphere of mutual sympathy and intimacy had evolved over the decade: "The united men, who at first numbered forty, hardly knew each other by name, but learned to respect and value each other as they gradually became closer and more friendly until the final, intimate friendship became an integrated totality."[39] Many brothers frequently credited Kohn for successfully bringing together not only strangers, but Jews from various religious and social backgrounds. In the words of one brother, Kohn was responsible for "uniting Judaism into a great, common, spiritual fatherland" and into "a common metapolitical system." According to the author of this obituary on Kohn, unity was his most fundamental principle: "The B'nai B'rith, nay, all of Judaism will become as you wanted it to become . . . a single nation of brothers."[40] Similarly, Wilhelm Knöpfmacher believed that the very essence of the B'nai B'rith was the reunification of the Jewish people. He felt that the emancipation of the Jews and the ensuing assimilation had threatened the idea and ideal of Jewish unity:

> It is now my firm belief that the actual reasons for the formation of the "B'nai B'rith" in Austria can be discerned and established only on the basis of a thorough investigation into and explanation of the destiny of the Austrian Jews . . . during the period after 1848. Only upon such a fundamental investigation do we arrive at the deepest essence of our union: It is my feeling that this is a reunification of all segments of Jewry who are disposed toward the ideal [of unity]. In the recent decades, the ideal of inner connection and the feeling of fellowship were missing.

For Knöpfmacher, Jewish reunification was not only the essence of the B'nai B'rith, but the essence of religion as well. Thirty years ago, he had defended the traditional practice and observance of Judaism. Now he claimed that religion was, in effect, the feeling of belonging together: "It is self-evident to interpret the word 'religion' only in its strict meaning found in its derivation from the Latin 'religare,' to tie back. It thus conveys the meaning 'reunification.' "[41] Both Kohn and Knöpfmacher took steps toward enhancing the spirit of fraternal fellowship, by introducing such functions as brother meals and orientation events for newly initiated brothers.

In financial respects, the establishment of Jewish welfare programs represented Wien's outstanding contribution to the Jewish community in Vienna. Within a few years after the founding of the B'nai B'rith in Vienna, these programs helped the society gain the esteem of the B'nai B'rith throughout Austria, making Wien the logical choice for becoming the district seat in 1911.

One result of the debate in the fall of 1897 was the creation of a *Humanitätsfond,* a fund procured from voluntary contributions of the brothers, to set up a job-placement agency for immigrant Jews. In the first years of its existence, the agency provided over 13,000 positions. The brotherhood set up other agencies, for lending money, treating the victims of tuberculosis, and establishing an orphanage. Kohn believed that these efforts embodied the highest principles of humanity. He felt that even if Jewish welfare programs were motivated by and directed toward Jews, they were, nevertheless, humane acts of charity that lifted the dignity of poor and deprived Jews. Conversely, the allocation of funds strictly to Jews was only a response to the inhumane neglect of poor Jews living in Vienna.[42] The support and success of the *Humanitätsfond* suggest how widely in the society the brothers held this interpretation of humanity. Ehrmann defended the limitations of the society and its charity for Jews: "This restriction exists only by necessity. It is a restriction based on the fact that the poor and oppressed Jew is not only poor and oppressed because this is his common human destiny, but is in a much more deplorable situation and is more oppressed than even the destitute of other faiths because he is a Jew."[43]

Besides its charitable endeavors, Ehrmann supported the society's stress on fellowship because he felt that, like Jewish welfare programs, Jewish fellowship was necessary. He argued that since those Jews who maintained their Jewish integrity were the victims of a "social boycott," they should have an opportunity for experiencing warm friendship, and for exploring the arts and sciences without fear or restraint.[44] He shared the sense of urgency with Kohn and Knöpfmacher. However, he was not satisfied with what he believed was their ultimately one-sided position. Freed from an obligation to reconcile or represent the brotherhood's differences of opinion in the years following his stating of the society's manifesto, Ehrmann wrote two major position papers in the *Quarterly Report* that defined a viewpoint, within the local lodge, opposing the tendency toward one-sidedness. Both of these papers – the first, a retrospective assessment of the B'nai B'rith (1899); the second, a response to a series of discussions on the goals and purposes of Wien (1902) – extended the logic of the humanitarian ideal beyond the interpretation that limited it to Jewish charity and fellowship. Whereas in the manifesto, Ehrmann attempted to achieve a consensus within the young Jewish society, by stressing the twofold importance of unity and universality, in the later two articles he explored their inter-relationship – on the one hand, establishing the position only vaguely suggested in his earlier resolve "to work on behalf of mankind," and, on the other, directing the society beyond its sectarian tendency.

The 1902 article, "Über die Function des Judenthums innerhalb der Menschheit und der B.B. innerhalb des Judenthums" ("The Function of Judaism within Mankind and of the B.B. within Judaism"), reaffirmed his earlier evaluation of Judaism. Rather than being an observance of laws and customs, he said, Judaism rests upon "the active support of the ideals of humanity which our prophets laid down but which have been ignored by European mankind." While he believed this was the function of Judaism generally, he felt the B'nai B'rith had an obligation to sustain it consciously:

> Until this glorious time [of freedom and unity] comes, it remains our function − as at the time of the prophets − to preserve the ideal of humanity through the period of moral degeneration. . . . In this world of insatiable lust for power . . . we must perform our inherited function: to prevent mankind from totally sinking into perverse hands as well as from succumbing to the worshipers of the Moloch of savage power and to the craving of reckless power-seekers.

This time, he explained the nomenclature of the B'nai B'rith in Austria without reference to the Jewish predicament: "We in Austria have not called ourselves *Humanitätsvereine* for nothing: we are the champions of the ideal of humanity." The ambiguity between the universal ideals and the desire for an isolated brotherhood of Jews thus recedes in this view of Jews as the sole defenders of the "proven ideals." In Ehrmann's opinion, the Jewish tradition not only was a noble tradition, but also was the only example in the present day of ideals promising democracy and peace.[45]

Ehrmann's emphasis on the unique, indeed the superior, quality of the Jewish people marked a shift from the position Jews had advanced during the previous decades. Though such Jews as Ehrmann, Königstein, and Freud, as well as several other members of Wien, belonged to the German-nationalist Leseverein and to other movements fostering the ideal of social integration,[46] they supported these movements with little, if any, regard for religion or their Jewishness. Indeed, they considered religion obsolete or, at most, ancillary. Even the Jewish humanitarian organization Chevra-Kadischa, to which Breuer belonged, differed in tone and stress, in the important respect that it never doubted German-Jewish compatibility. Though it was a separate Jewish group, Chevra-Kadischa evolved not as a response to social hostility or to social neglect, but as a positive effort aimed at improving the quality of life for fellow Jews, as its motto suggested: "Take care of your brothers who are weak or sick, honor your deceased, be merciful."[47] Moreover, the organization regarded the ethical heritage of the Jewish people as consistent with the ideals of European culture. Breuer himself expressed the dual identity in the way he signed his 1894 letter to Kadimah − "Josef Breuer, Jew by origin, German by nation." Affirming the German-Jewish balance, he wrote this neither in Hebrew nor in German, but in a neutral, transnational Latin.[48] As he implied in the letter, anti-Semitism was not a threat to German-Jewish congeniality. However precarious the balance might have seemed to him at the end of his life, he sustained a faith in − even, he admitted, an "illusion" of − amiable and equal social relations.[49]

In opposition to the position Breuer represented, Ehrmann, and those in Wien like him, believed that anti-Semitism had disturbed the German-Jewish balance. The brotherhood expressed the need to withdraw from the delirium of hate and intolerance. In many respects, this response to anti-Semitism paralleled another, across the park along the Ringstrasse, the nascent Zionist movement. In fact, in the months before the full-scale debate on the direction of the society, many brothers argued for some kind of liaison between Wien and political Zionism. The inherent differences between the two groups laid the issue to rest. Whereas the B'nai B'rith was an isle of refuge within a hostile environment, political Zionism sought refuge outside this environment. Moreover, the brotherhood's mission "to prevent mankind from totally sinking into perverse hands" differed from the political tone of Zionism. Ehrmann's position thus represented a compromise between an unrealistic perpetuation of congenial German-Jewish relations and the Zionist severance of these relations. In effect, this meant a retreat, but not a resignation, from the hope for genuine humanity and social equality. Conversely, it meant a preservation of these ideals, while the rest of Europe splintered into factional strife.

To be sure, this sense of uniqueness and superiority was not exclusivistic. Ehrmann felt that though the Jews were the only people in the current day capable of sustaining and exercising the noble ideals, this was the case because others chose to ignore them, not because they were incapable of achieving them. Indeed, the missionary inflection of his statement presumes only a temporary distinction between Jews and Germans before the "glorious time comes." On the other hand, the B'nai B'rith did not design or sponsor programs for mobilizing these sentiments into a tangible movement. Too many brothers, including Kohn and Ehrmann, hesitated to provoke any more hostility than already existed, as Ehrmann himself noted:

> As soon as Jews are ready as a group to raise the banner of love among men, which was at one time or another raised by men of all nations and confessions, the voices of the mob, who follow the course "from nationality to bestiality," make a loud noise about denationalization, the feeble stupor of humanity, Judaization [*Verjudung*], etc. . . . We have nothing to hide, but we have no reason to allow our cause to be thrown around in the street mud. . . . We do not shun publicity, but we do not seek it out either. We do not shun the crowd, but we do shun the profane crowd.[50]

Though the task of the B'nai B'rith did not develop into a defined procedure, it was more than a shared sentiment or a unifying idea. Several brothers felt that there was a way of transmitting the ideals from Wien to the rest of society. Ehrmann offered one explanation, by examining first the function of Judaism — he dismissed the term "mission" in describing the task, for he felt it implied a power the small, victimized, and only recently organized group of Jews did not have[51] — and then the function of the B'nai B'rith. Judaism, as "a principle of unlimited development and eternal progress," always had a liberating influence on the rest of mankind, especially in philosophy and in the sciences. Spinoza, for example, a "Jew even in his way of thinking," had contributed to excellence and freedom by pursuing knowledge and truth. Ehrmann noted that more recently, Jews had smoothed the way in all lands for the development of modern technology and remained in the forefront of biological research. In his praise of the influence of Jews and Judaism through the ages, Ehrmann pointed to Jewish culture as the basis of this influence. With his medical training in the currently popular Darwinian theories of evolution, it is possible he had in mind a Jewish élan vital. Certainly, he dismissed religion as insignificant, among the forces inspiring the Jewish contribution to the progress of mankind. He cherished the story of a Jewish convert who wrote, for the epitaph on one of the most important biologists of the day, a Jew, but also brought up without religion: "For his work, mankind is not yet ready."

"In our ranks," Ehrmann wrote, referring to the B'nai B'rith in the conclusion to his 1902 position paper,

> anyone involved in intellectual endeavors should realize that his work is nothing but idle ostentation if it fails to make man better, nobler, more sensitive to what is good and just. Pure scholarship surely has its place, but it also has its limits. He [the B'nai B'rith brother] should seize the opportunity for disseminating the ethical influences of his knowledge.[52]

About the time Ehrmann expressed these views, another brother, a founding member of Wien and president of the society between Kohn's and Ehrmann's terms of office, invoked the image of a fortress with "exiting gates" to describe the function of the B'nai B'rith. He remarked that within this bastion of ethical and humanitarian interests, the brother could gain the strength for stepping outside and, in the dissemination of these ideals, "become a blessing for all races of the earth."[53]

A NEW FORUM FOR MOVEMENT

From the addresses given by members of the Jewish society 24 years later, in celebration of Freud's seventieth birthday (May 6, 1926), it would seem that Freud adhered to this function of the B'nai B'rith in his development of the theory and the movement of psychoanalysis. Hitschmann, whom Freud enlisted for the brotherhood and for the psychoanalytic circle, regarded Freud's "extra-dimensional" or "universal" scientific achievement as a supremely Jewish contribution, and as an effective foil against the clamor of anti-Semitism: "In our time, it is the Jewish people who through Freud drown out the voices of the other people."[54]

Ludwig Braun (1867-1936), who joined the Viennese lodge Wien three years after Freud did, and served as its vice president in 1904-5, enlarged upon Hitschmann's observation. Braun had known Freud since the late 1880s, probably as a student, when Freud lectured at the university,[55] and became even closer to him as his private physician in the 1920s. His address, "Die persönlichkeit Freuds und seine Bedeutung als Bruder" ("Freud's Personality and His Importance as Brother"), was the first time anyone attempted to define Freud's Jewish identity. That Freud was, despite his lack of religion, "genuinely Jewish" was beyond Braun's doubt: "Can anyone even imagine Freud as not Jewish?" Braun divided his conception of what was Jewish into three dimensions. The first was a spirit of independence — independence from religious dogma, from conventional morality, and, for that matter, from the world. The only guide for the Jew was his inner morality. The second dimension brought the Jew back into a relationship with the world. This was his courageous determination to combat or oppose the rest of society, his enemy. Besides steadfast persistence, dignity, and composure, the struggle involved an optimism rooted historically in the Jewish will to survive millennia of ghettoization and persecution. According to Braun, this spiritual optimism constituted the "true religion of the heart." The third Jewish characteristic was the quality of wholeness (*das Ganze*). He said, "Wholeness means Jew precisely." The *Ganzjude* was able to discern, behind the fragmented and discordant surface, the unity and indivisibility of nature. Hitschmann and Braun described this ability, respectively, as an "extra-dimensional" insight and a "metapolitical" power. Braun believed that the unique capacity for wholeness enabled the Jew to recognize that "the mind and soul of every person have the same organization." The Jew sees all men equally. The three Jewish characteristics were all part of the dynamism of the Jewish personality that explained why Jews always have been martyrs in the cause of freedom.[56]

After defining the nature of Judaism, Braun made the connection between Freud's involvement in the Jewish society and in psychoanalysis. He felt that because Freud refused to devote himself to Zionism, to religious piety, or to any other partial expression of Judaism, he was "genuinely Jewish," a *Ganzjude*. Braun noted: "He is not just part of the whole. . . . As a *Ganzjude*, Freud's personality explains his natural relation to the B'nai B'rith." Moreover, the emphasis placed by the Jewish group, in lieu of the rest of mankind, on humanitarian ideals explained why "Freud feels at home here." Braun concluded that Freud's support of these Jewish ideals surfaced in his dedication to psychoanalysis. Seeking to understand nature's general laws and to "bring people together," Freud developed a science which affirmed "a perfectly Jewish conception of life" ("eine echt jüdische . . . Lebensanschauung"). Braun referred to Freud's claim for the convergence of life and death in the death wish as an example of Jewish insight, for the science "pulls back the curtain covering the depths of the mind and discloses the kernel of eternity."[57]

Freud recognized the exaggerated, ex post facto possessiveness of the brotherhood. "From all sides and places, the Jews have enthusiastically seized me for themselves," he wrote Schnitzler, a few weeks after the birthday celebration. He was embarrassed by the way they treated him, as if he were "a God-fearing Chief Rabbi," or "a national hero."[58] Yet, though Freud was aware of the tendency in the brotherhood to claim him and his work as "genuinely Jewish," now that psychoanalysis had achieved international attention, he did not dismiss the society's evaluation. Braun's words especially impressed him. They "cast a spell over the whole audience, including my family," he wrote. The remarks, which Freud read two days before the celebration, inspired the substance for his reply to the brotherhood. He had only to "add" to Braun's paper.[59]

While he felt it was difficult to pass overall judgment on Braun's insights, Freud confirmed his sentiments, and supported those in the Jewish society who urged Jews to regard themselves as mankind's champions of democratic and fraternal ideals. Recalling his decision to join Wien, he wrote: "It was only to my Jewish nature that I owed the two qualities that have become indispensable to me throughout my difficult life. Because I was a Jew I found myself free of many prejudices which restrict others in the use of the intellect: as a Jew I was prepared to be in the opposition and to renounce agreement with the 'compact majority.' So I became one of you [and] took part in your humanitarian and national interests."[60] The reference to his "Jewish nature" reflected a thorough Jewish self-conception that corresponded Braun's typological conception of the Ganzjude and with Ehrmann's notion of a Jewish élan vital. The two Jewish qualities, freedom from the limitations of bias, as well as an independence from, and an opposition to, the conventions of society, summed up, in succinct terms, Braun's three-point description of the progressive Jew fighting for equality, and Ehrmann's similar notion of the function of the B'nai B'rith.

Freud's expression of allegiance to the B'nai B'rith function came years after the initial development of psychoanalytic theory and the formation of the movement. Near the end of his life, in 1935, he expressed an even stronger adherence to the B'nai B'rith. He claimed that he "never lost the feeling of belonging" to the brotherhood. He said, "The total agreement [*die weitgehende Übereinstimmung*] of our cultural and humanitarian ideals, as well as the same joyful acknowledgement of Jewish descent and Jewish existence, have vividly sustained this feeling."[61] When he recalled his participation in the humanitarian ideals of the B'nai B'rith, Freud referred to a signficant and definitive tradition within the Jewish association, one that both supported a sense of Jewish moral superiority to the injustices of an intolerant, inhumane – indeed, anti-Semitic – society, and invoked the Jewish obligation not only to sustain the ideals of equality and the whole, but also to disseminate these ideals in the brother's own way.

Freud's adherence to the B'nai B'rith at the turn of the century was clearly as strong as his "feeling of belonging" later on. The date of his initiation into the society, the fall of 1897, indicates the fulfillment of a wish for Jewish fellowship, dreamt earlier that year. Less than three months after joining, Freud rejoiced at the "enthusiastic reception" of his first lecture. Not only did he continue his close association with the brotherhood, by presenting other addresses and by maintaining an active record of attendance, but he committed himself to the organization's growth, and, indeed, to the founding of Vienna's second lodge. With the exception of psychoanalysis itself, his work in the B'nai B'rith represented Freud's strongest commitment during this creative period of his life. Freud's close association with the brotherhood reflects an intense Jewish consciousness, as well as a sympathetic attraction to other Jews. In addition, it suggests a strong identification with the function of the brotherhood, from the very beginning of his active affiliation. The degree of this identification with the notion of Jewish ethical responsibility provides an important insight into the development of psychoanalysis, for it shows the extent of Freud's Jewish consciousness during his development of the theory and the movement of psychoanalysis. Moreover, the strength of Freud's adherence to the brother-hood's conception of a Jewish ethical elite suggests the importance of the Jewish society as an impetus for the psychoanalytic movement.

During the first years of his development of psychoanalytic theory, Freud utilized the B'nai B'rith as a primary intellectual forum for his germinating ideas. By being more accessible than Fliess, the society increased Freud's opportunities for intellectual exchange. Moreover, the B'nai B'rith filled the vacuum created by Freud's rejection of the professional and academic discussion centers between mid-1898 and late 1902, when he formed his own study group. Freud's affiliation with the brotherhood thus possessed the intimacy and uniqueness of this later study group. In response, the B'nai B'rith was a constantly supportive audience that provided Freud with the opportunity for presenting his views as well as for exploring ideas freely. In conjunction with the lectures on psycho-analytic topics, Freud's active interest in the expansion of the local B'nai B'rith indicates how highly he prized the Jewish society as a viable center for intellectual discussion. In the course of the first five years of membership, Freud played an important role in recruiting members for the Jewish lodge. He became an especially active recruiter for the second B'nai B'rith lodge in Vienna, *Eintracht* (Harmony). From 1900 to Eintracht's formation in 1903, Freud participated in the planning stages, serving, at the end of this period, on the search committee.[62] In addition to increasing his audience, he sought members sympathetic with his psychoanalytic views. Königstein and Rie, whom Freud recruited for Wien (1898) and for Eintracht (1901), respectively, were close friends of Freud's and supporters of his work. A third member Freud attracted to the B'nai B'rith (Eintracht), Hitschmann, was an extremely loyal follower of Freud in the psychoanalytic circle.

From 1897 to 1902, Freud brought his current scientific investigations to the brotherhood eight times. He addressed the B'nai B'rith three times before he published the results. On two other occasions, he explored themes in greater detail than he did in print.[63] Both his deliberate selection of the Jewish society for the communication of his discoveries, and the enthusiastic manner in which he pursued his ideas point to the central significance of Jews in his formation of a psychoanalytic following. Though all but one of his addresses have been lost, it is possible, from various notices, references, and reviews, as well as from the high degree to which the lecture titles and dates correspond with his published work, to reconstruct the themes he stressed. Moreover, this reconstruction and a close examination of the one extant lecture show the depth of Freud's intellectual esteem for the Jewish society.[64]

By the time Freud delivered his two papers on dream interpretation in mid-December 1897, he had presented his early findings to the Jüdisch-akademische Lesehalle (1896-97) and referred to his investigations on the subject in various letters to Fliess. However, the B'nai B'rith lectures represented his first mature expression of dream theory, since he only began a serious undertaking of his book on dreams at the time he delivered the lectures.[65] As the *Quarterly Report* indicated,[66] Freud began the lecture "Interpretation of Dreams" "with the familiar physiological causes of dreams," and then turned to "the psychology of dream life," which, the reporter wrote, "established the principles of a self-contained theory." The lecture contained the germ of the written text, which he completed in 1899. At the beginning of the book, Freud raised the question of "whether the explanation of the causation of dreams fell within the province of psychology or rather of physiology." The discussion of the sources of dreams that followed went beyond his lecture to the brotherhood, for it involved a survey of theories based on his current readings. Freud did not dismiss these theories. He doubted only the adequacy, not the correctness, of the view, for example, that "men dream of what . . . interests them while they are awake."[67] In devoting the remainder of the book to revealing other, unsuspected psychical sources of dream stimulation, Freud achieved the "self-contained theory" which he had posited earlier in his B'nai B'rith lectures.

At the conclusion of the second lecture on dreams, Freud proclaimed the intelligibility and the meaning of dream life. According to the reporter for the journal, Freud "characterized the great significance of his scientific theory; he said: whoever is occupied with the dreams of man and understands their true meaning peers into the secrets of the human mind as into a crater imbedded within the earth's dark interior." Freud's conclusion announced his intention of writing the book: Besides explaining the technique of interpretation, "I shall further endeavor to elucidate the [psychical] processes to which the strangeness and obscurity of dreams are due." In both cases, Freud conveyed the exhilaration of penetrating into hidden sources of life. In a similar vein, he wrote Fliess, two months after the B'nai B'rith lectures, "It has been left to me to draw the first crude map . . . [of] the psychical territory on which the dream process is played out." The lecture's conclusion affirmed not only the discovery of truth, but the common basis of life. Proof of the existence and primacy of psychic life impressed one brother for its revealing of what was of "general human interest."[68]

Freud's third lecture to the B'nai B'rith, "The Psychology of Forgetting," took place on February 3, 1899. Like his addresses on dreams, it reportedly had a "striking" effect on the brotherhood and "established new . . . points of view." As he was to do a few years later, in his own study circle, he not only contributed to the society's intellectual life, but played a leading role in it. Freud began his first serious exploration of parapraxes four months before his third talk to the brotherhood. In August 1898 he wrote Fliess about his growing interest in the common slip of forgetting a name and replacing it with part of another name. During the last week in September, Freud wrote a paper entitled "The Psychical Mechanism of Forgetfulness." It appeared in the December issue of a medical monthly, and eventually formed the basis of the first chapter of *The Psychopathology of Everyday Life* (1901). Most likely, Freud relied on the published article for his B'nai B'rith lecture. In this article, Freud discussed the emergence of threatening or repressed thought into the process of name recollection, which produced the phenomenon of memory lapses.[69]

A year later, on February 4, 1900, Freud delivered his fourth lecture, "The Psychic Life of the Child." This address, like the article with which it corresponded, "Screen Memories," was the sequel to his piece on forgetfulness. As early as January 3, 1899, shortly after he had published the first article, Freud wrote Fliess of his efforts to examine the relationship between the experiences of earliest childhood and the distortion of memories. By the end of May, Freud sent in the sequel for publication. It appeared in September, and later as the fourth chapter of the work on everyday psychopathology. The title of the address referred to the basic notion of the article: The "psychical functioning of children," that is, the first memories of fear, shame, pain, death, siblings' births, serve to distort the actual content of these events, but in a symbolic way, so that the analyst, through interpretation of the screened memory, can recover the original content as well as the sources of repression.[70]

Up to this time, Freud, in his lectures to the brotherhood, covered all his important published themes on dreams and parapraxes. In two subsequent talks, he explored ideas in greater detail, or with more certain freedom, than he did in print. Freud insisted on this practice of free discussion later in the psychoanalytic circle. Both lectures concentrated on the life of the contemporary French literary naturalist and public figure Émile Zola. On April 24, 1900, Freud discussed Zola's most recent novel, *Fécondité* (1899). His interest in Zola had emerged years before, in his interpretation of the revolutionary dream (Count Thun), and in a letter to Fliess in 1898. However, evidence of his fascination for this particular work appeared only years later, when in 1907, Freud listed "ten good books," in response to a colleague's inquiry. At this time, at the meetings of the psychoanalytic society, Freud frequently commented on the eccentric themes in Zola's novels. To Freud, Zola's work disclosed classical symptoms of an obsessional neurosis. This expression of interest explains Freud's immediate attraction to the novel in 1900. *Fécondité* (Fertility) was a wild celebration of the large family, and of procreation generally. Almost every chapter began, "Two years passed and Mathieu and Marianne had another child." An equally repetitive theme involved the censuring of sexual relations that did not result in procreation.[71] For the analyst, the book vividly clarified obsessional behavior and, in noting the absolution from wrongdoing in the act of procreation, expressed sexual guilt. Freud's review may have anticipated his paper on the resemblance between "Obsessive Actions and Religious Practices," written in 1907 when he renewed his interest in the French author, for Zola intended his novel to be the first of an evangelical cycle. He deliberately named the hero Mathieu, after the author of Christian gospel.

The second talk, entitled "Émile Zola," took place in the fall of 1902.[72] Freud's interest in Zola included an appreciation of the Frenchman's heroic rejection of incompetent and tyrannical authority. Twice in 1898, he had lauded the expression of revolt in Zola's *Germinal* and *La terre,* as well as his battle against the exponents of monarchy and anti-Semitism, during the dramatic Dreyfus affair. Jews strongly identified with Zola at that time. One recalled, "A Jewish lad in Vienna could not help but write a passionate letter to a friend about [Dreyfus's] unwarranted persecution. . . . Émile Zola stood up and declared: J'accuse!"[73] The fact that Zola died on September 29, 1902, and the simple title of the second talk suggest Freud's desire to commemorate Zola's accomplishments. This theme also permitted the analytic mind to explore the patricidal impulse in Zola's life, including the struggle against "feeble-minded" authority (as Freud found in *La terre*), against "the degeneracy of France" (as Freud referred to Zola's struggle in a letter to Fliess), or against obsolescence and repression in society (as other contemporary Jewish analysts perceived the fight against anti-Semitism).[74]

During the 18-month period preceding the founding of the Psychological Wednesday Society, Freud presented two lectures which expressed his primary concern for constructing comprehensive theories of dream life and parapraxes. On February 26, 1901, he delivered the paper "Chance and Superstition." This was the third talk on the topic of slips and lapses, and the third time a B'nai B'rith lecture preceded the publication of corresponding observations. Freud regarded parapraxes as good preliminary material for introducing nonmedical people to psychoanalysis. Three of his *Introductory Lectures* (1916-17), for example, were devoted to the subject. After he lectured on screen memories to the brotherhood in February 1900, Freud left aside the subject of parapraxes until the following fall, when he began to collect material for his book on the psychology of everyday life. On February 15, 1901, he reported to Fliess, "I shall finish with the every-day psychology during the next few days." The last chapter of *The Psychopathology of Everyday Life* was entitled "Determinism, Belief in Chance and Superstition: Some Points of View." The lecture on chance and superstition clearly incorporated this material. The chapter elucidated the psychological significance of superstitions and the force of the unconscious, which determines seemingly unintentional, accidental occurrences.[75]

On April 30, 1902, Freud gave the lecture "On Dreams." This was the first of the papers Freud gave to a B'nai B'rith audience outside Vienna. He delivered it to Moravia, a lodge in Brünn.[76] Freud apparently felt dreams were, like parapraxes, effective material for introducing his ideas to a lay audience. Five years earlier, he had succeeded in impressing the brothers of Wien with a discussion on the same subject. This time, Freud had available to him not only a completed and published account of the results of his investigations, but a 40-page précis that he contributed to the first number of a medical serial. The essay, "The Dream," appeared a year before the lecture.[77]

In connection with the B'nai B'rith lectures presented from 1897 to 1902, all indications point to Freud's serious concern for sharing the results of his scientific research with the brotherhood. However, because only traces of the lectures exist, the question arises as to the divergence between the lectures and the presentation of similar material in published form. Though Freud treated his audience with respect for its interest in his emerging theories and in human problems generally, to what extent did he adjust his presentation of theory to a lay Jewish audience? Since his publications were professional and concerned with scientific problems, it is possible that Freud's presentation of theory in this form differed from, more than resembling, his pronouncements to the B'nai B'rith. Though the one extant lecture, "We and Death," was given in 1915, years after the establishment of the movement, analysis of it affirms Freud's intellectual relation to the Jewish society.

Freud presented this lecture to the B'nai B'rith a few months before he published "Thoughts for the Times on War and Death" in the psychoanalytic journal *Imago.*[78] The second part of the essay "Our Attitude towards Death" corresponds with the 1915 B'nai B'rith lecture. Besides syntactical differences, there were three ways the lecture and the essay diverged. An example of the most obvious difference between the two appears at the very beginning of the lecture. Freud opened with the remark that Jews generally, and he personally, reacted in an unusual way to the pall of death brought on by the outbreak of international war six months before: "Instead of 'We and Death,' the title could read 'We Jews and Death,' for we Jews exhibit the attitude toward death, which I want to discuss with you, very frequently and in the extreme." He referred to the many occasions the brotherhood set aside for commemorating a deceased brother, and noted how the brotherhood dismissed or attempted to avoid the inescapable phenomenon by assuming that death was something accidental or personally remote. His observation was, at the same time, self-criticism. "When one asks a Jew how old he is, he answers, sixty (about) to a hundred and twenty!" Freud was then almost 59. To show how this fear of death had restricted life for Jews, he decided to use some anecdotes, because he knew that, like himself, "you are happy to hear jokes." He added, "I hope you have not become so preoccupied with the problem [of death] that you are not open to anecdotes here too." In a letter to a colleague two months later, Freud admitted the lecture contained "much grim humor." One such anecdote showed how the fear of death discouraged Jews from aspiring toward a better life: "The mother, seeing her son lying unconscious after falling from a ladder, runs to the Rabbi for advice and help. Tell me, the Rabbi says, why a Jewish boy on a ladder?"[79] Like the rest of this material on the problem of death for Jews, this anecdote did not appear in *Imago*.

Despite the concentration on Jews, the B'nai B'rith lecture was just as comprehensive as the *Imago* article. Even though he explored the Jewish reactions to death, Freud did not make a case for the high incidence of repression among the Jewish people. As in the *Imago* version, he maintained that it was a problem for everyone. By making a change in the wording of his title, he suggested that the problem of avoidance did indeed afflict Jews. But, by keeping the title "We and Death," he indicated that the problem was universal. Freud's isolating of the Jews in the lecture was an elocutionary device to sustain the interest of his audience. It did not limit his exploration into the responses to death. Indeed, the device made it easier for him to discuss the phenomenon of repression with the brotherhood.

The other ways in which the lecture and the essay diverged were procedural. These differences were matters of tone and approach. First, a sympathetic, tentative tone distinguished the B'nai B'rith lecture from the *Imago* version. For example, Freud apologized to the brotherhood for talking about a subject he knew would be uncomfortable for them to hear about. He also anticipated resistance from some brothers when he broached the subject of the death wish.[80] In the *Imago* article, he was more direct and argumentative in expressing his views. Secondly, in the *Imago* version, Freud left out various references he made, in his B'nai B'rith address, to his position in the society. An example of the respect he commanded from the brotherhood appeared in his discussion of the impulse of aggression. The impulse cannot be ignored, he said. Yet, "I cannot summon you to [aggressive behavior] as to something noble, for it is indeed a step backward, a regression." Also, he affirmed his critical attitude toward the Jewish religion when he reminded his B'nai B'rith audience that Judaism had repressed the impulse of aggression by dispelling the memory of the primal act of parricide.[81]

When Freud wrote his lecture on death for the B'nai B'rith, he presented substantially the same argument he presented in his *Imago* article. In both, he discussed the postulates of a death wish and its regression, as well as the therapy of recognizing its existence. The substantive similarities confirm his high regard for the society, expecially for its receptivity to ideas he felt were universal and progressive. The procedural differences are significant, too. The frequency and variety of such devices as making the topic relevant to his listeners, or anticipating the distress his topic might cause, reflected a desire to convince the brotherhood of the validity of his theory of human behavior, as well as of an effective method for overcoming problems due to unconscious responses. The effort to interest the Jewish society in the themes and teachings of psychoanalysis demonstrates the seriousness of his endeavors within the B'nai B'rith, as well as his intention of achieving an atmosphere of intellectual expression and theoretical exploration.

The two years directly preceding the formation of the psychoanalytic circle (1901-2) were Freud's most active years in the Jewish society. He concentrated most of his recruitment activity, and half of the ten lectures he presented from the time he joined the brotherhood, into this short period. Moreover, in the fall of 1901, and once again in the winter of 1902, Freud introduced two series of debates, both on the scope of the B'nai B'rith. Thus, besides forming a following and seeking discussion, Freud, now as chairman of the cultural committee, sought other ways to lead an attentive group in lectures and debate.

Seen as the antecedents of the psychoanalytic movement, Freud's accelerated recruitment, lecture, and leadership activity in the B'nai B'rith in 1901-2 points to the centrality of Jews in his development of a psychoanalytic school. By exchanging ideas with, and seeking advice from, fellow Jews, Freud promoted the view, commonly held in the brotherhood, that Jews played a primary role in affirming universal and humanitarian values. Freud also advanced the view that Jews played a responsible role in teaching these values to others. Many, believing this was the most important function of the B'nai B'rith, summoned the brother to "seize the opportunity for disseminating the ethical influences of his knowledge," as Ehrmann put it, or, as another brother urged, to "step outside" the society as a blessing for all mankind.

In the fall of 1901, Freud introduced a debate on the "Goals and Purposes of the B'nai B'rith Order." This debate inspired Ehrmann's statement on the function of Judaism within mankind.[82] Whether or not Freud himself directly affirmed, in his introductory remarks, the current B'nai B'rith belief in Jewish ethical responsibility, he did adhere to the belief in his development of the psychoanalytic movement. Until March 6, 1907, when Carl Jung (1875-1961) and another Swiss psychiatrist, Ludwig Binswanger (1881-1966), attended their first meeting in Vienna, every member of the circle — by this time, there were about 20 — was Jewish. The first non-Jew from Vienna to enter the circle was Rudolf Urbantschitsch (1879-?). He joined on January 8, 1908. Ernest Jones (1879-1958) came to the group four months later, on May 6.[83] As in the Jewish society, Freud surrounded himself with fellow Jews in the psychoanalytic circle, in the pursuit of his scientific ideas. His attraction to Jews was so strong that when non-Jews first entered the movement, he responded with an uncomfortable feeling of "strangeness." In a letter of 1908 to Karl Abraham (1877-1925), his colleague and a Berlin analyst, Freud expressed the concern that since Jung was not a Jew, he "finds his way to me only against great inner resistances." Even after several more non-Jews entered the movement, Freud continued to prefer a Jewish following because, as he remarked to Abraham, "it is easier for you than it is for Jung to follow my ideas."[84]

Nevertheless, Freud's decision to form the psychoanalytic circle in 1902 reflected his desire to go beyond a parochial setting for the development of psychoanalysis. Indeed, after 1902, his activity in the B'nai B'rith declined dramatically. If he searched for new members after he formed the circle, the commitment to B'nai B'rith ceased one year later, with the installation of the new lodge. Nor did he remain as active on the cultural committee. Since he no longer introduced debates to the brotherhood, an important function of the chairman, he probably retired from this position of leadership. Moreover, between 1907 and 1910, Freud began to miss lodge meetings on a regular basis. His interest in lecturing to the brotherhood decreased as well. After delivering ten papers during the five-year period preceding the formation of the circle, he gave an average of only one paper per year from 1902 to 1907, and one paper every two years thereafter. In the two statements given to the brotherhood after World War I, Freud explained simply that his psychoanalytic endeavors "took precedence" over his B'nai B'rith obligations.[85]

Freud's desire to broaden the appeal of the science intensified after 1908. In the same letter to Abraham in which he expressed his attraction toward Jews, Freud wrote about the "danger" of the movement's becoming a "Jewish national affair."[86] Two years later (1910), at the Nuremberg conference of the International Psychoanalytic Association, he defended his appointment of Jung to the group's presidency, against the protests of his Viennese colleagues: "It is absolutely essential that I should form ties in the world of general science." His effort at establishing the universal significance of the movement effectively checked the dangerous tendency toward sectarianism. However, neither the effort, nor his growing neglect of the brotherhood, affected his belief in Jewish ethical responsibility. He explained to his colleagues at the Nuremberg conference the distinction between a Jewish interest group and the unique, indeed the crucial, Jewish contribution to the psychoanalytic movement: "Jews must be content with the modest role of preparing the ground."[87] The position affirmed the view widely supported by the brothers of the B'nai B'rith (whom he never abandoned) — the belief in the pioneering function of the Jews.

The evidence of the depth of Freud's participation in the widely proclaimed Jewish mission is substantiated by his close identity with the Hebrew prophet Moses. For Jews seeking to articulate a deep sense of ethical purpose and a universal vision, Moses, the lawgiver and liberator of the Israelites, could serve as a supreme archetype. Freud's Moses identity, well known to us from his controversial publication from the 1930s, *Moses and Monotheism*, crystallized as early as the 1890s. In his Rome dreams (1897), when the Carthaginian general Hannibal emerged as the symbol of Semitic determination, Freud dreamt that "someone led me to the top of a hill and showed me Rome half-shrouded in mist; . . . the theme of 'the promised land seen from afar' was obvious in it."[88] His progress in the movement reinforced the identity. On January 17, 1909, he wrote Jung, "We are certainly getting ahead. If I am Moses, then you are Joshua and will take possession of the promised land of psychiatry, which I shall only be able to glimpse from afar."[89] During this period, his most thorough expression of this identity appeared in the essay "The Moses of Michelangelo." He wrote the essay in December 1913, during a fit of anger just after Jung defected from the movement. Aspiring toward Michelangelo's statuary conception of Moses, Freud attempted to maintain "the highest mental achievement that is possible in a man, that of struggling successfully against an inward passion for the sake of a cause to which he had devoted himself."[90]

Characteristic of his feeling about the Jewish mission, Freud expressed his attraction to the biblical figure in a reserved and unassuming way. He refused to discuss the obvious reference to Moses in his Rome dreams: "There was more in the content of this dream than I feel prepared to detail." He also resisted publishing his analysis of a parapraxis involving the name "Mosen." Even though his lapse in the recollection of the name led him to investigate not only the phenomenon of forgetfulness, but the field of everyday psychopathology generally, Freud refused to publish the experience because, as he wrote Fliess, "I cannot make it public." After completing the Moses essay, he, again, felt reluctant to publish it. When he finally decided to print it, he insisted upon his anonymity.[91]

Instead of indicating an ambivalence over his Jewishness,[92] the suppressed expression of his identity corresponded with the advice he gave his Viennese colleagues at the Nuremberg conference. The affirmation of the vital pioneering function of the Jew demanded public restraint in order to avoid confusing means with ends. He believed Jews were responsible for "preparing the ground," that is, for advancing the ideas and goals of psychoanalysis. If this meant that the Jewish task required public modesty, it also meant constant and firm inner resolve. That the Moses identity surfaced in his public writings is one indication of the vigor of his Jewish feeling.

One of Freud's close colleagues and a member of the circle from 1907 on, Hanns Sachs (1881-1947), regarded his mentor's attraction to Moses as a significant impetus for his endeavors in the movement: Freud "followed one of the oldest Jewish traditions. This is the belief that all Jews, born and unborn alike, were present on Mount Sinai and have there taken on themselves 'the yoke of the Law.' "[93] Besides indicating the significance of the Moses identity in Freud's work, Sachs was sensitive to the broad historical and cultural framework in which the Moses identity itself developed. This perspective is useful for explaining the meaning and scope of Freud's Jewish consciousness during the earliest phase of the psychoanalysis movement. Freud's identification with the archetypical visionary Jew received stimulation and reinforcement from his close adherence to the ideas of the B'nai B'rith. From this group, Freud gained a deep sense of Jewish fellowship, which, within a broader environment of anti-Semitism and eroding political liberalism, encouraged his feeling of a collective struggle. Moreover, the Jewish association fostered pride in a common Jewish destiny, promoting his commitment to the spread of universal ideals. The intimate Jewish circle inspired his desire for Jewish kinship and his belief in Jewish ethical leadership to such an extent that he looked to the brotherhood for his first psychoanalytic following.

In a yet larger context, the formation of the Jewish organization and Freud's search for fellow Jews were reactions to the breakdown of the liberal tradition of toleration, and, more directly, of toleration for Jews. In response to the anti-Semitism prevalent among students and teachers at the General Hospital, where he interned from 1882 to 1885, Freud built a basis of sympathy for Jews. He recognized, in the victimization of his colleague Carl Koller, the necessity of sharing the burden of self-defense. At the same time, he expressed a positive identification with his Jewish heritage. As he wrote Martha in 1886, the feeling of Jewish pride inspired his most passionate feelings.

The tendency toward Jewish solidarity and collective purpose began to surface a decade before Freud joined the Jewish society. The B'nai B'rith fulfilled his desire for fellowship and intensified his feeling of rebellion. Moreover, it was in the B'nai B'rith where these separate impulses came together, where the sort of mutual Jewish trust he enjoyed with Breuer, a trust deeper than his admiration for Koller, fused with the kind of response to anti-Semitism he respected in Koller, but could not find in Breuer. The Jewish society reinforced each aspect of his Jewish identity, integrated his Jewish pride and sense of solidarity with his vision of the whole, and thus oriented Freud, as a Jew, toward establishing the movement of psychoanalysis.

NOTES

1. The Nothnagel-Freud conversation about the proposal for promotion was reported by Freud in Sigmund Freud, *The Origins of Psychoanalysis: Letters to Wilhelm Fliess, Drafts and Notes, 1887-1902,* ed. Marie Bonaparte, Anna Freud, and Ernst Kris; trans. Eric Mosbacher and James Strachey (New York: Basic Books, 1954), 191 (hereinafter cited as *Origins*), and Sigmund Freud, *The Interpretation of Dreams,* trans. James Strachey (New York: Avon Books, 1967), 170-71 (hereafter cited as *Dreams*). For Freud's remarks on the professorship, see *Dreams,* 170, and *Origins,* 342.

Nothnagel had demonstrated against anti-Semitic intolerance from the beginning of the 1890s, when he joined the early efforts of the *Verein zur Abwehr des Antisemitismus* (Society to Combat Anti-Semitism). The organization was made up of Jews and non-Jews, primarily from the upper strata of society, who believed they could expose the immorality of the anti-Semitic movement. Nothnagel was also the first, and among the few, professors to call the attention of the public to such anti-Semitic practices at the university as the boycotting of classes taught by Jewish professors. At a protest meeting on October 13, 1892, he denounced anti-Semitism as "a crime against morality, justice, and humanity." Two years later, he published the complete text of this attack against anti-Semitism as the first part of his work, *Die Wahrheit über die deutsche Universität Wien und die Lage der deutsche akademische Jugend.* Bertha V. Suttner, *Lebenserinnerungen* (Berlin: Verlag der Nation, 1969), 244-50; *Jüdisches Volksblatt,* July 6, 1900, 5; Paul Molisch, *Politische Geschichte der deutschen Hochschulen in Österreich von 1848 bis 1918* (Vienna, Leipzig: Wilhelm Braumüller, 1939), 135.

2. Martin Freud, *Glory Reflected* (London: Angus and Robertson, 1957), 91. Königstein's *Dozentur,* recorded in *Jahrbuch der k.k. Universität Wien für das Studienjahr 1893-1894* (Vienna: Selbstverlag der k.k. Universität, 1894), 31. On his eventual promotion to a professorship in law, see Ernest Jones, *The Life and Work of Sigmund Freud,* vol. 1 (New York: Basic Books, 1953), 339 (hereafter cited as *Life*).

3. *Dreams,* 170-71.

4. *Origins,* 133; Peter Pulzer, "The Development of Political Anti-Semitism in Austria," in *The Jews of Austria,* ed. Josef Fraenkel (London: Vallentin, Mitchell, 1967), 434; *Dreams,* 226.

5. *Dreams,* 226-30.

6. This anecdote told the story "of a Jew who could not speak French and had been recommended when he was in Paris to ask the way to the rue Richelieu." *Dreams,* 228. When the Jew arrived in Paris, the story went on, he met a Parisian who happened to be a Jew. Being thoroughly confused in the language, he did not ask the way, but stated, "Je sais où est la rue Richelieu." The Parisian Jew recognized the gentleman as a fellow Jew who was obviously lost, and replied in Yiddish, "Men ken Shabes makhn mit dos" ("You can make the Sabbath with it"). See Alexander Grinstein, *On Sigmund Freud's Dreams* (Detroit: Wayne State University Press, 1968), 72-73. The remark made clear that, with an unfamiliar language, the Jew would get nowhere: like the Sabbath, a day of rest, his French is good for nothing. More important, communicated in Yiddish, the remark affirmed the common tie between the two gentlemen, implying that now the traveler could feel more at home and, with the assistance of this Parisian Jew, within reach of his final destination.

7. *Dreams,* 226, 229.

8. *Origins,* 190; Josef and Renée Gicklhorn, *Sigmund Freuds akademische Laufbahn im Lichte der Dokumente* (Vienna, Innsbruck: Urban und Schwarzenberg, 1960), 152-55, 187, and Figure 12. For two semesters during this period, the authors were not certain that Freud's classes were canceled. But given the pattern of eliminated courses, it is unlikely that Freud taught during these two terms.

9. Freud read a paper on sexuality and neurosis before the Doktorkollegium at the beginning of 1898. *Life,* 263-64.

10. *Dreams,* 651, 653; see *Origins,* 182-83, 211, 236.

11. *Origins,* 182-83.

12. Ernst Kris, "Introduction," *Origins,* 11-15, 43-45.

13. The date of Freud's induction into the B'nai B'rith is recorded in Edmund Kohn, "Bruder Freud," *B'nai B'rith Mitteilungen für Österreich,* 26 (May 1926), 136. The journal of the B'nai B'rith in Austria was published from 1897 to 1938, except for the years 1922-23, under the titles *Vierteljahrsbericht* (October 1897-April 1904), *Zweimonats-Bericht für die Mitglieder der österr. israel.* (June 1904-21), *Humanitätsvereine 'B'nai B'rith,'* and *B'nai B'rith Mitteilungen für Österreich* (1924-38); it will be henceforth cited as *BBJ.* The explanation Freud gives for joining the B'nai B'rith is in Sigmund Freud, *Letters of Sigmund Freud,* ed. Ernst L. Freud; trans. Tania and James Stern (London: Hogarth, 1961), 367 (hereafter cited as *Letters*), and in Sigmund Freud, untitled statement to the B'nai B'rith Wien, *BBJ,* 35 (November and December 1935), 193 (hereafter cited as "Statement"). His most active years in the B'nai B'rith were from 1897 to 1907. *Letters,* 368, and Kohn, "Bruder Freud," 137.

14. Martin Freud, "Who Was Freud?" in *The Jews of Austria,* ed. Fraenkel, 204, 206. Jung was the first non-Jew to visit Freud's psychoanalytic circle (March 1907). On Freud's card-playing enthusiasm, see *Life,* 329, and *Origins,* 312.

15. Official business for the society's fourth term began in January 1897. Wilhelm Knöpfmacher, *Entstehungsgeschichte und Chronik der Vereinigung 'Wien' B'nai B'rith für Österreich in Wien* (Vienna: Verlag Verband der israelitischen Humanitätsvereine 'B'nai B'rith' für Österreich in Wien, 1935), 21, 23.

16. Freud, "Statement," 193; Wilhelm Knöpfmacher, "Kritische Bemerkungen," *BBJ,* 1, no. 4 (October 1898), 154.

17. Solomon Ehrmann, "Über die Function des Judenthums innerhalb der Menschheit und der B'nai B'rith innerhalb des Judenthums," *BBJ,* 4 (January 1902), 100; Joseph Wortis, *Fragments of an Analysis with Freud* (Indianapolis: Bobbs-Merrill, 1963), 144. Ehrmann himself had to wait 12 years before he was promoted to a professorship in 1900. Ehrmann, "Der s.w. Verbandspräsident Br. Prof. Dr. S. Ehrmann," *BBJ,* 14, no. 3 (1911), 139-40.

18. Freud presented two lectures, titled "Über Traumdeutung," on December 7 and 14, 1897. The lectures are dated in a short review, from which the first quoted response of a

member is extracted, in *BBJ,* 1 (February 1898), 67. Record of Freud's delivery of papers on dreams to the Jewish academic society, for May 2, 1896, is in *Origins,* 162; for 1897, in *Jahresbericht der Jüdisch-akademischen Lesehalle in Wien über das Vereinsjahr 1897* (Vienna: Verlag der Jüdisch-akademischen Lesehalle, n.d.), 13. A sketch of his first lecture to this Jewish society was probably given to Fliess, but no trace of this paper is extant. See *Life,* 355.

19. *Origins,* 238.

20. A discussion of Freud's B'nai B'rith lectures appears later in this chapter and in Appendix A.

21. *Letters,* 368.

22. Freud's most active years in the B'nai B'rith were from 1897 to 1907. Ibid., and Kohn, 137. Reference to Freud's postfestivity remarks is in Karl Klemperer, "Erinnerungen an die ersten Jahre der 'Wien,' " *BBJ,* 35 (November and December 1935), 201, 203.

23. Freud knew Rie from the 1880s, when they worked at Max Kassowitz's public hospital for children. In 1891, they coauthored "Klinische Studie über halbseitige Cerebrallähmung der Kinder." At the same time, Rie was a student of Freud's at the university. In 1896, he married Fliess's sister. Josef and Renée Gicklhorn, 186-87; *Minutes of the Vienna Psychoanalytic Society,* vol. 2, ed. Herman Nunberg and Ernst Federn; trans. M. Nunberg (New York: International Universities Press, 1962, 1967, 1974, 1975), 1n (hereafter cited as *Minutes*); Grinstein, 23.

Freud's younger brother Alexander (1866-1943) joined the new Vienna B'nai B'rith lodge in 1901. *Festschrift anlässlich des fünfundzwanzigjähringen Bestandes des israel. Humanitätsvereines 'Eintracht' (B'nai B'rith) Wien 1903-1928* (Vienna: Selbstverlag des Vereines, 1928), 13. It is likely that Freud enlisted him, in addition to Königstein and Rie, for this lodge.

24. For Freud's recruitment of Königstein, see Freud, "Statement," 193. For his recruitment of Rie, see E. Kohn, "Bruder Freud," 137. I am grateful to Ludwig Markovits, Otto O. Herz, and David Becker, members or former members of the current Vienna lodge of the B'nai B'rith, for their assistance in uncovering the B'nai B'rith connection between Freud and Hitschmann. Freud became a member of the Gründungskomitee on February 26, 1901. Knöpfmacher, *Entstehungsgeschichte,* 37; E. Kohn, "Bruder Freud," 137.

25. Freud's contribution to the formation of the new society in E. Kohn, "Bruder Freud," 137. Rie was inducted on November 12, 1901. *BBJ,* 31 (October 1931), 322-23. Reference to Freud's service on the society's judicial and cultural committees is in E. Kohn, "Bruder Freud," 137, and in Ludwig Braun, "Die Persönlichkeit Freuds und seine Bedeutung als Bruder," *BBJ,* 26 (May 1926), 129. On the cultural committee, see Wilhelm Jerusalem, *Festschrift zür Feier des Fünfundzwanzigjährigen Bestandes von U.O.B.B. Humanitätsverein 'Wien' 1895-1920* (Vienna: Selbstverlag des Vereines, 1920), 56; Julius Katz, "Zweck und Bedeutung des Comités für geistige Interessen," *BBJ,* 4 (April 1902), 148-52; Julius Neumann, "Ein Programmvortrag," *BBJ,* 6 (December 1903), 104. The discussion on the B'nai B'rith is referred to in *BBJ,* 4 (January 1902), 107; Knöpfmacher, *Entstehungsgeschichte,* 38; Jerusalem, 127; and Ehrmann, "Über die Function des Judenthums," 99. The discussion on women is referred to in *BBJ,* 5 (March 1903), 104. Jerusalem wrote "Juden" instead of "Frau" in his 1920 chronicle.

26. Freud completed the Dora manuscript in January 1901. *Origins,* 325-26. Two months later, he showed it to Rie. *Life,* vol. 1, 362. Hitschmann joined the Viennese Psychoanalytic Society in 1905 and remained an active member for the following 30 years. The other two were not as involved. Königstein attended the Salzburg conference in 1908, and Rie became a member of the society the same year. *Minutes,* vol. 1, 390, and vol. 2, 1.

27. Freud, "Statement," 193. Some scholars have suggested that Freud's Jewish consciousness at the turn of the century, which could include his decision to join and remain an active member of the B'nai B'rith, developed as a reaction to the death of his father (October 23, 1896). According to Marianne Krüll, for example, Freud's Jewish

sensibility emerged from an attempt to reconcile himself to his father's Judaism. *Freud und sein Vater: Die Entstehung der Psychoanalyse und Freuds ungelöste Vaterbindung* (Munich: C. H. Beck, 1979), esp., 189, 245. No doubt this tragic event in Freud's life had a profound effect on his Jewish consciousness. Still, not all German Jews who asserted their Jewish pride at this time suffered from such a personal fate. The larger atmosphere of Jewish resurgence helped Freud in dealing with his ambivalent feelings over his father's death, and in affirming his Jewish pride.

28. Jerusalem, 21-24; Knöpfmacher, *Entstehungsgeschichte*, 1-6; S. Frankfurter, "Wesen und Aufgaben des Bundes B.B.," *BBJ*, 34 (October 1934), 220-21; Ehrmann, "Über die Function des Judenthums," 100; Edmund Kohn, "IV Festrede aus Anlass des zehnjährigen Bestandes der 'Wien,' " *BBJ*, 8, 6 (1905), 202-3.

29. See E. Kohn, "Bruder Freud," 136-38. Material on the formation of Wien is in Edmund Kohn, "Festrede," 203-5; Knöpfmacher, *Entstehungsgeschichte*, 6-9; Arnold Ascher, "Grosspräsident Dr. Edmund Kohn," *BBJ*, 26, 6 (1929), 185-86. On Kohn, see Ludwig Braun, "Trauerrede zum Andenken an den Grosspräsidenten Br. Dr. Edmund Kohn," *BBJ*, 29 (June 1929), 193-94.

30. Kohn referred to the principle he used in soliciting members for Wien in "Festrede," 204. Though he did not mention the preamble specifically, his phrases correspond exactly to passages in the document. The preamble cited in the text was taken from *B'nai B'rith News*, 11 (September and October, 1918). Freud acknowledged Kohn in "Statement," 193.

31. Excerpts of the speech were printed in Jerusalem, 25-27. Jerusalem was present, but, like Freud, he waited to join. Kohn also attended the lecture. E. Kohn, "Festrede," 204. Ehrmann and Knöpfmacher were two of the first 25 who were inducted directly into Wien on the installation date, October 13, 1895. Knöpfmacher, *Entstehungsgeschichte*, 14; their interest in the B'nai B'rith dates from the speech in March. See Jerusalem, 24.

32. Braun, "Trauerrede," 196; E. Kohn, "Festrede," 203.

33. *Letters*, 368; see also Freud, "Statement," 193.

34. Solomon Ehrmann, "In diesen Tagen . . ." *BBJ*, 26 (May 1926), 102-3. Ehrmann and Freud met in the class of Karl Claus, professor of zoology at the medical school of the University of Vienna, in the fall of 1874. They remained friends from then on. Solomon Ehrmann, "Meine persönlichen Beziehungen zu Sigmund Freud," *BBJ*, 26 (May 1926), 132 34. He joined the Leseverein a year later than Freud did, in the fall of 1874, but left the society some time before the summer of 1876, two years before the society was dissolved. *Jahresbericht des Lesevereines der deutschen Studenten Wiens, über das Vereinjahr 1874-1875* (Vienna: Selbstverlag des Lesevereines der deutschen Studenten Wiens, 1875), 23. No *Jahresbericht* for the following year is extant. Freud's own membership is documented in the membership lists of the *Jahresberichte* (1873-78). "Was Wir Wollen" appeared in *BBJ*, 1 (October 1897), 3-7. It was signed, "Im Auftrage des Hum.-Ver. 'Wien' B'B': Die Redaction."

35. Ehrmann, "Was Wir Wollen," 3-7.

36. E. Kohn, "Festrede," 207; Knöpfmacher, *Entstehungsgeschichte*, 25-26; idem., "Kritische Bemerkungen," 153.

37. Jerusalem, 20, 38.

38. E. Kohn, "Festrede," 218.

39. Ibid.

40. Braun, "Trauerrede," 193, 196-97, 199.

41. Knöpfmacher, "Kritische Bemerkungen," 156.

42. E. Kohn, "Festrede," 203, 208-11.

43. Solomon Ehrmann, "Betrachtungen über den Stand der 'B'nai B'rith' am Ende des Jahrhunderts," *BBJ*, 2 (December 1899), 148.

44. Ehrmann, "Betrachtungen über den Stand der 'B'nai B'rith." 139.

45. Ehrmann, "Über die Function des Judenthums," 103-5.

46. A comparison of the membership lists of the Leseverein in its *Jahresberichte* (1871-78) and the lists of the B'nai B'rith Wien (1895-1910) in Knöpfmacher, *Entstehungsgeschichte,* reveals a substantial overlap, considering the 20-to-30-year lapse in time and the short existence of the Leseverein. Over ten members of Wien had belonged to the student political society.

47. Cited by Sigmund Hirschler, "Toast auf die neueingetretenen Mitglieder," *Zur Erinnerung an die General-Versammlung des Vereines für fromme und wohlthätige Werke: Chevra-Kadischa am 10. Adar 5633/9. Marz 1873* (Vienna: In Selbstverlage des Vereines, 1873), 32.

48. Henri Ellenberger, *The Discovery of the Unconscious* (New York: Basic Books, 1970), 424.

49. Two years before his death in 1925, Breuer questioned the possibility of a congenial relationship between Germans and Jews. Josef Breuer, "Curriculum Vitae" (MS., Archiv der Akademie der Wissenschaft in Wien, Vienna, 1923), 10. But, as he wrote in his 1894 Kadimah letter, he refused to accept the socially disintegrating implications of anti-Semitism. He preferred, instead, to rise above conflict, writing, on May 18, 1912: "Man lives not by bread alone, but by his illusions. These are just as holy as bread, with however various differences and limitations." *Marie von Ebner-Eschenbach-Dr. Josef Breuer, Ein Briefwechsel: 1889-1916,* ed. Robert A. Kann (Vienna: Bergland Verlag, 1969), 122-23.

50. Ehrmann, "Betrachtungen," 148. Ehrmann was citing Austria's great dramatic poet Franz Grillparzer (1791-1872). The quote is part of the phrase, "from humanity by way of nationality to bestiality."

51. Ehrmann, "Über die Function des Judenthums," 102.

52. Ibid., 102-5.

53. The brother responsible for this example was Albert Kuh. Ehrmann cited his ideas in ibid., 105.

54. Eduard Hitschmann, "Sigmund Freud und seine Lehre," *BBJ,* 26 (May 1926), 106-7.

55. See Ludwig Braun, "Br. Sigmund Freud," *BBJ,* 36 (September and October 1936), 126, and Josef and Renée Gicklhorn, 169.

56. Braun, "Die Persönlichkeit Freuds," 126-28.

57. Braun, "Die Persönlichkeit Freuds," 128-31; idem., "Dr. Sigmund Freud," 126.

58. Sigmund Freud, "Briefe an Arthur Schnitzler," *Die Neue Rundschau,* 66, 1 (1955), 99-100: May 24, 1926; *Letters,* 369: to Marie Bonaparte, May 10, 1926.

59. Freud could not attend the festivities because of failing health. His younger brother Alexander delivered Freud's statement. *BBJ,* 26 (May 1926), 101, 103.

60. *Letters,* 368: to the B'nai B'rith, May 6, 1926.

61. Freud, "Statement," 193.

62. The search committee was organized on February 26, 1901. Knöpfmacher, *Entstehungsgeschichte,* 37. Evidence of Freud's involvement in the planning stages of the second lodge is in E. Kohn, "Bruder Freud," 137.

63. A complete chronological list of Freud's B'nai B'rith lectures (1897-1917) appears in Appendix A. Actually, Freud addressed the brotherhood ten times between 1897 and 1902. The two papers he presented on topics apparently unrelated to psychoanalysis were "Goals and Purposes of the B'nai B'rith Order" (fall, 1901) and "The Role of the Woman in Our [B'nai B'rith] Union" (between January 14 and March 4, 1902). During this four-year period, the three lectures he delivered to the B'nai B'rith before he published them were the two on dream interpretation (1897) and "Chance and Superstition" (1901). Freud's two lectures on Zola represented a complete discussion of the Frenchman. He referred to Zola only briefly in *The Interpretation of Dreams,* in letters to Fliess, and at meetings of the Vienna Psychoanalytic Society.

64. With the exception of the one lecture, none of Freud's lectures exists in Vienna, neither in the Freud Museum, nor in the library of the current B'nai B'rith lodge, nor in

the repository of the Viennese Jewish community. Nor does any lecture show up in Freud's literary estate (according to a personal communication with Kurt Eissler, February 19, 1975), or in the followup lodge to Wien, the Jacob Ehrlich Lodge (Tel Aviv). The one lecture that is extant appears in the eighteenth volume of the society's journal, a volume only recently uncovered in Vienna's Jewish collection, and existing, until now, in obscurity at the Leo Baeck Institute. Despite its publication, there has been no reference to the address outside the B'nai B'rith. Even the editor of the *Standard Edition* of Freud's works, who knew that Freud delivered the lecture in 1915, did not actually see it. See *The Standard Edition of the Complete Psychological Works of Sigmund Freud,* ed. and trans. James Strachey (London: The Hogarth Press, 1953-1974), vol. 14, 274 (hereafter cited as *SE,* followed by the volume number and the page[s]).

65. See *Origins,* 244: February 9, 1898.

66. *BBJ,* 1 (February 1898), 67. Freud delivered the lectures, titled "Traumdeutung," on December 7 and 14, 1897.

67. Freud, *Dreams,* 56. 73. In addition to discussing the physiological sources of dreams in Chapter I, Freud discussed the "somatic" sources of dreams in Chapter V, 253-74.

68. Freud, *Dreams,* 35; *Origins,* 244-45: February 9, 1898. Knöpfmacher was the brother who commented on Freud's lectures. Idem, *Entstehungsgeschichte,* 25.

69. Sigmund Freud, "Zur Psychologie des Vergessens," referred to in *BBJ,* 2 (December 1899), 156. For the publication history of this piece, see *Origins,* 260-62, 264-65, 328: August 26, 1898, September 22 and 27, 1898, and February 15, 1901. See also *SE* 3, 289-97.

70. Sigmund Freud, "Das Seelenleben des Kindes," referred to in *BBJ,* 3 (April 1900), 52; *Origins,* 270-71, 281: January 3, 1899, May 28, 1899; *SE* 3, 303-22.

71. Sigmund Freud, " 'Fécondité: von Émile Zola," referred to in *BBJ,* 3, 4 (1900), 38. For Freud's interest in Zola, see *Letters,* 278: to Hugo Heller, 1907, and *Minutes* 3, 103, 204: January 13 and April 7, 1909.

72. Sigmund Freud, "Émile Zola," referred to in *BBJ,* 5 (March 1903), 104. The *Quarterly Report* printed only the year of this lecture (1902). But it is clear that Freud gave the paper after March, since the title "Professor" appeared before his name for the first time, and probably after September, since Zola's death in late September would have prompted an occasion for eulogizing a man whom Freud respected.

73. Freud praised Zola in *Dreams,* 247 and 250-51n (the revolutionary dream took place in early 1898), and in *Origins,* 245: February 9, 1898. The Jew who commended Zola's courage was Richard Bermann (1883-1939). He expressed the praise in *Die Fahrt auf dem Katarakt: Autobiographie ohne einen Helden* (MS., Memoir Collection #191 of the Leo Baeck Institute, New York, n.d.), 13.

74. For a discussion of the connection between Zola and the oedipal revolt in *The Interpretation of Dreams,* see Grinstein, 111-24.

75. Sigmund Freud, "Zufall und Aberglaube," referred to in *BBJ,* 4 (January 1902), 107; *Origins,* 325, 328: October 14, 1900, February 15, 1901; *SE* 6, 239-79.

76. Sigmund Freud, "Über Träume," referred to in *BBJ,* 5 (October 1902), 62. Freud presented the other lecture, "Über den Witz" ("On Jokes," November 2, 1907), to both of the lodges in Prague. *BBJ,* 11, no. 1 (1908), 23-25.

77. Freud printed the piece in *Borderline Problems of Nervous and Mental Life;* see *Life* 1, 362. James Strachey, the translator of Freud's works into the English edition *SE,* translated "Über den Traum" as "On Dreams." See *SE* 5, 631.

78. Sigmund Freud, "Wir und der Tod," *BBJ,* 18, no. 1 (1915), 41-51; see *Imago,* 4, no. 1 (1915), 1-21, and *SE* 14, 274-302.

79. Freud, "Wir und der Tod," 41-42, 43, 49. Freud's comment on the lecture is in *Life* 2, 370: to Sandor Ferenczi, April 8, 1915. Freud had often utilized anecdotes, in previous lectures to the B'nai B'rith, to illustrate his arguments. See the discussion of his addresses on the unconscious (1905) and on wit (1907) in Appendix A.

80. See Freud, "Wir und der Tod," 41, 48.

81. See ibid., 45, 51.

82. Ehrmann, "Über die Function des Judenthums," 98-99. Ehrmann referred to "the excellent remarks about the purposes of the union 'Wien,' " which comprised the substance of a discussion held the year before. Only one discussion of this nature was held in Wien in 1901, the one Freud introduced. See Jerusalem, 127; Knöpfmacher, *Entstehungsgeschichte,* 38.

83. Jones mentioned that the Swiss were the first Gentiles in the movement. *Life* 2, 43 and 398. On Urbantschitsch and his Catholicism, see his autobiography, *Myself Not Least* (London, New York: Jerrolds, 1958), 12. The dates when Jung and Binswanger, Urbantschitsch, and Jones joined the movement appear, respectively, in *Minutes* 1, 138, 276, 392.

84. Sigmund Freud and Karl Abraham, *A Psycho-Analytic Dialogue: The Letters of Sigmund Freud and Karl Abraham 1907-1926,* ed. Hilda C. Abraham and Ernst L. Freud; trans. Bernard Marsh and Hilda C. Abraham (New York: Basic Books, 1965), 34: May 3, 1908 (hereafter cited as *Dialogue*). Freud's expression of discomfort with Jones is in Sigmund Freud and Carl Jung, *The Freud/Jung Letters: The Correspondence between Sigmund Freud and C. G. Jung,* ed. William McGuire; trans. Ralph Manheim and R. F. C. Hull (Princeton: Princeton University Press, 1974), 145: May 3, 1908.

85. See Knöpfmacher, *Entstehungsgeschichte,* 43; Jerusalem, 50; E. Kohn, "Bruder Freud," 157; *Letters,* 368: May 6, 1926; Freud, "Statement," 193.

86. *Dialogue,* 34: May 3, 1908.

87. Fritz Wittels, *Sigmund Freud: His Personality, His Teachings, and His School,* trans. Eden and Cedar Paul (New York: Dodd, Mead, 1924), 140.

88. *Dreams,* 227. In an enlightening discussion, Max Schur, Freud's physician during the 1920s and 1930s, argued that evidence of Freud's Moses identity appeared in the Fliess correspondence as early as 1893. Idem, *Freud: Living and Dying* (New York: International Universities Press, 1972), 72, 90, 102-3, 207, and 466. He cited one passage from a letter to Fliess (August 16, 1895) as an example: "Shortly after . . . one of the foothills had been climbed, I saw new difficulties before me and did not think that my breath would hold out for [further psychological research]."

89. *The Freud/Jung Letters,* 196-97.

90. *SE* 13, 233; see *Life* 2, 365-67.

91. *Dreams,* 227. On Freud's reluctance to publish the "Mosen" parapraxis, see *Origins,* 261-62: August 26, 1898. On his desire to remain anonymous in 1914, see *Life* 2, 366, and Ernst Simon, "Sigmund Freud, the Jew," *Leo Baeck Institute Yearbook,* 2 (1957), 302-5.

92. See, for example, Martin S. Bergmann, "Moses and the Evolution of Freud's Jewish Identity," *The Israel Annals of Psychiatry and Related Sciences,* 4 (March 1976), 3-26.

93. Hanns Sachs, *Sigmund Freud: Master and Friend* (Cambridge: Harvard University Press, 1944), 152.

4

THE PSYCHOLOGY OF THE FOLLOWER:
OTTO RANK

On December 13, 1905, Otto Rank (1884-1939), one of Freud's followers, wrote an essay on the relationship between Judaism and psychoanalysis. The adolescent essay, "Das Wesen des Judentums" ("The Essence of Judaism"), appeared at the end of a year during which he discovered and first applied Freud's theories. By the time he wrote the piece on Judaism, Rank had completed his first extensive psychoanalytic study, *Der Künstler* (*The Artist*), and received his teacher's praise for the work.

Basing the first part of the Judaism essay on the results of his work on *Der Künstler*, Rank asserted that the history of mankind had evolved from an original state of complete sexual gratification into the neurotic state of sexual repression. The essay reaffirmed, and at the same time was more specific than, the conclusion of his study of the artist. Psychoanalysis indeed provided the method for restoring mankind to the original state, but he felt only the Jews could engineer the struggle against repression: "The Jews thoroughly understand the *radical* cure of neurosis better than any other people. . . . They brought matters to such a point that they could help others, since they have sought to preserve themselves from the illness. This is not the least part of their task."[1] The essay defined Rank's approach to psychoanalysis and anticipated his membership in the psychoanalytic circle. He felt that due to their uniquely favorable position, Jews were preeminently qualified for fulfilling the psychoanalytic mission.

Rank's statement on the role of the Jews in the psychoanalytic movement is an explicit example of the penetration of Jewish consciousness into the movement's earliest phase of development. More than indicating the broad existence of this consciousness in the early circle, Rank's perspective provided a view of the role of the Jews that was different from that held by Freud. After experiencing a difficult home life, Rank joined Freud's movement in 1906, four years after the circle's formation. Rank's views on the value of the Jews to the movement thus reflect the experiences of a young man searching for his individuality as well as for meaningful and persuasive ideas.

Rank's perspective is especially valuable for specifying, from the point of view of a follower, the dimensions of the Jewish missionary consciousness in the psychoanalytic movement. In every aspect of his young life, Rank exhibited the characteristics of a follower. Though he had an inventive mind, Rank required a structure for defining and guiding his life and work. This is apparent in his varied relationships with his Jewish heritage. Like Freud and many other German Jews living in Vienna during the last several decades before World War I, Rank went through a period of assimilation. But, whereas Freud continued to accept his Jewish heritage even during the 1870s when he gravitated toward broader cultural currents, Rank desired to participate completely in the surrounding culture. After formally repudiating the Jewish religion in 1903, Rank followed the persuasive teachings of his adopted intellectual mentor, Friedrich Nietzsche. His adherence to Nietzsche had the quality of a son's attachment to a father.

The same demand for structure informed his later decision to join the psychoanalytic movement, as well as his renewal of interest in his Jewish heritage. He discovered that psychoanalytic ideas gave a definition to his need for self-respect and self-expression, while Freud himself provided him with educational, financial, and personal stability. As he pursued some of his ideas beyond Freud's theoretical framework, Rank gained substantial reinforcement for his work by affirming the redemptive resources of the Jews. Rank thus demanded more from his Jewish heritage than did Freud. For the leader of the movement, Jewish pride primarily served to strengthen his quest for a firm basis for humanity and his positive rebellion against social injustice, whereas for his closest follower, Jewish consciousness came to define and give substance to his redemptive aspirations. Whereas Freud regarded his Jewish heritage and the feeling of Jewish solidarity as important vehicles for his search for the whole, Rank went much further in attaching significance to his Jewishness — for to him, Jews were not only in the vanguard, but constituted the essence, of redemption.

THE ART OF PSYCHOANALYSIS

The paucity of scholarship on Rank's early life, and the large corpus of his published work that remains untranslated, do not reflect the importance of the contribution he made to the psychoanalytic movement and to the vigorous intellectual life of turn-of-the-century Vienna. An appraisal of this contribution not only shows his significance to the movement and to psychotherapy generally, but underscores the fertility of his late adolescence (1899-1906), when Rank laid the basis for his creative and influential work.

When Rank joined the circle in 1906, he was the youngest member. This fact, and the 28-year age difference between him and Freud, formed the basis of their mutually close father-son relationship. Indeed, according to Sachs, another member of the circle, Rank was the closest to Freud among Freud's protégés.[2] Immediately impressed by *Der Künstler*, Freud encouraged Rank to devote himself to the nonmedical or aesthetic side of psychoanalysis,[3] and entrusted him with numerous practical and scholarly responsibilities. Upon Rank's induction, Freud made him the secretary of the circle. Sachs remarked that Rank eventually assumed responsibility for "Lord Everything Else," with the exception of conducting the meetings and keeping financial records.[4] In the two years before World War I (1912-13), Freud appointed Rank as founding coeditor of *Imago*, the psychoanalytic journal of the arts, and of the *Internationale Zeitschrift für Psychoanalyse*, the most important periodical of psychoanalytic literature published in German. Freud also invited Rank to revise and contribute to later editions of *The Interpretation of Dreams* (1914-22). In the view of Paul Roazen, the author of a study on Freud's circle, Freud's trust in, and generous support of, Rank shows that he not only adopted Rank as a son, but also regarded him as even more loyal than a son. Freud himself made this point in a letter written in 1913. Rank's devotion showed him a "filial love" without the "negative aspect" of jealousy or animosity.[5]

Freud's estimation of Rank as a dutiful follower was accurate, for, indeed, Rank was an industrious and dedicated follower of Freud and his theories. Sachs recalled how he and Rank eagerly pursued ideas with Freud well after the adjournment of psychoanalytic meetings. In addition, Rank always seemed eager to discharge his responsibilities. As Ernest Jones observed, "He never complained of any burden put upon him." Some within the circle felt Rank's attachment to Freud and to the movement was excessive, an opinion supported by Rank's uninhibited display of devotion. For example, during the meetings, Rank would serve Freud obediently by bringing him water or lighting his cigar.[6] In 1913, Rank assumed the leading position in the five-man "committee," the group which declared steadfast loyalty to Freud's theories, after Carl Jung, a few weeks earlier, became the third member of the movement to defect. Rank recalled in the 1920s, "I was in the deepest of all."[7]

Rank's enthusiastic involvement in the movement is evident from the sheer quantity of his intellectual output. During the four years before the outbreak of the war (1910-13), Rank published 46 pieces, including three major contributions to the psychoanalytic literature. He possessed unusual analytic abilities for the interpretation of legends and myths, as well as of individual artists or their masterpieces. In *Die Lohengrinsage* (1911), Rank explored Wagner's identification with his operatic hero Lohengrin, arguing that through the swan-knight's relationship with Elsa, Wagner achieved a reunion with the pure and holy mother of his childhood.[8] The following year, Rank submitted this study as his doctoral thesis, the first dissertation utilizing the psychoanalytic method of interpretation. Two other studies, *Das Inzestmotiv* (1912) and "Die Nacktheit in Sage und Dichtung," applied the theme of progressive universal repression, which he had developed in *Der Künstler*. In these two works, Rank argued that as repression increased in civilization, literary interest in incest or nakedness became more and more restrained, though it never disappeared entirely. Instead of concentrating on the family romance, the artist turned to the father in the oedipal triad, exploring the themes of patricide and revolution. Rank concluded these studies along the lines of his other work. He showed that the motivating impulse of the artist, no matter how disguised in his work, had been the desire to achieve sexual gratification.[9]

As a member of the movement and as a scholar, Rank contributed widely to the development of psychoanalysis. In 1911, Freud commented that of all the members of the Viennese circle, "only 'little Rank' had any scientific future."[10] This remark, taken together with his appointment of Rank to the editorship of two important journals, suggests the germ of Freud's interest in Rank as his successor to the leadership of the movement, an interest that intensified in the early 1920s when Freud became seriously ill. In turn, Rank exhibited the most convincing signs of loyalty, at least among the Viennese. Besides leading the "committee," he dedicated his work to Freud either directly (e.g., *Das Inzestmotiv*) or through profuse acknowledgment (e.g., *Der Künstler*). But Rank's relationship with Freud was more complicated, or more truly filial, than Freud was willing or able to admit. In fact, as Jones noted, no one in the movement before World War I had suspected Rank's "vigor," his unique and independent analytic point of view, which finally isolated Rank from orthodox psychoanalysis in 1926.[11]

The signs of Rank's uniqueness are apparent in all of his writings, which were themselves closely connected with the values and objectives of his life. Two related concerns distinguished Rank from Freud. The first was the phylogenetic idiom in which Rank wrote. Whereas Freud explored the psychological conflicts of his patients, Rank analyzed human behavior as it emerged in culture or in history. For example, Rank regarded repression as a collective malaise, and abreaction, even for the individual, as an early stage of social liberation. Rank's second distinguishing area of exploration was psychology of the artist. This interest reflected the deepest division between Rank's and Freud's work. Rank attributed considerable significance to the artist because he felt that only the artist, through creative expression, escaped repression. Artistic affirmation was, for Rank, the hallmark of human development, and each artistic achievement seemed to voice mankind's yearning for freedom from repression.

Like Freud, Rank valued the conscious awareness of instinctual impulses. But, whereas Freud believed in the therapeutic value of knowledge, Rank preferred to regard psychoanalysis as a practical method of instinctual release. To Rank, psychoanalysis was just an advanced stage of artistic affirmation, the most mature appreciation of human nature. To Freud, on the other hand,

Rank's interest in cultural psychology was simply the "nonmedical" side of psychoanalysis. This distinction between the art and the science of psychoanalysis provoked the final rift between the two analysts.

Rank's most direct challenge to conventional psychoanalysis, *Das Trauma der Geburt* (*The Trauma of Birth*), appeared in 1924. In this work, he argued that the basis of neurosis was not oedipal, but preoedipal, the separation of the child from the mother. Instead of the father, the mother formed the center of his theory. Rank thus described neurosis as the ambivalence occurring between the desire to return to prenatal existence and the fear of repeating the separation trauma. He claimed that this insight into the etiology of neurosis would expedite the analytic situation. The analyst could recapitulate the conditions of prenatal existence and, by asking the patient to "act out" his fantasies, produce the patient's rebirth.[12]

The Trauma of Birth manifested Rank's interest in man's creative longing for self-expression. In contrast to Freud's strong emphasis on intellectual insight in the therapeutic process, Rank stressed the return to the natural condition as the only viable method of human liberation. He felt the emotional release allowed truly individual expression and development. At the same time, this major work established Rank's own independent development. The birth-trauma theory did not in itself isolate Rank from psychoanalytic psychology. Indeed, Rank intended to make a substantial contribution to psychoanalysis. As in previous works, he dedicated the study to Freud. Initially, Freud praised the work as "a thoroughly original achievement in the analytic field."[13] However, the work did precipitate the final schism. During the following years, the negative aspect of Rank's filial relationship with Freud fully emerged. Rank directly attacked Freud's rational approach to clinical therapy because he felt it inhibited free expression and thus contributed to the patient's neurotic illness. "I believe [orthodox Freudian] analysis has become the worst enemy of the soul," he told his close associate, Anais Nin, in 1933. "It killed what it analyzed. I saw too much psychoanalysis with Freud and his disciples which became pontifical, dogmatic."[14]

Rank's intellectual legacy rests primarily on the studies and lectures he produced during the last 16 years of his life, from 1924 to 1939. Though a small group in America studies closely Rank's ideas on the preoedipal relationship with the mother, the separation crisis or primal anxiety, and acting out in analysis, there is no Rankian school as such: Rather, Rank's significance for psychoanalysis has been the introduction of these ideas into the mainstream of the field. They are especially noticeable in object-relations theory, the work of Melanie Klein, and in the brief, dynamic technique of psychotherapy (Gestalt and existential), favored widely in America.

Our interest in these ideas goes back to an earlier period of his life, when his desire for natural self-expression, and his struggle for emancipation from his father as well as from convention were beginning to germinate. The impact that his adolescent search for freedom had on his later life is dramatically illustrated by the gift Rank decided to give Freud in 1926 on his seventieth birthday. Rank sent the gift from Paris, where he had established residence after breaking with Freud. The birthday gift was a lavishly bound edition of the works of Nietzsche.[15] With this gesture, Rank paid tribute to the most important force working in his youth, to affirm his independent search for progress in psychotherapy — the Nietzschean summoning up of individual expression. As we shall see, Rank's youthful attraction to Nietzsche also helped in forming his Jewish sensibility, an important basis of his dedication to the psychoanalytic movement.

NIETZSCHE AS SURROGATE FATHER

Rank's rebellion against his family and culture emerged in 1899 when he was 15. On one level, there was nothing unusually difficult about his life that could alone explain this reaction. The environment in which he lived resembled the environment of most Viennese youths growing up in Vienna's second district at the turn of the century. Rank, going by the family surname Rosenfeld, until his rebellion, grew up on the Czerningasse, as the youngest in a family of four (a sister died when she was a few months old). Both his parents observed Jewish practices, but, as natives of the western provinces of the empire, and exposed to the secular influences of cosmopolitan life in Vienna, they were far from being devout. Like other assimilated Jews of the time, the Rosenfeld family attended synagogue during the High Holy days and observed a few other customs, but it was, for the most part, unaffected by the traditional or moral imperatives of the religion.[16]

The tone of the family was set by the father, Simon (1849-1927). Because of his meager wages as an artisan jeweler,[17] he focused his energies, and the energies of his family, on achieving material security. Thus, like the fathers of other lower-middle-class families residing in the Leopoldstadt ghetto, Simon transmitted to his sons the burden of survival. He relieved his elder son Paul (1881-1921) from some of this pressure by permitting him to pursue a professional career in law. But he made certain that Otto pursued a practical education leading to a practical career. Thus, upon his completion of Volksschule, about 1894, Rank was sent to Bürgerschule, a terminal institution, for technical training. After serving one year (1898-99) as a locksmith's apprentice, Rank was sent to the Maschinenbau-Abteilung der Höheren Gewerbeschule, to learn the trade of machine construction. He received his diploma from the advanced technical school in 1903. For the following two years, Rank worked irregularly in various machine factories.[18]

In his exertion of control over the affairs of his family, Simon was imperious and frequently callous. His forceful manner often brought his wife, Karoline (née Fleischner, 1856-1935), to tears and oppressed his children. As his mother vented her grief, Paul occasionally expressed his anger. But the young Otto, who portrayed his father as a loud and ominous figure, felt overwhelmed. Frightened by Simon's authoritarian inflexibility, he suffered inwardly.[19] In a manuscript written during an early stage of his rebellion, the tormented Rank described his painful adherence to his father's expectations: "If someone expected me to learn, I would be a diligent student. If someone expected me to be productive, I would be a tireless worker." He believed that his obedience was so complete that "if someone expected love from me, I would love."[20]

Rank's unexamined acquiescence to the will of his father may itself seem unremarkable. But the fear that accompanied such submission penetrated him so deeply and painfully that he appeared to live his youth in dreadful terror. On several occasions, in his diary, Rank vividly communicated the horrible image he had of his father. "I believe it was a drunken rage," he wrote in October 1903, recalling a terrifying moment once when he was alone at home with him. Rank noted: "I still remember clearly how he roared until he was hoarse and how he struck his hands against the table until they bled, while I sat in a corner without moving as if I were not alive but rather part of the furniture. I followed him with only my eyes." The nightmare of Rank's youth was the feeling of being trapped in a corner by his father. In an inscription entered in his diary in November 1904, he revived the memory of an incident which occurred when he was seven: "My father strode with ludicrous exaggeration through both rooms and shouted. I cowered in a dark corner of the bedroom and trembled in fear."[21]

The depth of Rank's agony filled him with a yearning to escape. One of his dreams, which he had a few days before describing his dark-corner anxiety, dramatically portrayed the psychological texture of his adolescent desire for a way out. In the dream, Rank found himself in a house like his own, except that there were many doors. When a friend asked him to close the doors, Rank hesitated, then complied. Rank explained in the analysis that the doors meant "ways enough — ways out." The request to close the doors, his resistance, and his final compliance symbolized both the desire for freedom and the fear that no way out existed.[22]

Occurring late in 1904, the dream described not only his desire to escape from his home, but also the enduring quality of his despair. Although Rank did not actually move away from home until 1905 or 1906, he was psychologically prepared for escape several years earlier. Rank first broke from the unpleasant atmosphere of his home in 1899 when he began to attend performances at Vienna's principal theater, the Burgtheater. "I was rarely at home in the evening," he recalled in 1903. "I owe much to the four theater years, for, besides consuming many an evening, the evening theater created an illusion which diverted me [*mich . . . hinwegtäuschte*] from the raw reality of the day." Shortly after abandoning his home at night, Rank, along with his brother, finally fell out with his father. Due to "differences of opinion" and his father's intransigence, the brothers "no longer greeted him."[23] This early effort at escaping from the suffocating grip of his father released other pent-up desires for freedom.

Increasingly, he affirmed the wish to get out of the technical school. His wish became so intense that even a year after his graduation in 1903, he dreamt about how anxious he was to leave the unpleasant school atmosphere.[24]

In another expression of his desire for freedom and of the growing breach with his father, Rank formally severed his ties with the Jewish confession on March 18, 1903.[25] He could no longer tolerate the religion, for, as he wrote in his diary in July, he found it irrelevant and hypocritical:

> The observance of the laws in the Old Testament was very simple at the time of its inception. . . . Today it is utterly impossible to live in accordance to the viewpoints of that time. The last "Jew" has been dead for a long time now; yet, the descendants, with a mixture of obstinacy, arrogance, malice, and self-conceit appropriate to their race [*Stamm*], hold fast to their inherited laws and prejudices.

At the time of the High Holy days in October, Rank ridiculed "observant" Jews who, "out of boredom go to the synagogue and reduce it to a place of business, as if it were a branch of the stock exchange. The women show off their dresses, or what is beneath them; the men discuss petty affairs, but not what is beneath them." Rank explained that Jews were petty and restless because they were essentially "lazy" people.[26]

As a gesture of his rebellion against his past and his father, Rank gradually avoided the use of his surname, Rosenfeld. Although he used the name Rosenfeld until late 1905, on rough drafts of his early writings, including one addressed to Freud, he replaced it with "Rank" on his earliest completed draft, the play "Götzen" (November 1903), and on his diaries, which he began in January 1903. His increasing avoidance of the name Rosenfeld (he never used it in connection with his psychoanalytic activity, and in 1909 he legally changed it),[27] was both a sharp repudiation of his father and his family, and an act of dissociation from Judaism.

Rank's change of surnames was decisive in severing his ties with the past. Aware of the Jewish sound of "Rosenfeld,"[28] he dropped it for a name that affirmed the intensity of his escape. As the phonetic equivalent of the German *rang* – the past tense of the verb "to struggle," "Rank" conveyed an image of a Nietzschean overcoming that prepared the way for renewal.

Rank's endeavor to escape from his father and from Judaism was only part of his strong assimilationist thrust during the period of his late adolescence. With similar intensity, Rank searched for guidance and support in his break with the past. His eagerness to follow a direction leading away from his home and from his religion intensified in the fall of 1903 as he became thoroughly familiar with the works of Friedrich Nietzsche (1844-1900).[29] In his first document showing Nietzsche's impact, his nine-page piece "Autobiographie," Rank directly acknowledged the German philosopher as the one influence in his life that provided him with the resolve for rebellion. The depth of Rank's dependence on Nietzsche is clear from an extended play with his names: In two of his literary pieces, he strongly identified with Nietzsche by adopting "Friedrich" and the diminutive "Fritz" for the names of his protagonists.[30]

In their rebellious tone, Nietzsche's works — especially *The Birth of Tragedy from the Spirit of Music* (1872), *Schopenhauer as Educator* (1874), and *Twilight of the Idols* (1889) — appealed directly to Rank's psychological needs. Nietzsche's description of the decline of liberal culture provided Rank with a vivid and convincing expression of the contempt he had for the familial, educational, and religious institutions of his world. With relentless force, Nietzsche had stressed the complete exhaustion of the existing order: "How then does the philosopher view the culture of our times? . . . When he thinks of the general bustle, the increasing tempo of life and the lack of all leisurely contemplation, it almost seems to him as though he detected the signs of a complete uprooting and destruction of culture. . . . Never was the world more worldly, and never was it poorer in love and goodness." The focus of his critique was the liberal institutions of the modern day. Working within the Schopenhauerian philosophical perspective of noumenal and phenomenal reality, Nietzsche argued that modern institutions lost the "will," "instinct," or Dionysian power to stimulate a full and satisfying life. Modern life, remote from the emotional impulses of the noumenal, undifferentiated will, was characterized by a "decrease in vitality" and "atomistic chaos." The secular "laissez faire spirit" of worldly concerns allowed selfishness and greed, the fragmented will of phenomenal reality, to prevail. Modern morality was an essential feature of cultural degeneration, for, as an attempt "to organize everything anew from itself outward," it was also alien to the creative and harmonizing power of primordial reality. The rational organization of the modern family — "the smallest structure of domination" — of "neighbor-love" in religion, or of democratic equality and freedom in politics undermined the will for self-assurance and self-responsibility.[31]

Nietzsche's opposition to liberal culture, and the enormous impact he had on German and Austrian intellectuals from the 1870s on, reflected the political and cultural crises in German Europe at the end of the nineteenth century. Many who were exposed to the waning influence of liberalism during their youths, and thus especially distrustful of the liberal order, regarded Nietzsche's work as an important primer for the postliberal era.[32] More than most other analyses of cultural malaise during this time, Nietzsche's ideas inspired a following, not only because they formed a coherent critical ideology, but also because they summoned those alienated from liberal ideals to active rebellion. Nietzsche stressed that conventions in the family, in religion, and in politics had made people timid and insecure. He noted, "What alone can be our doctrine?: that no one gives man his qualities — neither God, nor society, nor his parents and ancestors, nor he himself," referring, in the last instance, to the selfish manifestations of individuation. Nietzsche assailed the "ideal of humanity" or the concept of "God" as forms of enslavement. Education, too, turned men "into machines" and accomplished this by means of "the concept of duty." The perfect citizen of the modern state was the "civil servant."[33]

By being "anti-liberal to the point of malice,"[34] Nietzsche was preparing for the final liberation from the hostile forces within modern man and culture. As he wrote in *Schopenhauer as Educator,* freedom meant "virility of character, early knowledge of human nature, an absence of scholarly education, of patriotic restrictions, of compulsion to earn one's bread, of connections with the State." The first step toward freedom was the denial of conventional or familiar values: "It is necessary to get really angry for once in order for things to improve. . . . [Man] has to be hostile even to the people he loves and the institutions in which he grew up; he may spare neither people nor things, however much it hurts him."[35]

Nietzsche's tragic view of contemporary culture and his compelling appeal to final liberation gave form and intensity to Rank's revolt against the oppressive restraints in his young life. His "Autobiographie" was indeed a document of bitter worldly denial. The first line alone indicates an acquired Nietzschean perspective: "It is astonishing how most men lead the same empty and worthless lives." Throughout this document, Rank conveyed the senseless superficiality of his existence by placing references to his education, his friends, and, indeed, to life, in quotation marks, and by using the indefinite pronoun "one," as in the phrase "one must make a profit from his sons," in referring to his father. Within a month of making the autobiographical entry into his diary, Rank completed his first literary piece, a play entitled "Götzen: Vier Acte aus dem Schauspiel des Lebens" ("Idols: Four Acts Taken from the Spectacle of Life"). The title and the setting for the first act — dusk in late autumn — suggest the extent to which Nietzsche, and specifically, his *Twilight of the Idols,* influenced Rank. The suggestion is supported by the name of the protagonist, Fritz, as well as by the play's hostile tone of denial.

The first half of the opening act poignantly illustrated Rank's intense rebellion against his father. As a vivid expression of generational revolt common in Central European families at this time, this portion of the play deserves particular attention. After briefly conveying an atmosphere of tension in the home, Rank opened the scene with the father, Adolf Kerrmann, confronting his son with the news that his sister has not yet returned home:

Fritz (lightly): Then she probably has gone out.
Kerrmann (urgently): She's already been away from home for two days and a night.
Fritz (makes a jeering motion)
Kerrmann: Stop making a joke of this please and show that you are a man.
Fritz (laughing): I think I've proven that already, just ask the...
Kerrmann: To the devil with you! For once make some sense! Haven't you a feeling in your body?
Fritz: Of course! But it must be aroused the right way; just ask the...

Kerrmann (enraged): Oh, pooh! I really think you're drunk, boy (goes up to him...grabs Fritzy by the coat and shakes him, screaming) Do you hear me? *Your sister has run away!* Has...run...away... from...home! Do you hear me! How one...

Fritz (somewhat roused, pushes his father away from him): What gives you the right to treat me this way, huh? Do you think I am your slave? Behave yourself please, otherwise...

Kerrmann [to his wife]: You let me be; I will have the boy done with.[36]

Later in the play, we learn that Fritz's sister has left home to participate in a social cause, thus vindicating Fritz's nonchalance. But this is an incidental point of the play. More important, Fritz's nonchalance was an expression of disrespect, reinforced by derision and, by use of the personal form *"du"* for "you," condescension. Moreover, by defining the relationship between his father and him as master-slave, Rank made his revolt legitimate and necessary.

In the second half of the play, Rank shifted the scene to a meeting place for serious intellectual discussion. Fritz, escaping from his father's control, is the society's president. The group's positive search for the "joy of life" and for the "power of creation" is preceded by sharp challenges to the economic, religious, and educational constraints that constituted the institutional dimensions of Rank's existence. Speaking through one member of the group, Rank objected to the limitations imposed by the compulsion to earn an income. "I have great, bold, and original thoughts," the member proclaimed. But he could not become a "philosopher" since he had to worry about the next meal: "Each day I am worked to exhaustion so that at no time do I have the energy to do my own thinking." Another member opposed the dogmatic posture of religion, refuted the existence of God, and affirmed "the great doubt" as being the necessary preparation for the superior form of belief — belief in the self. A third character challenged the method of education that avoids the student's needs and "contradicts his nature." Following Nietzsche especially closely in this portion of the play, Rank expressed, through this member, contempt for the conception of education that teaches the individual "to accept the customs, manners, views, and prejudices of his milieu." Such training is false and deceptive, another example of "the curse of so-called civilization." Like economic imperatives and formal religion, false training produces a modern form of slavery, the "civil servant."[37]

In February 1904, Rank wrote, in his diary, that he conceived of "Götzen" as an anticivilization piece. Reflecting on the play, he wrote, "Our needs are truly deprived in a world in which they cannot be satisfied."[38] Reinforced by Nietzsche's powerful polemic, Rank attempted to resolve the misery of his home life by renouncing his father, his technical education, and his Jewish religion. However, escape alone would not be sufficient relief. He recognized the need for compassion and support as well as for distance from hostile forces. He tried to gain comfort from his mother, but, in Rank's eyes, she fulfilled only the minimal needs of providing the family with food and clothing. She appeared indifferent to his search for protection. Rank also turned to his brother for support, but Paul rarely offered him satisfaction. His older brother preferred to associate with his own friends, or to spend time on his studies. As a consequence of this frustrated need for solace within the family, Rank nurtured the wish that his sister were alive. In "Götzen," Rank portrayed a close and sympathetic relationship between Fritz and Lilly, his sister. Moreover, Fritz refused to accept his father's contention that Lilly had left home.[39]

Rank also expressed the painful absence of friends in his life, as well as the disturbing lack of a religion "to which I would be able to cling."[40] Thus, while he eagerly denied all that oppressed and enslaved him, he became, by the fall of 1903, restless over the rootlessness brought about by his rebellion against the past. He felt an intense but frustrated need for structure and support. His decision to keep a diary helped to fulfill his desire for understanding. "I begin this book for my own instruction," he wrote on the first page, in January 1903. The diary would serve as a reflection on his readings and as a means of relating the insights of authors, philosophers, and playwrights to his own search for a "comprehensive knowledge of mankind that explains the riddles of our thinking, behavior, and speaking, and leads back to certain basic characteristics."[41] Judging by the frequency and length of his entries, Rank's search for clarity became compulsive in the fall of that year, when he began to analyze the works of Nietzsche.

As Rank wrote in his autobiographical sketch, Nietzsche became his first truly inspiring teacher, "a model, guide, and leader" (*Vorbild, Führer und Leiter*). The German philosopher not only assisted the young Rank in his rebellion against the past, but explained to him the meaning of the riddles he confronted in his life. Moreover, Nietzsche fulfilled Rank's psychological need for the kind of support he sought from his mother and brother: He "should protect me for the present against external attacks."[42] Indeed, in Nietzsche, Rank discovered a means not only to combat the crude forces of his time, but to restructure his life and to recover the "basic characteristics."

Nietzsche's philosophy comprehended a systematic analysis of, and program for, cultural regeneration that spoke directly to Rank's search for renewal. Many of these views are contained in *The Birth of Tragedy* and in *Twilight of the Idols,* as well as in *Thus Spoke Zarathustra* (1891). His most succinct and authoritative expression of these ideas, however, appeared in *Schopenhauer as Educator.* In these works, Nietzsche asserted that the individual seeking liberation from the oppressive forces of contemporary culture must, at some point, begin to replace superficial existence with a new foundation for personal and cultural development. That point began with the recognition and constant affirmation of the universal will or "daimon" (genius) within each individual: "This is the fundamental idea of culture, insofar as it sets but one task for each of us: to further the production of the philosopher, of the artist, and of the saint within us and outside us, and thereby to work at the consummation of nature." Only the production of genius would restore vitality and fullness to life and bind man to man.[43]

Nietzsche believed that the process of regeneration required certain procedures in order to bring out the individual's daimon and to sustain his contact with pure and eternal nature. Above all, the individual needed someone to educate him: We cannot "achieve this momentary surfacing by our own efforts; we have to be lifted — and who are they that lift us? They are those true men. . . . With their appearance, nature, who never jumps, makes her only jump, and it is a jump for joy."[44] In *The Birth of Tragedy,* Nietzsche argued that the dialectical complement of Dionysian ecstasy was Apollonian form, for the Apollonian spirit completed or "discharged" the Dionysian condition through similitude or through a particular artistic image. He said, "It parades the images of life before us and incites us to seize their ideational essence." In *Schopenhauer as Educator,* Nietzsche defined the philosopher, representing the truest expression of nature, as the "image of man." He "could raise one above the insufficiency of his times and teach him to be simple and sincere in his thinking and living."[45] Later, in *Zarathustra,* Nietzsche referred to the philosopher-genius as the "overman."

The importance of "true men" in the regeneration process is clear from his belief that "only he who has given his heart to some great man receives the first consecration of culture." Nietzsche's ideal thus demanded that man be devoted to the philosopher or the artist or the saint, in order to overcome selfish existence and to achieve unity with nature and all mankind. Those who contemplate this great man "will presumably, for a long time to come, derive the incentive to transfigure their own lives."[46] By "presumably," Nietzsche meant to convey that devotion alone could not produce self-transcendence. One needed a further impetus for sustained development. He felt that only "a strong organization" would prevent the consecrated "from being swept away and dispersed by the crowd . . . or even from being diverted from their great task." In addition to an "inner kinship with the genius," the first consecration of culture requires "a mighty community which is held together not by external forms and laws but by a fundamental idea. This is the fundamental idea of culture."[47]

In order to reach the highest state of development, Nietzsche maintained, the individual must go through a second consecration of culture. He must make the transition from inner renewal to judgment of the outer world. "Culture demands from him not only inner experience . . . but finally, and chiefly, action. This means fighting for culture and being hostile to the influences, laws, and institutions in which he does not recognize his goal: the production of genius." In this struggle for culture, the individual leads the noblest life obtainable, the heroic life. He "fights against very great odds for what is beneficial to all."[48] The regeneration of culture thus required the redemptive struggle as well as inner development. When Nietzsche wrote *The Birth of Tragedy,* he recognized Richard Wagner as the one who would awaken the Dionysian spirit in the modern world. Nietzsche believed Wagner understood the metaphysical significance of art. Through his operatic dramas, Wagner achieved the fruitful interaction between the Dionysian and Apollonian spirits. The Dionysian music "incites us to a symbolic" intuitive understanding of the limitless power of the universal will. The word, the tragic Apollonian myth, "rescues us from the Dionysiac universality and makes us attend, delightedly, to individual forms."[49]

By describing the prospects of renewed vitality in modern life, and by establishing a coherent method of regeneration, Nietzsche offered Rank stimulating ideas in his search for meaning and structure. Several features of Nietzsche's philosophy were directly relevant to Rank's situation. The stress on the viability, indeed the necessity, of inspired leadership gave dramatic expression to Rank's need for psychological support. By paying homage to Nietzsche, in his autobiographical statement, in late October 1903, and by identifying with him, the next month in "Götzen," Rank quickly responded to the impression Nietzsche protrayed of spiritual guidance, by regarding the philosopher himself as his mentor. There is evidence that Nietzsche's emphasis on the true man fulfilled Rank's desire for a surrogate father, for Nietzsche's discussion of the educator conveyed and, at times, directly pointed to a son's need for a father. When referring to Schopenhauer as his educator, Nietzsche wrote that he was among those who "will listen to every word he had to say . . . and if one wants to imagine a listener, let him think of a son whom his father is instructing. It is sincere, firm, good-natured speaking before a listener who listens with love."[50]

Similarly, the procedures Nietzsche defined in the regenerative process appealed, in form and substance, to Rank's search for meaningful religious satisfaction, for Nietzsche conceived the process as religious inspiration. Nietzsche indeed demanded devotion to a fundamental idea and referred to this idea as the consecration of culture. Moreover, the first consecration of culture consisted in devotion to some great man and to the mighty community. He referred to the existing order as "sin" or as "secular," and to mankind's Dionysian disposition as "holy." Regarding his philosophy as a "religious way of thinking," Nietzsche thus appealed to Rank's desire for a religion to which he could cleave.[51]

Finally, Nietzsche's emphasis on education satisfied Rank's intense desire for learning. After reading Nietzsche in the fall of 1903, Rank resorted more frequently — almost daily — to his diaries. He reflected on the philosopher's work and adjusted his own perspective of life to the Nietzschean view. The clearest indication of Rank's reliance on Nietzsche for renewed inspiration is, again, found in his first artistic endeavor, "Götzen." That Rank turned to art to express his longing for renewal itself indicates the extent of Nietzsche's influence on Rank's earliest positive development. Though the play oscillated between venomous denunciations of civilization and urgent appeals for something new and for mankind's redemption, its general direction pointed toward the latter. The discussion group's name alone revealed Rank's germinating interests — "The Society for the Awakening and Promotion of Individuality and Its Application for the Salvation of Mankind."

Rank followed Nietzsche's call for the recognition of inner strength, by making individuality the focus of the society. Rejecting the external constraints in civilized education and religion, Rank expressed, through the society's members, the primacy of self-responsibility and self-respect. One member, arguing that conventional education deprived the young person of the chance to "be calm and live for himself," advocated the radical reversal of this civilizing tendency in education, before "new illnesses" occurred:

> Let each young person live for a certain period of time entirely according to his own discretion. From this recognize his inclination, abilities, weaknesses, habits, and passions. According to these traits, direct his education. Teach him to make good use of his abilities, indeed even of his weaknesses. Direct his attention to what he does best; . . . awaken young people to great and beautiful things. Show them the sea, the sun, and the stars!

When exchanging views on the nature of belief, in the segment of the play on religion, one member articulated the need for a new religion based on self-belief. He added: "Create a strong, unshakeable belief and stubbornly hold on to it!"[52]

As in Nietzsche's process of regeneration, a "great, powerful, wholesome man" played the crucial role in Rank's conception of renewal. Given the name Josef Frei (free), this character in the play resembled the redemptive figure Nietzsche variously called the philosopher, the genius, the artist, the saint, or the overman. Frei was "the first [in the group] to devote himself wholly to individuality and personality." Promising that those who "follow me will feel already my influence," Frei functioned as the spiritual leader of the society. He offered members guidance and direction, often reminding them that their task was not limited by mere discussion of human problems or of their solution: "I believe we already have enough free spirits and free thinkers. Now on that basis and once for all, strive to realize freedom through action."[53] This final appeal to the members of the society reflected the Nietzschean call for the second consecration of culture. Fritz, who has escaped from his father's ruthless domination to devote himself to a great man as well as to a noble organization, is called upon to commence the final stage of the regenerative process, the heroic struggle for universal salvation. Rank stressed the Nietzschean ideal of the production of genius. Those who are "moved, by spirit, by an impulse to be free, and by human dignity," to fight against the civilizing process become the rare "geniuses" of humankind. Their task is to preserve the way of life that promises mankind's renewal.[54]

Until the spring of 1904, Rank sustained the Nietzschean struggle for culture by opposing all the inherited ties that inhibited personal development, and by promoting creative self-expression. He continued to separate himself from his father, noting, in December 1903, that his father lacked his "inner calling."[55] In January, Rank cited a passage from Otto Weininger's *Über die letzen Dinge* (1904), to reaffirm his own contempt for the shallow Jew: "The Jew will not burden himself with responsibility (and for this reason avoids problems); he is thus unproductive. The only obligation he has is . . . to avoid purpose and the demands of life [*Weltprocess*]."[56] Rank's criticism of the superficial and the conventional was unyielding. A month later, he wrote that civilization produced the "loathsome illness" of intellectual "paralysis." As he rejected conventional life, Rank emphasized the value of inner strength or "self-respect," calling it "the first condition of [real] life." Referring again to Weininger, he proclaimed in February, "I stand alone, am free, am my own master."[57]

Rank's search for artistic expression increased during the early months of 1904. Inspired by Nietzsche's glorification of the power of Wagnerian operatic drama,[58] Rank increasingly attended performances at the Vienna Opera. According to many contemporary observers, the performances of Wagnerian theater under Gustav Mahler's direction (1897-1907) brought out the deeply metaphysical qualities of the composer's art and thus exercised a religious effect on audiences. One observer, Richard Specht, commented in 1913 that, in performing Wagner, Mahler had expressed "longing for the hidden essence of true and unitary, meaningful humanity . . . and he wanted others to experience [this]."[59] Rank indeed experienced the rapture of Wagner's operas. Several times in his diaries, from early 1904 on, he expressed total admiration for the composer's redemptive vision. As a student of the Nietzschean-Wagnerian credo, Rank endeavored "to comprehend completely the artist through the man." Frequently, during the preliminary stages of his own writing, Rank claimed that he experienced tension between worldly moorings and artistic elevation involved in self-transcendence. He felt "dizziness, confusion [*Schwindel*], a mixture of disgust for life and joy in creativity, indifference and concern, thoughts of death and plans for the future."[60]

A RADICAL CURE OF NEUROSIS

Though Rank's search for renewal continued through the spring, he began to feel something less than the complete fulfillment Nietzsche and Wagner promised in their work. Expressions of artistic self-affirmation, as well as of the Promethean struggle for universal regeneration, inspired hope and the recognition that he was part of a powerful intellectual revolution. But, as he painfully discovered throughout the remaining months of the year, intellectual or theatrical assurances — though exhilarating in themselves — could not protect him completely from external pressures, the way he imagined they would when he first devoted himself to Nietzsche.

A dream Rank had in mid-February reflected intense sadness and anticipated deepening despair. "Last night I dreamt that fire broke out in the house where I lived. I am on the top floor; there is no possible rescue for me. I burn completely, along with all my possessions. *No one knows I have ever lived.*

Everything has disappeared without trace."[61] As in his writings, the theme of rescue from an enveloping threat at home is paramount. But unlike before, this dream expressed the feeling of hopelessness — there is no escape this time. Neither Nietzschean-Wagnerian ideology nor artistic engagement could have saved Rank in this instance. He demanded personal and direct liberation. In the weeks after the dream, he reflected upon his loneliness, exclaiming at the end of the month, "I am always anxiously seeking to understand important individuals in a *complete* way." Rank's description of this search echoed the need for emotionally immediate contact. By reading everything authors had written, including letters and diaries, Rank attempted to become familiar not just with their ideas, but with "their course of life."[62] As he soon realized, however, even extensive reading could not completely satisfy his desire for direct inspiration.

Nor could his reading sufficiently rescue him from other developments in his young life. On March 19, Rank reluctantly took a job at a machine factory, a decision no doubt prompted by his father. "I suffered terribly," he wrote that evening. A week on the job was more than he could take. The drudgery of work, compounded by the loss of his freedom and of the opportunity to cultivate his artistic talent, led him to the brink of despair. At the end of March, he wrote, "When I awake in the morning, the first thought that enters my consciousness is the hollowness, emptiness, and aimlessness of my present life. The feeling is dreadful. I would like to go to sleep again immediately and forever." For the following ten weeks, Rank could barely endure the feelings of loneliness, and of enslavement to the chore of machine construction. In an expressive passage dated April 17, Rank communicated his sorrow as well as his growing anxiety. He wrote how he was driven to tears out of sympathy for a dog "who had lost his master." The dog's "pathetic helplessness," his "anxious and breathless" search, had touched Rank deeply.[63] At the end of the month Rank expressed, in a letter to an acquaintance, the desire "to make an end of the whole thing." He explained that either he would realize his suicidal intent, or he would leave his job and his parents to devote himself to writing. Rank's appeal for support was tentatively phrased, for even though he recognized the acquaintance as the one person to whom he could turn, he felt distant even from him.[64]

Rank appeared to have lost the struggle for artistic renewal when, on May 14, he bought a weapon, with the intention of killing himself.[65] Though he emerged from this crisis, the pain of solitude persisted. Responding to this pain like the dog who appeared lost and helpless, Rank cried out in despair, for lack of meaningful encouragement and support: "I haven't yet met a living man whom I could regard in every respect as more complete than myself, although I have felt a deep need for association with such a man."[66] This remark, written on May 20, formed the central idea of a short story he finished on June 8. Entitled "Der Freund" ("The Friend"), the story resembled closely the main point of a parable Nietzsche presented in *Zarathustra*. Nietzsche wrote that the true friend was neither slave nor tyrant, but someone who could redeem others. "What he loves in you is the unbroken eye and the glance of eternity."[67] In "Der Freund," Rank portrayed the brilliant but unstable relationship between Friedrich and Maximilian. As in "Götzen," Rank identified with Nietzsche, the one source of inspiration in his life, by examining, through Friedrich's eyes, the needs, gratifications, and disappointments involved in the search for a superior individual.

After a short Nietzschean critique of existence and the appeal for creative life, Rank concentrated on Friedrich's rejection of his immediate world — the institutional crutches of family and religion — aimed at cultivating fully the powerful resources of his own inner nature. To accomplish this, Friedrich said he needed "a man to whom he could cling. In his entire life, he had met no one to whom he could look upon with respect." In Maximilian, Friedrich found an elder friend who appeared "uncommonly mature, witty, and intelligent." Though Friedrich at first defended himself against Maximilian's inclination to dominate, he eventually gained enormous inspiration from the friendship. "He inflamed and stimulated Friedrich to do excellent work. He inspired self-confidence and hope in him especially when [Friedrich] was being eaten and rooted up by despair in his knowledge or when he was on the verge of collapse. Moreover, he reprimanded and corrected him when he saw him possessed by the holy zeal for creation, in order to moderate his impetuousness."[68]

"Der Freund" shows that Rank continued to find Nietzsche's conception of regeneration attractive. He recognized that encouragement and discipline were necessary for inspiring and completing the artistic process of renewal. However, reflecting his despair in meeting such an individual, and thus his doubt in the practicality of Nietzsche's philosophy, Rank ended the story with Maximilian's ultimate betrayal. He turned out to be just another ordinary individual. More important to Maximilian than artistic creation was the pursuit of worldly pleasure — women easily distracted him from aiding Friedrich's work. Moreover, he was not a true friend in the Nietzschean sense. He did not educate Friedrich; he trained him. As Friedrich discovered after leaving Maximilian, he could not perform his work alone. Crushed by disillusionment, Friedrich escaped from the city to natural environs, where he finally killed himself.[69]

Throughout the following months, Rank looked again to Nietzsche, this time to derive periodic strength from the philosopher's portrayal of the suffering, lonely artist. With frantic intensity, Rank concentrated, for two days in late June, on the life of Napoleon. Rank felt he was a great man who "wanted to accomplish and possess *everything alone.*"[70] A few days later, he affirmed that the success of Jesus consisted in his belief in himself and in his work. He said Wagner manifested "the will to [gain and assert] power." Nietzsche's own stoic solitude impressed Rank as well.[71] However, it was a summer of unhappy endurance for Rank. In addition to the difficult trial of loneliness, he found the life of artistic creation difficult to sustain. For someone in need of direct stimulation and discipline, the Nietzschean ideal of an artistic perception of the universal will seemed too remote and inaccessible. Frequently, Rank complained that neither the process nor the results of his writing offered lasting inspiration.

In August and September, Rank took increasing interest in the psychology of the child. An observation in late September was typical of earlier remarks: "A child frequently has the same expression for two different things."[72] His concentration on the undifferentiated or timeless quality of the child's mind provided Rank with another method of apprehending the regenerative forces of man's inner nature. His germinating interest in psychology did not diminish his appreciation for Nietzschean ideals. Rather, it served to reinforce or define the philosopher's vision. "We must understand [Nietzsche] correctly," he asserted in early September. Relying on his acquired knowledge of child psychology, Rank gained direct insight into the production of genius. "One mark of genius is the capacity of recalling . . . the inner significance of these [childhood] events and their necessity for further development."[73]

One of the books Rank read in October, to increase his understanding of man's vital resources, was Freud's *The Interpretation of Dreams.* Rank discovered the work through his family's physician, Alfred Adler (1870-1937), whom he had been seeing about a persistent rheumatic condition.[74] It was Rank's good fortune that by means of this medical consultation, he came into contact with one of Freud's earliest and most brilliant pupils. Freud's book on dreams had an immediate impact on Rank. In a manuscript he addressed to Freud six months later, he recalled, "I read [the book] through and was completely inspired. Naturally, I understood it for the most part, that is, only as far as the isolated theories interested me."[75] The remark makes clear that *The Interpretation of Dreams* furnished Rank with fresh psychological insights into areas he had been exploring the past twelve months. Thus, his earliest quotes from the dream book reflected his desire for illumination of mankind's inner reality. On October 29, for example, Rank cited Freud twice — on thought association or the interconnection of perceptions in the memory, and on the permanent, eternal quality of dreams and the unconscious.[76]

Freud's intellectual stimulation is evident in practically every one of Rank's diary notations or manuscripts written after his introduction to *The Interpretation of Dreams* in October. The concept of the unconscious, and especially the interpretation of dream life as an authentic expression of man's inner nature, provided Rank with a focus for his interests in the creative process, in inner renewal, and in universal redemption. Moreover, Freud's scientific method of exposition appealed to Rank's need for a more complete and practical definition of the regenerative process than Nietzsche's metaphysics of artistic renewal. Though Rank continued to write prose and poetry after October, he now became attentive to psychological processes and studious about psychological explanations. For example, reflecting in early November on a poem he had just completed, he wrote, "Poetry is nothing more than dreaming awake." Rank applied his understanding of dream life to sharpen, also, his appreciation of Wagner. After reading *The Interpretation of Dreams,* Rank felt prepared to interpret the operas' symbolic expression of redemption, and thus more confident about his own development. He remarked, at the end of November, that an understanding of dream life could clarify the function of Wagnerian theater. Both dreams and the dramas make "latent, unconscious thoughts free. The affects, suppressed 'during the day,' burst forth [*toben sich aus*] . . . . We can morally extend ourselves with its word, breathe fully again, and be as we are."[77]

Using dream analysis as a method of interpreting or grasping the renewal process, Rank applied the method to his own dreams. On November 24, he came out with his first analytic study, an eight-page interpretation of three dreams he had the night before, entitled "Träume und Versuche ihrer Deutung" ("Dreams and Attempts to Interpret Them"). Rank followed the format of *The Interpretation of Dreams* — a description of each dream, followed by an analysis of details and an elaboration of their meaning. The first dream took place in a classroom setting at the Gewerbeschule. Rank, called upon as head boy to solve a difficult problem of construction at the blackboard, proceeded to invert the design. He was afraid he would have to take the year over again for making the mistake, and thus be deprived of his free time. Finally, Rank took the problem to his friend Johann Stur, who was sitting at the back of the room. According to Rank's interpretation, the dream expressed the desire for self-respect. His inversion of the design represented the wish to impress the instructor with his cleverness and superiority, as well as with the intention of doing "what I wanted." His relation to Stur was significant, too, for he reversed the seat positions (the mark of academic rank) they actually had held when they had gone to school together. Rank wanted to "outshine Stur."[78]

In the other dreams, the wish for self-esteem again emerged. The second dream involved a debt Rank owed another friend, A. Later, Rank felt uneasy when he asked A to conceal from a mutual friend, W, his desire to postpone repayment. W overheard the conversation between Rank and A. The dream concluded with a vague reversion to an earlier period in his life. In the interpretation, Rank believed the dream expressed self-respect on two levels. He remarked in the analysis that, as a latent part of the dream sequence, W was in debt to him. According to Rank, by placing him in the creditor's position, the dream expressed his wish to gain control over his financial and personal affairs. Secondly, the feeling of uneasiness that emerged in his dealings with A expressed, by means of pain, the dream's discouragement of moral laxity. As Rank explained, the dream made him uncomfortable because his request for the postponement of repayment of his debt to A involved a plan of deception. Recalling his dream awareness of W's presence at the time he had addressed his request to A, Rank observed that behind the request was the desire to dupe W into believing he really needed money and thus to extort from W the money he owed A. By expressing aversion to the scheme, the dream attempted to restore Rank's integrity. The time reversion in the dream stressed the moral regressiveness of his deceitful intentions. Like the quality of uneasiness that accompanied the scheme, this dramatic reversion in time expressed the dream's "revenge" against a moral infraction.[79]

The final dream portrayed a physical fight between Rank and a person he did not recognize. It ended with a prelude to the final confrontation. His opponent asked Rank to close the doors behind him. One door closed by itself, which frightened Rank. In the analysis, Rank explained that the fight was a "struggle" for preserving his "ego." His faceless opponent, whom he identified in the interpretation as Stur, suggested the advantage he had over an "average" contender.[80]

Rank's interpretation of the symbol of the doors emerges as the central feature of his dream analysis. The mysterious self-closing door, and the anxiety this created, meant to Rank that the "personality," which his dreams attempted to preserve, faced overwhelming forces. Rank noted that the threats in the previous two dreams — his uncomfortable position in relation to Stur in the first, and the practice of deceit in the second — left the ego room for self-preservation, but that the threat to the ego at the end of the third dream was so enormous that the ego had only one route of escape left. Since "I knew no more ways out [through the doors], I awoke to prevent [the ego] from succumbing." To Rank, the dream was an inner struggle of the ego's "self-creating radiance," to pierce the "web of lies" of superficial reality. On the day he wrote this manuscript, Rank went on to explain that the dream was the psychic response to the "ruling opposition," to the "negating elements (reality) . . . which seek to reduce one's ego, abilities, successes, hopes, and to attack one's honor. . . . [The dream] wants to strike back in order to defend the personality."[81]

More than signifying a reaffirmation of self-respect, these careful dream analyses mark a critical turning point in the perspective Rank brought to the search for inner renewal. That he interpreted his dreams as the struggle of the ego for existence indicates that he had discovered a new way of defining and giving expression to his desire for freedom. Allusions to the former ways of achieving inner strength, and the summary rejection of them, highlighted the transition to the new way. Rank recalled his "close friendship" with Stur and their "harmonious collaboration" on projects. He also recognized a wish "to be like Stur." Rank indicated his total disaffection with the past, in an analysis of the final part of the third dream. He noted that besides the door which closed by itself, one door completely disappeared. This was the door through which Stur entered the room for the fight. Explaining the disappearance, Rank remarked, "That is *his* way, which I do not [any longer] recognize."[82]

Indeed, Rank expressed a strong revolutionary impulse in the dreams and in their interpretations. His inversion of the construction problem in the first dream was a literal "revolution," or "reconstruction" of the reality facing him. Moreover, he regarded the clever gesture as evidence of his superiority over his instructor, the most apparent authority figure in the dream. Other observations he made in the analyses reflected the feeling of qualitative change in his life. In the first and the third dream analyses, Rank declared his academic and physical superiority over Stur. In the second dream analysis, Rank claimed control over his financial affairs. His references, at the end of this analysis, to the ego's act of revenge against moral negligence lent an aspect of principle to the revolt. The dynamism of Rank's search for renewal in this study betrays something more than a restatement of inner strength. The revolutionary solution to the construction problem, the repulsion of immorality, and the multiple reversals of life conditions point to Rank's replacement of the past by a renewed and invigorated view of life.

Despite his profound discovery of strength in the psychoanalytic perspective of inner renewal, Rank recognized the vulnerability of the ego to the "ruling opposition." At the end of the study, Rank left the impression that negating forces continued to threaten him. Even as he proclaimed his advantage over Stur in the struggle for physical supremacy, Stur still appeared invincible to him. Rank would beat his rival furiously, but Stur would not bleed.[83] The discovery of Freud's theory of dreams, and its intensifying effect on his search for inner power, were only initial steps in his struggle for renewal. It would be several more months before Rank could make the irrevocable break from his father and establish the conditions of financial and intellectual independence. Yet, his enthusiastic response to *The Interpretation of Dreams,* as well as his eager application of its theoretical insights, show that psychoanalysis offered Rank a meaningful conceptual structure and a language for articulating the creative forces of human nature. Rank recognized the difficulties of the struggle ahead, but he had found a framework for overcoming the obstacles which threatened his sense of honor and hope.

The recognition of Stur's invincibility, at the end of the study, did not shake Rank's faith in the strength of his own ego. Though he admitted that he could not defeat him, he also believed he would not lose either.[84] Feeling overwhelmed by Stur at the end of the third dream, Rank finally preserved his freedom by appealing to the wisdom of psychoanalysis. He recognized that the dream itself asserted the power of inner strength. This recognition gave Rank confidence in the eternal regenerative possibilities of man's nature, in the face of the most formidable social pressures. Just a little over a month after reading Freud's dream book, Rank rejoiced in the redemptive power of psychoanalysis. Like artistic creation, dream analysis could spur inner renewal, he observed on November 30, 1904. However, analysis had the distinct advantage of conscious insight. He noted that the analyst can "disentangle all the fine meanings, suggestions, and threads of connections," and thus elucidate the "real" life of the patient. "For the dream has its origin deep in the childhood memories; but only through interpretation will those be awakened since the dream alone does not allow these memories beyond the threshold of consciousness."[85]

Looking to psychoanalysis for instruction, and regarding the science as a source of regeneration, Rank revered Freud in the same way Nietzsche revered Schopenhauer — as an educator. He had found a superior figure who realized his longing for guidance and discipline. In Rank's mind, Freud was the practical extension of the character Josef Frei or of the positive features of the character

Maximilian, for Freud offered him insights into the creative energy of man's nature. The nature of this relationship with Freud points to the basis of their intellectual differences as well as to their similarities. First, while both shared an interest in the interpretation of dreams, Rank viewed dream analysis as only a preliminary fulfillment of man's creative striving. He felt that even when analysis was most effective, it only performed in the service of man's longing for creative expression. The continuing influence of Nietzsche is apparent here — the objective of education was: the unification of man with eternal nature, or the production of genius. Unlike Freud, then, Rank viewed analysis as a necessary but limited means of renewal. Secondly, while both Freud and Rank aspired toward the ideal of the whole, their criteria for achieving the wholeness of humanity differed. Having grown up during the constitutional era of the 1860s and 1870s, Freud possessed considerable faith in liberal ideals. Though he was sensitive to the decline of liberalism, as well as to the growing stress on emotion and self-assertion in culture, he continued to regard reason and toleration as humanitarian objectives. Rank was deeply critical of reason and suspicious of the human capacity for toleration. His belief in the whole emerged from the concept of human nature or of the universal will. In short, by seeking to preserve man's "self-creating radiance" as well as his community with mankind, through the evocation of the will, Rank manifested the artistic or antiliberal tendencies in psychoanalysis.

During the winter months of 1904-5, Rank's interest in the psychoanalytic interpretation of the creative personality intensified. The fascination he expressed for creativity anticipated his decisive devotion to psychoanalysis, beginning within the following months. Selecting the features of Freud's theories that were most attractive to him, Rank endeavored to define the function of artistic creation. In December, he wrote that the structure of the drama followed the format of dream life because the dramatist expressed, in artistic form, the inner wishes that also sought fulfillment in dreams. Thus, Rank interpreted dramatic form as the struggle of the hero, against opposing forces, for "distinction and glory, the fulfillment of the wish to be his own person."[86]

In January and February 1905 Rank dedicated a portion of his diary to studying the psychological processes of creativity. Though he originally regarded this segment as a "supplement" to his diary, he referred to the study, on February 10, as "Artist" (*Künstler*). His immediate inspiration was Wagner. Rank believed that the composer showed the clearest transition from unconscious dream life to musical artistic expression. Thus, the hero in Wagnerian opera impressed Rank as an expression of wish fulfillment; power, as a manifestation of sexuality; love, as a form of sublimation; and so forth. Near the end of the "supplement," Rank did a summary of his research, the thesis for the book *Der Künstler,* which he began to write in the spring: "Just as the dreamer not only opposes [his] affirmative promises and hopes to negative voices (the repressed), but treats his wishes as facts, so the artist not only opposes his power of resistance, his capabilities, his individuality, and his genius to oppressive life, but incorporates all this in the deed — in the work of art." Rank continued with the analogy between dreams and artistic creation. Defining the dream as the wish of the will for the universal, he similarly conceptualized art as the wish of the genius for the universal and pure human (*das allgemeine und reine Menschliche*).[87]

Rank interrupted his sketch of *Der Künstler* in mid-April, to devote more time to the study of Freud's theoretical work. As he wrote, a month later, about this revived interest in psychoanalysis, "I wanted to study the work once again, although this time with thorough attention to every aspect." Unable to procure a copy of *The Interpretation of Dreams* for himself, he read Freud's and Breuer's *Studies on Hysteria* (1895) and several articles by Freud. He finally went back to Adler, a week later, to borrow his copy of the dream book.[88] This renewed interest in the principles of theory, and the desire for contact with Adler, reflected a need Rank had not yet entirely fulfilled. Though his previous study and application of psychoanalysis provided him with a focus for his work, it did not bring him the kind of direct or personal satisfaction he had been seeking. On April 6, he complained in his diary that he had no one with whom he could speak, nor anyone to whom he could write. "*I am so alone, so entirely alone!*" The next night, Rank had the following dream. He was absorbed by a moving performance of an actor playing the part of a priest. From where he was sitting in the theater, he had trouble seeing the play. Even more frustrating, he could not hear the final words of the actor-priest. The dream brought to the surface Rank's strong need for spiritual guidance, as well as the profound anguish of his isolated existence. The desire for meaningful association emerged again on April 13 when he questioned whether he should remain "entirely dependent on myself."[89] His intensified study of psychoanalytic theory in mid-April was thus a response to the need for immediate stimulation. As is clear from the introduction to *Der Künstler,* he began to read everything Freud had written.

In addition to his contact with Adler, Rank also attempted to contact Freud. On May 12, he addressed an eight-page, untitled manuscript to the movement's founder. There is no evidence that Rank ever sent it to Freud, but the gesture itself indicates the need for immediate communication. After reading *The Interpretation of Dreams* for a second time, Rank felt inspired to respond to Freud's Frau Doni dream. His careful examination of Freud's treatment of the dream, his frequent quoting from the dream book, and his praise for Freud's astute psychological understanding indicate the extent of Rank's appreciation for Freud. He felt that his study of Freud had "deepened" his knowledge of the psyche.[90]

Rank's analysis also betrayed his own unique development, for again he utilized dream theory for confirming the discoveries he made about man's inner striving for creativity. The Frau Doni dream involved Freud's concern for his children. At the beginning of the dream, Freud followed an acquaintance, P, to a hospital and toward a restaurant. Later, he asked for a Frau Doni and was told she lived with three children at the back of the restaurant. Before he got there, he met an indistinct figure with his two little girls. He stood with them for a while, then reproached his wife for leaving them there. Freud believed that the dream expressed his "satisfaction . . . with the fact that my marriage had brought me children." He ended the interpretation by suggesting that the recent birthday of his eldest son prompted the dream, adding parenthetically that his son "seems to have some poetic gifts."[91]

Rank did not accept Freud's interpretation of the dream. It is revealing that he based his criticism on Freud's final remarks about his son, for Rank was indeed sensitive to the needs of a son for protection. He raised these questions: Why did Freud emphasize the importance of his son, if he appeared neither in the dream nor in the interpretation? Why did Freud attribute poetic gifts to him? Immediately upon reading this dream in late April, Rank recorded his suspicion about Freud's interpretation: "F's son cannot become a poet since [Freud] has protected him beyond puberty from all dangers or threats. . . . [The son] can never come into any painful conflict with the 'world,' which is necessary for making an artist of him."[92] Rank referred to Freud's own observation, appearing on the page preceding the Frau Doni dream, to explain the emphasis Freud placed on his son. Since the judgments made after the dream recall the feelings which incited the dream, the interpretation itself forms part of the latent content of the dream.[93]

Rank believed that the appearance of the final remarks about the gifted son was the result not of the interpretation of the dream, but of a wish, the wish for immortality. The problem he found with this confusion between wish and interpretation was that Freud totally neglected the wish which emerged in the dream. According to his reinterpretation, Rank felt the dream expressed Freud's dissatisfaction, not satisfaction, with the fact that his marriage brought him children. He explained: In the dream, Freud identified his wife with Frau Doni, for their differences were indistinct. As Freud commented in the interpretation, Frau Doni was an approximation of the name Frau Dona A---y, a woman whose death in childbirth he read about the day before the dream. The dream identification with Frau Doni thus expressed Freud's wish that his family would cease growing. Moreover, Freud's identification with P, at the beginning of the dream, represented his desire for freedom from the responsibilities of raising a family, for Freud noted in the analysis that P's life "lay for some time alongside mine; [he] then outdistanced me socially and materially, but [his] marriage was childless."[94]

Rank concluded that Freud's interpretation was an example of "scientific disguise," a concealment of the unconscious. He claimed that Freud ignored his desire for no children and, instead, fulfilled his wish for immortality through the circuitous and less painful route of interpretation. Rank insisted that this dream interpretation was typical of the rest of the work: "The book is an unconscious defense against fear. . . . The wish fulfillment of the book is this: my theory is true, right; it has scientific value. Consequently I am not really neurotic." Rank claimed that Freud exhibited neurotic characteristics by failing to deal comprehensively with his unconscious: "You have not put your doubts and fears to rest." He summarized the meaning of the book by interpreting its enigmatic Latin motto, "If I cannot move the powers above, I will move the powers below," as, "If I cannot convince people of the correctness of my theory, I will at least soothe my 'unconscious.' "[95]

To Rank, Freud's book both proved the correctness of his theory and demonstrated the temptation of withdrawing into reason and resolution too quickly. As he wrote in his introduction to the reinterpretation of the Frau Doni dream, while the book deepened his knowledge of the psyche, only his own work "opened my eyes completely."[96] Rank thus affirmed the belief that "the satisfaction of the sexual instinct [in creative self-expression] is the main thing," even as he devoted himself to studying psychoanalytic theory in the spring of 1905.[97] From early May to late August 1905, when he referred, for the first time, to his personal contact with Freud,[98] Rank concentrated on the development of his own theory of creativity. This period, a period of enormous self-confidence for him, brought to light the heroic or universal dimension of Rank's struggle for creative self-expression.

On three separate occasions after reading Nietzsche in the fall of 1903, Rank had expressed enthusiasm for the positive regeneration of mankind. He stressed the theme of mankind's salvation in "Götzen." During the winter of 1904, he became fascinated with Wagnerian drama because of its redemptive vision. The following fall, Rank saw, in dream interpretation, the potential for universal renewal. In each instance, Rank expressed concern for humanity only after he found a source of inspiration for inner renewal. The pattern suggests Rank's close adherence to Nietzsche's concept of change. Deriving inner strength from Nietzsche, Wagner, and Freud, Rank made the crucial transition to experiencing the second consecration of culture. The final notations in his diary anticipated his involvement in the psychoanalytic movement. In them, he proclaimed that the power of psychoanalytic interpretation to affirm man's longing for creativity would bring about the "purification" of, or "cure" for, the human race.[99]

Der Künstler was Rank's first contribution to this movement for redemption. In it, after describing the evolution of the human organism from the original state of complete gratification to increasing states of repression, Rank discussed the forms of resisting neurosis or of expressing repressed instincts. Consistent with the Nietzschean view of renewal, Rank advanced two important concepts. First, in each successive state of renewal, only a small minority was able to affirm unconscious powers of expression. Secondly, just as artistic expression preserved the original state of gratification, the artistic minority kept the rest of mankind from succumbing to massive hysteria. Regarding the work of art as the satisfaction of the will that was yearning for liberation, Rank thus stressed the significance of the heroic minority, as well as the destiny or mission of this minority.[100]

Rank believed that the artist's chief limitation in his task was his subjectivity. While he was capable of producing an affective response in his audience, the effect could only be temporary. In order to bring about a permanent change, the *Künstler* must become a *Heilkünstler,* an artist capable of curing neurosis. This required sustained, conscious, analytic affirmation of the unconscious striving for creativity.[101] Analysts, or "physicians," thus formed, in Rank's view, the new vanguard of universal, artistic regeneration.

Characteristic of Rank's need for practical affirmation of his involvement in the regeneration process, he wrote a five-page essay, in December 1905, defining the redemptive elite. The essay, "Das Wesen des Judentums," was actually his third contribution to the movement for redemption, for in July he wrote a two-page study entitled "Die Barttracht" ("The Beard as Dress"), an interpretation of folk tradition and, specifically, of the concentration of hair on the face as an example of sexual repression in contemporary culture.[102] It is clear, just from his use of *Der Künstler* as an introduction to the essay on Judaism, that Rank regarded Jews as an integral part of the psychoanalytic movement. Indeed, as an event in his intellectual development, the essay brings out the central significance of his Jewish consciousness in his growing devotion to Freud and to the movement.

The essay appeared at the beginning of a one-year period when he finally rejected his home life for more enriching and promising contacts. From August 22, 1905, the date of his first reference to meeting Freud, until October 10, 1906, the first day he is known to have attended psychoanalytic meetings, Rank drew extremely close to Freud. He moved from the second district, where he had always lived with his family, to an apartment in the ninth district, not far from Freud's residence.[103] The act of irrevocable separation from his father acquired symbolic permanence via the name of the street to which he moved — Simondenkgasse, a street in the memory of Simon. Soon thereafter, Rank and Freud saw each other almost daily. In agreement with Freud's wishes, Rank entered gymnasium and, upon graduation in 1908, the University of Vienna. No doubt, Rank felt honored by Freud's intention of preparing him for a dozentur at the university. Reinforcing this emergence of an accessible and caring father surrogate in his life was Freud's willingness to support Rank financially. This support, including Freud's assignment of Rank to the position of salaried secretary for the psychoanalytic circle, increased Rank's devotion to Freud during 1905-6.[104]

As he developed ties with Freud and the movement, Rank elaborated the view that Jews, "more than any other people," were capable of curing neurosis. They were the "physicians" for mankind. This conception of the Jewish task resembled the theories he formed of the artist and of the dream, which ultimately reflected the Nietzschean conception of the philosopher-genius. According to Rank, Jews possessed special creative powers since they had been able to maintain a "direct relation to 'nature,' to primitive sexuality." To explain this phenomenon, Rank pointed to the "numerous difficulties" that prevented Jews from entering the arena of civilized morality. He noted, Jews "do not have their own 'culture.' " Like women, they have "preserved themselves," and thus "remained 'unchanged.' " Rank concluded the first part of the essay with the highest praise he could confer on any people: *"The essence of Judaism is its stress on primitive sexuality."*[105]

The concept of struggle emerged as the central feature in this essay, as it did in Rank's stories and other studies. Rank believed that for the Jews, struggle was only a recent condition of life, a reaction to both an external and an internal repression of sexuality. Like the negative forces of reality that prompted his dream about preserving the ego, the strength of these pressures incited the Jews to strike back. Rank indicated the magnitude of the pressures threatening Jewish existence in two ways. He found that the fear of sexuality existed even among artists like Schopenhauer and Nietzsche, who made it their task to combat sexual repression. Their direct attack on the Jews offered him the evidence for this claim, for anti-Semitism was "nothing more than the expression of the denial of sexuality." Rank indicated that the other serious threat to Jewish existence was the development of sexual repression among the Jews themselves. He argued that "suddenly and without transition," Jews began to deny their own vibrant sexuality: "Through a painful suppression in which the Jews resigned themselves to a parasitic existence among the people with whom they were living, and through merging with these people, repression of sexuality mounted among the 'cultivated' Jews as well." Rank believed that this psychic interpretation of the assimilation process explained why Jews became neurotic along with the rest of civilized humanity.[106]

The remainder of the essay described not only the Jewish efforts at resisting neurosis, but the unique advantage they had in overcoming nervous illness. Rank argued that the choice of a way out of this difficult situation depended on the "bent of the psyche," as well as on the degree of consciousness attained through resistance. Most of those who resisted repressive influences sought relief by contributing to cultural achievements. The production of art, philosophy, and the newspaper succeeded in "discharging affect." However, the enduring Jewish stress on nature and the suddenness of their search for renewal "attracted [them] to a few extreme cases." Rather than merely seeking momentary relief, Jews led the way toward creating the conditions for regeneration. Rank asserted that Jews were superior to the rest of mankind because they attempted to go beyond the momentary to the "radical cure" of neurosis. The Jewish struggle was more than a subjective reaction to the illness. Jews were distinguished by being in a position to "help others."[107]

In this short, significant piece on Judaism, Rank addressed himself to the major themes which preoccupied many German Jews in Vienna at the turn of the century. His view of the Jewish reaction to the social pressures of assimilation and anti-Semitism provides critical insight into the complicated relationship between Jews and Germans. On one level, Rank regarded these pressures as morally and spiritually destructive. Indeed, he regarded anti-Semitism as a prominent restriction of freedom in Jewish life. But Rank placed less emphasis on the role of anti-Semitism in Viennese culture than did many other Jews, including Freud, for he believed the phenomenon was only the symptom of a highly repressive culture. This relatively moderate estimate of anti-Jewish hostility may be explained in part by Rank's obliviousness to the liberal currents of toleration that dominated Viennese culture in the generation before his birth. Because anti-Semitism prevailed throughout his early life, Rank possessed neither the nostalgia for an era free of anti-Jewish hatred, nor the view that such hatred brought about the atmosphere of restricted freedom.

Because he regarded repression as the fundamental impediment to cultural liberation, Rank blamed repressed Jews as well as non-Jews for creating the conditions of general malaise. He continued to hold contempt for superficial Jewish conventions and customs. In fact, in August 1905, only a few months before he wrote the essay, Rank summarily dismissed Judaism as an "out-of-date point of view."[108] He was careful to point out that Jews, as much as Germans, were responsible for the repressive process of assimilation. Yet, despite his criticism of the process, Rank recognized that on a deeper level, the pressures of assimilation and anti-Semitism promoted Jewish cultural development. He perceptively observed that these pressures provided the necessary stimuli for inspiring a positive, redemptive reaction. Just as the artist needed painful conflict with the world for poetic creation, he felt Jews needed direct pressure to stimulate their struggle for creative freedom. Rank believed that the reaction of Jews to the threats of external and internal repression prompted them to preserve their relationship with nature and, in the process, to gain consciousness of this special relationship. This conception of assimilation is valuable for defining the dynamic, dialectical quality of the process. In contrast to the more popular deterministic view, Rank believed that Jews contributed to the climate of repression, and that, at any rate, this climate favored the development of inner renewal.

His conclusion to the essay affirmed the notion, current in German-Jewish intellectual circles, that beside the faults of conventional Jewish habits, there existed a significant reserve of strength and purpose in Jewish life. This reconciliation with Judaism was a practical fulfillment of his search for meaningful religious experience. Already familiar, through Nietzsche's writings, with the "holy zeal for creation," as well as with the concepts of the spiritual community and of redemption, Rank was prepared for reexamining Judaism and for investing it with meaning. Moreover, having appreciated the value of heroic minorities, such as the community of geniuses or artists, Rank was attracted to the prevailing image of Jews as a socially peripheral and persecuted group.

Similar to the reconciliation other German Jews made with Judaism, Rank's reconciliation implied much more than a sectarian revival. In the first place, he attached universal meaning to Judaism, regarding it as the foundation of mankind's regeneration. His concept of the Jewish task resembled Nietzsche's ideal of education, for, since the essence of Judaism was the stress on sexuality, the

Jewish mission was the consummation of nature. Rank could have given the essay on Judaism the subtitle "Jews as Educators." Secondly, his dedication to the Jewish task compressed effectively the direction of his thought, intensifying his germinating feelings of self-assertion, of a collective struggle, and, most significantly, of redemption. In this concise statement, Rank coordinated his previous personal achievements as well as his missionary tendencies, and gave them definitive form.

As with his previous efforts at clarifying the regenerative process, the effect of this concentration on the meaning of Judaism was crucial to his intellectual development. The essay not only intensified his continuing commitment to the values of rebirth and of a missionary movement, but articulated a deeper commitment to these values than ever before. He discovered, in Jewish existence, a source of inspiration that even psychoanalysis could not fully supply. Rank's need for stimulation and discipline did not cease within the intellectual and spiritual universe of psychoanalytic psychology. Of course, child psychology and psychoanalysis provided him with more effective methods for defining Nietzsche's intuitive vision than did his literary imaginings of spiritual guidance, as evident in "Der Freund" (1904). Indeed, Freud had a profound impact on Rank's search for clarity. In a diary entry of May 13, conveying ecstatic joy, and squared in bright orange crayon, Rank exclaimed, "Now I see everything clearly. I no longer find the process of the world a riddle. I can explain all of culture, indeed everything."[109] Yet, writing this on the day after his reinterpretation of Freud's Frau Doni dream, Rank was aware of the limitations, as well as of the power, of psychoanalytic interpretation. To Rank, though psychoanalysis gave definition to Nietzsche's philosophy, it threatened to withdraw dangerously into reason and "scientific disguise."

Cognizant of the limitations of psychoanalysis, Rank developed, in *Der Künstler,* a more promising conception of the heroic minority. His concept of the *Heilkünstler* implied a power that exceeded the power of the artist, who, in Rank's view, was unable to effect a permanent cure for neurosis. The idea went beyond his understanding of the analyst as well. As in the case of Freud, the power of the analyst appeared to him as potentially subverting artistic supremacy. Though a necessary intellectual achievement, the concept of *Heilkünstler* created a psychological vacuum for Rank, for it lacked a point of reference. He could not identify with this model of strength and vision as he could with an artist or with an analyst. The ideal of Jewish existence filled this immediate psychological vacuum. Moreover, the ideal filled a larger vacuum created by his critical view of psychoanalysis. Where psychoanalysis failed to sustain the essential relation to nature, his identification as a Jew succeeded in this regard. The image of the sexual and uncivilized Jew who acquired consciousness through his struggle against the repressive influences of civilization provided Rank with a more reliable basis of renewal than did the concepts of artistic or analytic redemption. Even more than crystallizing his belief in the movement for universal redemption, Rank's Jewish sensibility prepared him for deeper engagement. His Jewish self-conception inspired him to proclaim the possibilities of the "radical cure" for neurosis.

NOTES

1. Otto Rank, "Das Wessen des Judentums" (MS., The Otto Rank Collection at Columbia University, 1905), 4-5. See Appendix C for the English translation.
2. Hanns Sachs, *Sigmund Freud: Master and Friend* (Cambridge: Harvard University Press, 1944), 14-15.
3. Sigmund Freud, *The Standard Edition of the Complete Psychological Works of Sigmund Freud,* trans. and ed. James Strachey (London: The Hogarth Press, 1953-1979), vol. 14, 25.
4. Sachs, 62.
5. Lou Andreas-Salomé, *The Freud Journal of Lou Andreas-Salomé,* trans. Stanley A. Leavy (New York: Basic Books, 1964), 98. See Paul Roazen, *Freud and His Followers* (New York: Alfred A. Knopf, 1975), 395. See also Sachs, 60, and Anais Nin, *The Diary of Anais Nin 1931-1934* (New York: Harcourt Brace Jovanovich, 1966), 279.
6. Sachs, 62; Ernest Jones, *The Life and Work of Sigmund Freud* (New York: Basic Books, 1953, 1955, 1957), vol. 2, 160.
7. Jesse Taft, *Otto Rank: A Biographical Study* (New York: The Julian Press, 1958), xvi.
8. Otto Rank, *Die Lohengrinsage: Ein Beitrag zu ihrer Motivgestaltung und Deutung* (Leipzig, Vienna: Verlag von Franz Deuticke, 1911).
9. Otto Rank, *Das Inzestmotiv in Dichtung und Sage: Grundzüge einer Psychologie des dichterischen Schaffens* (Vienna: Deuticke, 1912); idem, "Die Nacktheit in Sage und Dichtung," *Imago,* vol. 2 (1913), 267-301, 409-46.
10. Jones, vol. 2, 86.
11. Jones, vol. 2, 160. Freud was uneasy with Rank's early interest in the preoedipal stage of human development, dismissing his pupil's different course of investigation as a digression from the main themes of the subject. See *Minutes of the Vienna Psychoanalytic Society,* ed. Herman Nunberg and Ernst Federn; trans. M. Nunberg (New York: International Universities Press, 1962), vol. I, 10.
12. Otto Rank, *The Trauma of Birth* (London: Routledge and Kegan Paul, 1929); German original: *Das Trauma der Geburt und seine Bedeutung für die Psychoanalyse* (Leipzig, Vienna, Zurich: Inter. Psycho. Verlag, 1924).
13. Jones, vol. 3, 65.
14. Nin, 277.
15. Roazen, 412.
16. Otto Rank, "Tagebücher" (MSS., The Otto Rank Collection at Columbia University, 1902-5), vol. I, 40: October 26, 1903. Hereafter cited as "Tagebücher," followed by the volume number, the page, and the date of entry. The information about his religion appeared in a lengthy diary inscription, which he entitled "Autobiographie" ("Tagebücher," I, 39-47: October 26, 1903). Because this diary segment provides much information about his early life, material taken from this segment will be henceforth cited as "Autobiographie," followed by the diary page(s). Rank had five volumes of diary notations from late 1902 to 1905: I, January 1, 1903-February 22, 1904; II, February 22-December 30, 1904; III, January 1-April 8, 1905 (including material from the summer and fall of 1904); IV, April 10-July 1, 1905; V, c. October 1902-August 21, 1905 (poems).
17. Matrikelamt Zivil Magistrat Wien (Records Office of the Vienna City Hall); Matrikelamt Israelitische Kultusgemeinde Wien (Records Office of the Viennese Jewish Community), 2609 (1927).

18. Otto Rank, "Curriculum Vitae" (MS., Niederösterreichisches Landesarchiv [Archive of Lower Austria, in Vienna] k.k.n.ö. Statthalterei Z., IX – 2749/3, November 15, 1909), 2. This was Rank's application for a state-managed stipend for study at the University of Vienna. The foundation rejected his application two months later.

19. "Tagebücher," II, 89: November 28, 1904; "Autobiographie," 43-44. Karoline Fleischner was born on December 10, 1856, in Hausbrünn, Moravia. Matrikelamt Zivil Magistrat Wien.

20. Otto Rank, "Tagebuchblätter eines Totgeborenen" (MS., The Otto Rank Collection at Columbia University, n.d.), 4-5. Though the manuscript is undated, its themes, especially those dealing with the purposelessness of life, indicate that he wrote it between 1899 and 1903.

21. "Autobiographie," 46; "Tagebücher," II, 89: November 28, 1904.

22. Otto Rank, "Träume und Versuche ihrer Deutung" (MS., The Otto Rank Collection at Columbia University, November 24, 1904), 7-8.

23. "Autobiographie," 42-43.

24. "Tagebücher," II, 20: April 29, 1904; Rank, "Träume," 2, 5.

25. Matrikelamt Israelitische Kultusgemeinde Wien, 2700 (1884).

26. "Tagebücher," I, 7: July 20, 1903; 23: October 6, 1903.

27. Magistrat Stadtsarchiv Rathaus Wien (Archive of the City of Vienna), Konscriptionsamt Zahl, 39350 (1909); Niederösterreichisches Landesarchiv, k.k.n.ö. Statthalterei Zahl XVII – 1502/2 (hereafter cited as Nöla).

28. Rank expressed his awareness of the Jewish sound to the authorities who legalized his change of names in 1909. See ibid. Rank's rejection of, and possible discomfort with, the Jewish name Rosenfeld was not the only, or even the chief, reason he legalized the name Rank. According to Austrian law at the time, an author who did not use a legally recognized name would lose royalties on published material. The stipulation of this law appeared in his legalization papers (Nöla): "As a result of strict legal regulations conerning the rights accorded to authors, the disagreement of the name of the writer and the real name means substantial financial disadvantages." In 1908, when he first applied to the authorities for legal adoption of his pseudonym, Rank had *Der Künstler* in print and anticipated publishing two other works – *Der Mythus von der Geburt des Helden* (completed, 1908; published in Vienna and Leipzig by Deuticke in the spring of 1909) and *Das Inzestmotiv* (completed, 1906; published in 1912). For these dates, see Otto Rank, analysis of writings, 1906-30 (Untitled ms., The Otto Rank Collection at Columbia University, 1930), 4, 8.

The process of legalization was complicated for Rank, involving a legal religious conversion. At first, the authorities resisted Rank's application because they felt that his new name would be confused with the name of the then well-known author Josef Rank (1816-96). Furthermore, they advised him that the reasons he gave for the change were insufficient. (See Nöla.) Rank thereupon appealed for, and was granted, permission to convert. The Roman Catholic ceremony took place on October 20, 1908, at the Pfarre Schotten. Matrikelamt der Pfarre zu den Schotten (Records Office of the Schotten Benedictine Parish, in Vienna), *Geburts* und Taufbuch 1905-1915, tom 61, fol. 86. Upon Rank's return to the civil offices in February 1909, the authorities recorded that Rank had, "on the basis of this conversion to the Christian confession [requested] the change from the pronounced name Rosenfeld to 'Rank.' " Reversing their opinion about the confusion of names, the authorities proceeded to make the change legal. (It became legal on March 20, 1909). See Nöla. This pressure on Rank to convert is a good illustration of the nature and extent of official discrimination against Jews at the time. Though the authorities asked Rank to notify the Pfarre Schotten of the name change, Rank neglected the order, for he had accomplished his original intention of qualifying for the royalties.

On the books, Rank remained a Roman Catholic until 1918, when he formally returned to the Jewish confession. Like his conversion ten years before, this return was a result of ulterior circumstances which required an appropriate religious affiliation. During the last two years of World War I, Rank was stationed in Cracow, then in the northern part of the Habsburg Empire. There, he worked for, and intermittently edited, the official journal of the Austrian army, the *Krakauer Zeitung.* In the fall of 1918, Rank decided to marry a woman whom he had met a short time before in Cracow, Betty Münzer. The decision to have a Jewish marriage was probably Münzer's since she had lived her life in the tradition-bound Jewish pale of Austrian Galicia. Rank's withdrawal from Roman Catholicism and return to Judaism on October 24, 1918, just two weeks before their marriage, would have reflected Münzer's preferences. Moreover, the policy of the military office of Jewish affairs, where they were married on November 18, stipulated that no Jewish ceremony could be conducted without the prerequisite documented proof that both partners were Jewish. For the record of Rank's withdrawal from Roman Catholicism, see *Trauungs-Buch* k.u.k. Militarkommando Krakau 0549, 98 (Izarelicka Ksiega Sluba, 1917/1918 Krakow Tom II, Bestätigung: Magistrat Krakau Z. 105681/18/IV). For the record of his marriage and return to Judaism, see ibid., Bestätigung: Matrikelamt der isr. mil., Seelsorge der Mil. Kommando Krakau E586/18. Münzer was born in Neu Sandez, Galicia (near Cracow) on February 16, 1896. The *Trauungs-Buch*, located in the Records Office of the Military (a division in Vienna of the Austrian Federal Ministry of the Interior), shows that the military office of Jewish affairs required documents of Jewish affiliation.

29. The diaries show an increasing concentration on Nietzsche beginning in the first week of October 1903.

30. A discussion of these two works will be given later in this chapter.

31. Friedrich Nietzsche, *Schopenhauer as Educator,* trans. James W. Hillesheim and Malcolm R. Simpson (Chicago: Henry Regnery, 1965), 37-39; idem, *The Birth of Tragedy and the Genealogy of Morals,* trans. Francis Golffing (Garden City, New York: Doubleday, 1956), 105-12; idem, *Twilight of the Idols,* in *The Portable Nietzsche,* trans. Walter Kaufman (New York: The Viking Press, 1966), 539-44.

32. See William J. McGrath, *Dionysian Art and Populist Politics in Austria* (New Haven and London: Yale University Press, 1974), 33, and H. Stuart Hughes, *Consciousness and Society* (New York: Vintage Books, 1958), 339-40.

33. Nietzsche, *Schopenhauer as Educator;* idem, *Twilight of the Idols,* 500-1, 532.

34. Nietasche, *Twilight of the Idols,* 543.

35. Nietzsche, *Schopenhauer as Educator,* 43-45, 92.

36. Otto Rank, "Götzen: Vier Acte aus dem Schauspiel des Lebens" (MS., The Otto Rank Collection at Columbia University, November 1903), 2-3. Only act one is extant. It is possible that he never intended to finish the play. Rank continued to work on the first act after completing it in November 1903. "Tagebücher," I, 76: January 24, 1904.

37. Rank, "Götzen," 9-10, 14-16.

38. "Tagebücher," I, 89: February 16, 1904.

39. "Autobiographie," 40-44; Rank, "Götzen," 1-9.

40. "Autobiographie," 40, 44.

41. "Tagebücher," I, 1: January 1, 1903.

42. "Autobiographie," 45, 47.

43. Nietzsche, *Schopenhauer as Educator,* 2-3, 56.

44. Ibid., 54.

45. Nietzsche, *Birth of Tragedy,* 38-39, 56, 128-29; idem, *Schopenhauer as Educator,* 12, 28, 40.

46. Nietzsche, *Schopenhauer as Educator,* 40, 61.

47. Ibid., 56, 81-82.

48. Ibid., 45, 62.

49. Nietzsche, *Birth of Tragedy,* 16-17, 101, 128.

50. Idem, *Schopenhauer as Educator,* 13.

51. See ibid., 27, 35; idem, *Birth of Tragedy,* 139.

52. Rank, "Götzen," 9-10, 14-16.

53. Ibid., 6-7, 12, 18.
54. Ibid., 15.
55. "Tagebücher," I, 56: December 7, 1903.
56. Ibid., I, 77: January 28, 1904. The quote was taken from the end of "Letzte Aphorismem," in *Über die letzten Dingen* (Vienna: Whilhelm Braumüller, 1903).
57. "Tagebücher," I, 73, 88: January 22, February 16, 1904; II, 1: February 22, 1904.
58. See "Autobiographie," 45.
59. McGrath, 243.
60. "Tagebücher," II, 4: February 29, 1904; II, 8: March 12, 1904.
61. Ibid., I, 87-88: February 15, 1904.
62. Ibid., II, 2-5: February 29, 1904.
63. Ibid., II, 9, 11, 17: March 19, March 30, April 17, 1904.
64. "Entwurf zu einem Brief" in ibid., II, 19-24: April 29, 1904.
65. Ibid., II, 28: May 14, 1904.
66. Ibid., II, 30: May 20, 1904.
67. Friedrich Nietzsche, *Thus Spoke Zarathustra*, in *The Portable Nietzsche*, trans. Walter Kaufmann (New York: The Viking Press, 1966), 167-68.
68. Otto Rank, "Der Freund" (MS., The Otto Rank Collection at Columbia University, June 8, 1904), 4-5, 8-9.
69. Rank, "Der Freund," 10-13.
70. "Tagebücher," II, 40-46: June 18-19, 1904. Cf. Nietzsche, *Twilight of the Idols*, 547-49.
71. "Tagebücher," II, 49: June 23, 1904.
72. Ibid., II, 70: September 28, 1904. See ibid., II, 60-73: August 6-October 8, 1904.
73. Ibid., II, 66: September 10, 1904; II, 72: October 6, 1904.
74. Otto Rank, "Im October vorigen Jahres . . ." (Untitled unpub. ms.: The Otto Rank Collection at Columbia University, May 12, 1905), 1. The rheumatic condition intensified during the summer of 1904 and through the following fall and winter. See e.g., "Tagebücher," II, 58: July 25, 1904, and III, 7: January 15, 1905. Rank's early medical relation to Adler is mentioned in Nin, 278-79, and in Roazen, 393.
75. Rank, "Im October vorigen Jahres," 1.
76. "Tagebücher," II, 75-76: October 29, 1904.
77. Ibid., II, 76-78, 90-91: November 3, 10, and 29, 1904.
78. Rank, "Träume," 1-5.
79. Ibid., 1-2, 5-7.
80. Ibid., 2, 7-8.
81. Ibid., 5, 7-8; "Tagebücher," II, 85-86: November 24, 1904.
82. Rank, "Träume," 3, 4, 8.
83. Ibid., 8.
84. Ibid.
85. "Tagebücher," II, 94: November 30, 1904.
86. Ibid., II, 94: December 8, 1904.
87. Ibid., III, 39-42, 45-46: February 1905.
88. Rank, "Im October vorigen Jahres," 1.
89. "Tagebücher," III, 53, 56, and IV, 10: April 6, 8, 13.
90. Rank, "Im October vorigen Jahres," 1.
91. Sigmund Freud, *The Interpretation of Dreams*, trans. James Strachey (New York: Avon Books, 1967), 483-84.
92. "Tagebücher," IV, 20: April 29, 1905.
93. Rank, "Im October vorigen Jahres," 3; Freud, *The Interpretation of Dreams*, 482.
94. Rank, "Im October vorigen Jahres."

95. Ibid., 5-7.
96. Ibid., 1.
97. "Tagebücher," IV, 22-23: May 1, 1905.
98. Otto Rank, Sketchbooks, source for "Tagebücher" (MSS., The Otto Rank Collection at Columbia University, October 8, 1903-August 24, 1905), V, 84: August 22, 1905. Rarely did Rank's sketchbooks deviate from his diaries, though the last book included entries postdating the last volume of his diaries (i.e., July 1-Aug. 24, 1905).
99. See esp., "Tagebücher," IV, 23, 27, 29: May 2, 4, 31, 1905.
100. Otto Rank, *Der Künstler: Ansätze zu einer Sexual-Psychologie* (Vienna, Leipzig: Hugo Heller und Cie, 1907), chap. 1.
101. Ibid., 55-56.
102. Otto Rank, "Die Barttracht: Eine Studie" (MS., The Otto Rank Collection at Columbia University, July 20, 1905).
103. All five sketchbooks (October 8, 1903, to August 24, 1905) are inscribed with the address Rothe Kreuzgasse 5, the second district. On the first day minutes were kept for the psychoanalytic society (October 19, 1906), Rank's address was listed as Simondenkgasse 8, the ninth district, a few blocks from Berggasse 19, where Freud lived and the society met. *Minutes of the Vienna Psychoanalytic Society,* vol. 1, 3.
104. Rank, "Curriculum Vitae," 2-3; Freud, *The Standard Edition,* vol. 14, 25; Jones, vol. 2, 92, 98, 160, 163; *Minutes of the Vienna Psychoanalytic Society,* vol. 1, 7.
105. Rank, "Das Wesen des Judentums," 2-3.
106. Ibid., 3-4.
107. Ibid., 2-3.
108. Rank, Sketchbooks, V, 63: August 8, 1905.
109. "Tagebücher," IV, 29: May 13, 1905.

5

CONCLUSION

A JEWISH MOVEMENT

During Freud's active affiliation with the B'nai B'rith, and one year before Rank expressed his belief in the psychoanalytic-redemptive mission of the Jews, Fritz Wittels (1880-1950), then an intern, and, within a short time, the enfant terrible of the psychoanalytic movement, wrote the provocative pamphlet *Der Taufjude* (*The Convert Jew,* 1904). The essay expressed the exhilaration and the sense of purpose that his psychoanalytic writings and lectures conveyed during his intensive three-year association (1907-10) with Freud and his circle. During this association, Wittels advocated a freedom of sexual expression to a degree that neither Freud nor many of his supporters could accept. When, for example, Jung reviewed *Die Sexuelle Not* (*The Sexual Need,* 1907), a passionate entreaty for uninhibited instinctual gratification, he wrote, "I have not read a book on the problem of sexuality that so harshly and mercilessly tears to pieces our present-day morality."[1] As Wittels wrote near the end of his life, it was his extreme delight "to hurl the importance of sex into the teeth of society."[2] Despite the unabashed impudence of the remark, Wittels maintained that his purpose was creative, not destructive. In 1908, he argued that the elimination of repression and the satisfaction of sexual needs would evoke man's "supreme achievements" and establish the conditions for ethical and legal reform. Like Rank, he recognized, in this vision, the psychoanalytic task of universal redemption. "Some of us believed that psychoanalysis would change the surface of the earth . . . [and introduce] a golden age in which there would

138

be no room for neuroses any more. We felt like great men. . . . Some people have a mission in their life."[3]

When he wrote *Der Taufjude,* Wittels was already influenced by Freud's writings, especially by *The Interpretation of Dreams.*[4] He exhibited the two-fold psychoanalytic concern for honest expression and for mankind's liberation from forces inhibiting honest expression. His essay examined the psychological disability of hypocrisy, the way of life of the convert Jew, and proclaimed the strength and moral integrity involved in positive Jewish identity. Though he addressed himself to other Jews who had felt the temptation to convert, the polemic was clearly a piece of personal history. He expressed the bitterness of being the victim of discrimination and insult, of being treated no better than a dog. He desired his freedom. He understood the "irresistible compulsion" to convert. Moral resolve was not the reason for, but the result of, resisting the temptation to convert. The reason originated from a recognition as perspicacious as Theodor Herzl's: that conversion and other forms of assimilation were bankrupt methods of personal and social liberation. Wittels observed that the history of the double monarchy had been one of systematic official and popular prejudice against the Jews.[5]

The convert Jew, by his timid and naive act of conversion, prolonged the injustice of discrimination and his own moral weakness. Arguing against a reliance on "natural right" or on the theoretical guarantees of the state (the *Staatsgrundgesetz* of 1867), Wittels encouraged the Jew to be responsible first to himself and, through his own efforts, to strive for emancipation and justice. He noted that the Jews are "one of the few groups which, in the process of securing their own interests, must swing the sword of the ideal to secure at once the rudimentary conditions of a decent life." He stressed that only this "lofty passion of the oppressed" will elevate the Jews from the position of the dogs of society to that of men.[6] With the exuberance of recent discovery, Wittels announced "the struggle for justice" — the title of his final chapter — as the "life purpose" of the Jewish people.

The germ of Wittels's psychoanalytic mission to "change the surface of the earth" is found in *Der Taufjude.* He wrote about the Jewish responsibility for stimulating the Aryan people toward the truth and nobility of self-assertion as well as toward the struggle against passivity and the accepted standards of conduct. Since the Jew, in opposition to the obsolescence of traditional society, seeks renewal and can comprehend, if not revive, "eternal life," it is his obligation to bring about a new order of human dignity and freedom, equality, and social peace (*Frieden*). As Wittels concluded, the Jew intimately and immediately "yearns for final redemption."[7]

The number of psychoanalysts who shared the discovery of value and meaning in Jewish existence with Wittels, Freud, and Rank, as well as with other Viennese Jews discussed in the first chapter, argues for the interpenetration of the Jewish redemptive vision with the psychoanalytic movement's redemptive hope for the eradication of neurosis. For at least part of their tenure as members of Freud's circle, Eduard Hitschmann and Oskar Rie were active leaders in the B'nai B'rith. Hitschmann's simultaneous membership in the second Viennese lodge, Eintracht, and in the psychoanalytic movement indicates, in conjunction with Freud's own parallel allegiance, the common concerns of the two enterprises. His involvement in both circles intensified after World War I, when he presented several lectures to the B'nai B'rith on psychoanalysis and became the first director of the psychoanalytic clinic in Vienna. It was during this time that he praised Freud and the psychoanalytic movement as supremely Jewish and therefore superior to the rest of society.[8] Rie, who, like Hitschmann, joined the B'nai B'rith through Freud, was less active in psychoanalysis, though he remained a member of the movement beyond the two years of his close association (1908-10). During part of this period of his association, Rie served as vice president of Eintracht.[9]

Two other members of the psychoanalytic movement acknowledged the ethical superiority and universal responsibilities of the Jewish people. Though Isidor Sadger (1867-194?), a relative of Wittels's and the one who introduced him to Freud, criticized the aggravated obsessional neurosis of East-European Jews, he endorsed the German-Jewish student struggle for humanitarian achievements, by lecturing to the *Jüdisch-akademische Lesehalle* and to the *Lese- und Redehalle jüdische Hochschüler.*[10] Victor Tausk (1879-1919) asserted, a few years after joining the movement in 1909, that the "progress of psychoanalysis" rested with the Jews. He explained that the unique position of the Jews as society's outcasts furnished them with a special sensitivity to the collapse of the traditional political and moral order, as well as with a capacity for discerning the foundations of a more stable order: "It is understandable that in ancient, neglected palaces, with crumbling walls, we [Jews] can see the inner structure and can gain insights which are inaccessible [to those living] in beautiful new houses with polished facades."[11]

The common belief in the value of Jews to the development of psychoanalysis is evidence of the circle's intense Jewish self-consciousness in the decade before World War I. Believing Jews were chiefly responsible for the analytic redemption of mankind, the early analysts regarded the psychoanalytic movement as a Jewish movement. In the case of Freud, this belief can be seen to underlie his deep involvement in the B'nai B'rith. His communication of the earliest results of his scientific investigations to the brotherhood, and his search for new members sympathetic to his germinating psychoanalytic theories, indicate that the psychoanalytic movement began, in embryonic form, within the B'nai B'rith. Even after 1908, when Freud attempted to reverse the tendency toward Jewish exclusiveness within the circle, he maintained the belief in Jewish ethical responsiblity. This belief surfaced both in his identification with the Hebrew prophet Moses, and in his communication, to his followers, of the idea that Jews played a crucial pioneering role in disseminating the redemptive insights of psychoanalysis.

The belief in the revolutionary significance of the Jews was given one of its most intensive expressions in Rank's essay on Judaism, "Das Wesen des Judentums." Until he wrote the essay in late 1905, Rank looked in vain for a source of renewal that could sustain his struggle against family and social pressures, as well as his search for final redemption through the affirmation of nature. His image of the natural Jew struggling against the repressive forces of civilization revitalized his personal struggle for creative self-expression. The image also made possible his deep commitment to the heroic struggle of the psychoanalytic movement, for he believed that only the Jews were able to bring about the cure for neurosis.

The Jewish consciousness of Freud, Rank, and other psychoanalysts had both a formative and a cohering effect on the development of the psychoanalytic movement. Affirming the value of Jewish existence, Jews in the movement discovered a source of positive individual pride and a basis for collective solidarity. In addition to strengthening their Jewish self-consciousness, the affirmation of the value of Jewish existence renewed the consciousness of hope in the reconciliation of social differences. This *Zielbewusstsein*, the term used frequently by the Jews of the time to denote a constant awareness of the ultimate goal of social integration or wholeness, was as important a part of Jewish consciousness as the emphasis Jews placed on self-dignity or on mutual support. In fact, this universal dimension of Jewish consciousness was the vital sensibility that animated German-Jewish life in Vienna at the turn of the century. No matter how sensitive Jews were to the necessity of self-determination, they maintained as strong an emphasis on humanitarian ideals as assimilationist Jews did, or as many of them did when they grew up in the liberal atmosphere of the constitutional era. The affirmation of a national pride was the new contemporary idiom in which many Jews expressed, or rather, found renewed strength to express, their faith in the social whole.

THE PARTICULAR AND THE UNIVERSAL

The effect of the assertion of Jewish pride on the development of the psychoanalytic movement was powerful, but it was not completely positive. The stress on individual and collective Jewish pride that supported the formation and growth of the movement tended to inhibit the success of the movement as well, for the expressions of inner and mutual Jewish strength served to distract many, within the circle, from their universalistic intentions, and to give a sectarian impression to many both within and outside the circle. These disruptive results seem especially paradoxical in light of the value Jews placed on social reconciliation.

Freud's sensitivity to his followers' Jewish or non-Jewish affiliations created an atmosphere of tension within the movement. This sensitivity was so intense that it seriously marred his effort at constructing a truly universal movement.

On the one hand, the closeness he felt toward fellow Jews influenced his belief that psychoanalytic ideas flowed more easily among Jews. Thus, in a letter sent to Karl Abraham on May 3, 1908, expressing his pleasure at having Jews in the movement, Freud explained their intellectual affinity with reference to their "racial kinship."[12] On the other hand, he felt a deep, indeed a "racial," separation from non-Jews. Just a week after meeting Ernest Jones in 1908, Freud noted that Jones gave him a feeling of "racial strangeness." This feeling of strangeness with the non-Jew also aggravated relations with Jung. Even as he tried to win Jung over to the movement, Freud sensed a racial barrier between them, a feeling that surfaced in the letter Freud sent to Abraham on May 3, 1908. Unable to restrain his feeling of racial distance, he wrote to Jung, the same day, about Jones's "racial strangeness," conveying directly to Jung the separation he felt from non-Jews.[13]

Other terms used by Freud and his colleagues reflected the deep division they felt between Jews and non-Jews. Instead of viewing their differences with non-Jews as national or religious, Freud and Wittels frequently distinguished themselves as Jews on the basis of race, by referring to the non-Jew as an Aryan, instead of as a German or a Christian. In *Der Taufjude,* Wittels reaffirmed his racial feelings by using the term "blood" in describing the nexus of the Jewish people. Rank believed that the civilized repression of sexuality made the non-Jew "abnormal."[14]

The tendency to place the Jew and the non-Jew in a relationship of fundamental opposition imbued even the expressions of redemption with an adversary quality. In one of his most poignant passages, Wittels maintained that Jews not only participated in, but completely "Judaized" (*verjudeten*) the revolutionary movements for freedom and democracy. He concluded *Der Taufjude* with the promise that "the spirit of the Jews would conquer the world." Freud's identification, in his Rome dreams, with the Semitic general Hannibal brought to the surface his desire for a Jewish conquest of social forces that impeded the struggle for justice. Similarly, Rank asserted, in 1903, that the sine qua non of mankind's development was the prevailing influence of Jewish ideas.[15]

The emphasis on race and the allusion to racial superiority that appeared in the writings of those Jews attracted to psychoanalysis emerged in the writings of many Jews outside the movement as well, indicating a wider circle in which the separatistic inclination of Viennese Jews could be found. No Jew emphasized the racial composition of the Jew more than Otto Weininger. He defined the Jewish character in terms of "protoplasm." Richard Beer-Hofmann used the term "blood" in referring to his fellow Jews.[16]

More so than most German Jews of the time, Arthur Schnitzler was sensitive to the depth of sectarian feelings among his contemporaries, as well as to the ambivalence the sectarian stress evoked in German Jews who cherished, above all, the ideal of universality. In *The Road to the Open,* Schnitzler suggested the high priority Jews gave to their collective pride — one non-Jewish character, after listening to a Jewish tirade against Germans, observed: "And he dares . . .

to hold forth about anti-Semitism. . . . He has asserted on one occasion that he felt there was no one with whom he had anything in common. It is not true. He feels he has something in common with all Jews and he stands nearer to the meanest of them than he does to me." Schnitzler examined, with special care, the problem this recently acquired Jewish pride created for Jews. He frequently portrayed his Jewish characters as vacillating between the desire for social integration and the impulse to separate. "I am as much a German as you," the converted Jew Schreimann proclaimed in *Professor Bernhardi.* Yet his dueling scar, received years before he converted, when he belonged to a Jewish student society, betrayed the evidence of his Jewish allegiance. "You are more proud today of your Jewish scar than of all your Germanism," he is told. Schnitzler ended the scene without resolving Schreimann's ambivalence: "We live in such muddled times — and in such a muddled land."[17]

Compared with the confusion of those who were unable to reconcile these expressions of Jewish pride with the Jewish desire for integration, the vacillation of Freud, and of his Jewish contemporaries, between sectarianism and universalism caused minor disturbances in the development of humanitarian movements like psychoanalysis. The feeling of Jewish superiority alienated many non-Jews within the movement and encouraged many outside the movement to dismiss as hypocritical the humanitarian claims of the psychoanalysts. Jones was especially unhappy about the manifestation of Jewish pride within the circle. He felt that despite the warm welcome Freud extended to Jung and to himself in 1907-8, and despite his genuine interest in attracting non-Jewish followers, Freud maintained a "certain mistrust" for non-Jews. The determination of Freud, and of other Jews in the circle, "not merely to regard themselves as different from other people," but to "impose" on other people "the superiority of their intellectual powers . . . tended to confuse the issue" of promoting the "truth" of psychoanalysis. Jones added that, even more so than Freud, the majority of his followers were responsible for this confusion. He conveyed his belief in the depth of their suspicions about the non-Jew, by explaining their early prediction of Jung's defection from the movement, with the remark, "Hate has a keen eye."[18]

Many non-Jews, as well as Jews, who were uninvolved in the Viennese psychoanalytic circle reacted to the appearance of Jewish superiority, racial opposition, national pride, or Jewish solidarity, in a manner that was more damaging to the success of the movement than was Jones's critical view. While Jones intended his criticism of the partisan impulse to be a constructive effort at preserving psychoanalytic truth, those outside the Viennese movement concluded that the science was an exclusive preserve of the Jewish people. A. A. Roback, an American-Jewish admirer of Freud from the 1920s, argued that the analytic and introspective method, as well as the stress on realism and on the concrete, were manifestations of "the Jewish bent of mind," or of the "racial" inclinations of the Jews.[19]

The argument often used to denounce psychoanalysis utilized substantially the same logic Roback used in praise of the science. Those detracting from the science, especially those sympathetic with national socialism, but including many before World War I, suspected that the missionary intention of the movement implied a universal *Verjudung,* a term popularized as early as 1881 when Eugen Dühring condemned the "exclusive dominion of the Jewish element" in German life and culture. While the term entered the vocabulary of many Jews as an ironic expression of pride, it gained wide currency, at the turn of the century, as the classic expression of repugnance for the term *unverschämte Antisemiten.* The prefix "ver" emphasized the exceptionally sinister influence of the Jew and conveyed the impression which the English "Jew" connotes when used as a verb. Disagreement with psychoanalytic theory, especially with its concentration on sexuality, often summoned the specter of *Verjudung,* thus degenerating into an attack on Jewish perversity or, as one author, writing in 1943, expressed it, on "the decadent influence of Judaism in Viennese society." In his three-volume history of Vienna (published 1940-44), Friedrich Walter typically vilified Freud and other Jews for exposing to public view "the filth of the gutter." The perception of psychoanalysis as having an immoral or politically subversive Jewish influence on German culture resulted in the final dissolution of the psychoanalytic movement in Vienna. When the Nazis identified Freud as a member of the B'nai B'rith, in 1938, they ordered his removal from the city and the abolition of the Internationaler Psychoanalytischer Verlag.[20]

Even critics who never doubted the humanitarian intentions of Freud and his Jewish contemporaries have commented on the regnant Jewish national loyalty of many Viennese Jews at the time,[21] and thus pointed to the possibility that movements like psychoanalysis were not only inspired by Jews, but, in effect, were directed toward fulfilling the needs of their fellow Jews. Instead of regarding the Jewish stress on humanity as a deliberate deception, many sensitive to the Jewish struggle for self-determination, even when the struggle first emerged, suggested that Jews were the victims of self-deception. They believed that, contrary to their universalistic intentions, the feelings of superiority and longing for Jewish sympathy, as well as the very remoteness of their vision, transformed the Jewish movements for social integration into movements for the social advancement of the Jewish people.[22]

The stress on Jewish pride that surfaced in Vienna at the turn of the century and, specifically, in the nascent psychoanalytic movement thus proved detrimental to the German-Jewish cause for social reconciliation. While Freud's close affiliation with the B'nai B'rith, and the two essays on Judaism by Rank and by Wittels, reveal sources of renewed strength in the movement, these expressions of racial superiority also provoked tensions within the circle as well as the suspicions of the critics of psychoanalysis. An observation by Jones in his memoirs captured the conflicting impulses involved in the expressions of Jewish pride. In a disapproving tone, he remarked that the Jewish emphasis on superiority, including their "peculiar belief of being God's Chosen People," fostered, among the early analysts, the idea that psychoanalysis was not only a science, but a movement as well.[23] He perceptively recognized that the feeling of inner and collective Jewish pride formed the matrix of the psychoanalytic movement, thus providing analysts with a vehicle for transmitting to others their insights into the cause of and cure for neurosis. His objection to the confusion caused by making a science into a movement reflected a sensitivity to a development which, as well, threatened the success of the psychoanalytic movement. Jones suggested that the private bombast and public condescension of the Jewish analysts would lend credence to the allegation that psychoanalysis was a science designed either for the benefit of the Jews or for the conquest of the non-Jewish world.

No doubt, Freud was aware of the "danger" involved in the movement's "becoming a Jewish national affair." In an essay entitled "The Resistances to Psychoanalysis" (1924), he expressed the belief that "the personality of the present writer as a Jew who has never sought to disguise the fact that he is a Jew may . . . have had a share in provoking the antipathy of his environment to psychoanalysis."[24] Freud did not explore the reasons for this resistance; by attributing this antipathy toward his work to general anti-Jewish hostilities, he understood the resistance to his work as a fact of life for Jews living in Vienna. An examination of some of these reasons makes clear that the non-Jewish resistance to Freud's "Jewish science" reflected a fundamental conflict between Jews and non-Jews, one rooted in the political climate of fin de siècle Vienna as well as in the historical relations between the two groups.

The interpretation of the psychoanalytic movement as being the work of a Jewish interest group reflected the general atmosphere of skepticism and distrust that crystallized in Vienna and throughout Europe with the breakdown of political liberalism at the end of the nineteenth century. For the same reasons Freud and other analysts doubted the claim to objectivity, when the claim referred to truth as self-evident or as the genuine concern of the state, those critical of psychoanalysis were quick to question the psychoanalytic claim to truth. The breach, within the political liberal tradition, between theory and practice made clear to many, regardless of their intellectual or political disposition, that behind the facades of neutrality lurked the interests of class or nationality. As H. Stuart Hughes characterized the outlook of the era, "No longer could one remain content with easy assurances of the rationalistic ideologies inherited from the century and a half preceding – liberal, democratic, or socialist as the case might be. The task was rather to penetrate behind the fictions of political action. . . . Behind these conventional facades, one could postulate the existence of the actual wielders of power, the creative minorities, the political elites."[25]

By the end of the century, observers of contemporary political reality, now aware of the narrow self-interests of the German middle class, could no longer accept political liberalism at face value. This critical view of political liberalism produced a sensitivity to subjective states and, specifically, a psychological mode of interpretation that focused on the power of unconscious motivations.[26] Indeed, Freud and his Jewish followers became sensitive to their own subjective impulses and affirmed the value of self-determination, as other national and ethnic groups of the time were doing. The cultural sensitivity to inner states was taken to extremes by many outside the psychoanalytic circle and by those hostile toward Jews. Their obsession with subjective states blinded them to genuine aspirations toward objectivity. The expressions of Jewish pride thus struck them as manifestations of the movement's narrow Jewish interests.

The severe fragmentation of the political and ideological liberalist consensus in Austria produced a climate of mutual skepticism that considerably intensified the fundamental differences between Jews and non-Jews. In his study of the effect of the Enlightenment on European Jewish life, Jacob Katz concluded that the tensions between Jews and non-Jews emerged from the opposing ways the two groups interpreted Enlightenment ideals. While Jews expected a society based on the shared values of genuine equality and humanity, many non-Jews, envisioning an egalitarian society, expected the Jews to relinquish their distinctive characteristics and to adopt fully the dominant characteristics of their environment. "The Gentile mind did not expect these enlightened Jews to continue remaining Jews. . . . The different anticipations harbored by donor and recipient of Jewish emancipation are perhaps not unnatural, but the fact that this social contract is accompanied by conflicting hopes on the part of both participants augurs ill for a smooth implementation."[27]

During the brief period of liberalist supremacy in Austria, Jews went far in fulfilling non-Jewish expectations by actively assimilating to German culture. Jews as well as non-Jews overlooked their remaining differences over the practical implementation of democratic ideals, in favor of enhancing the prospects of peaceful and equal relations. The breakdown of the liberal order during the closing decades of the nineteenth century brought back to the surface the opposing assumptions about social integration that had distinguished the Jewish from the non-Jewish sensibility. Annoyed by the parochial attachments of other people, and unreceptive to the idea of a pluralistic state, many non-Jews interpreted the Jewish assertion of pride as a subversion of the "enlightened" or egalitarian state. The Jewish stress on national or racial pride reinforced the non-Jewish perception of the Jew as a disruptive social force. Thus, many of those who were aware of the Jewish composition of the psychoanalytic circle, and of the national consciousness of the Jewish analysts, tended to exaggerate the manifestations of sectarian pride. Already sensitive to the interests of class or nationality, and consequently skeptical of the universal objectives of psychoanalysis, many redoubled their suspicions when they realized that the psychoanalytic movement was dominated by Jews.

The studies by Hughes and by Katz are valuable for explaining why many reduced the Jewish struggles for social reconciliation to diabolical enterprises that posed a Jewish threat to the German state. Because of the postliberal-era climate of social tensions, many translated the expressions of self-determination into expressions of self-interest. The affirmation of inner and collective Jewish pride appeared especially inimical to those who expected Jews to assimilate to German culture. It is ironic that, by adopting a national consciousness and a racial rhetoric, the German Jews exhibited a degree of dependence on Viennese culture. However, Jews never regarded their national distinction or their use of racial terminology in the same way that German nationalists did. Instead, they either regarded themselves as uniquely progressive or supported the pluralistic idea of the enlightened state, and thus saw no contradiction between the expression of self-determination, or even of self-interests, and the desire for social reconciliation. To Jews asserting their uniqueness, superiority did not imply an insurmountable distance between Jews and non-Jews, as it did for many non-Jews. On the contrary, the feeling of superiority instilled in them the sense of redemptive purpose aimed at overcoming the severe rupture in social relations that plagued the world in which they lived.

Unquestionably, the psychoanalytic effort at restoring a balance to the fragmented social order promoted Jewish self-interests. Even if the Jewish analysts were unaffected by the feelings of superiority or by the desire to conquer, and stressed only the value of genuine humanity, they would have devoted themselves to the psychoanalytic mission because this value immediately benefited the victims of discrimination and abuse. However, neither the particular desire for preserving Jewish dignity, nor the stress on Jewish superiority, conflicted with the universal desire for social reconciliation. A few examples of the way Jews expressed their partisan interests illustrate how the consciousness of the self and of the social whole coexisted.

The racial conceptions shared by many German Jews in Vienna at the turn of the century transcended the narrow view of race commonly held by non-Jews. To Beer-Hofmann, Jewish blood differed from the blood of other people because, chosen "for a torch," it exalted Jews above selfish, partisan conflict. Weininger regarded the Jews as a race contaminated with the degenerate traits of Judaism. But he believed Jews would overcome these negative tendencies. In contrast to the exclusivistic connotation of race, when many non-Jews used the term, Weininger argued that the burden of the Jewish race would stimulate the regeneration of the Jews and ultimately the regeneration of all mankind.

A strong emphasis on separation and on the particular interests of the Jews is found in the writings of Solomon Ehrmann, Freud's close friend and the principal voice of the B'nai B'rith Wien. He prophesied, in 1902, that at the time of the "glorious period . . . not only the B'nai B'rith, but all of Judaism will have fulfilled its task. They will disappear as a self-contained community, because all of mankind will have been judaized [*verjudet*] and joined in union with the B'nai B'rith."[28] Ehrmann's use of *Verjudung* contrasted sharply with the way many non-Jews used the term. Instead of implying a unilateral conversion of mankind to Judaism, *Verjudung,* as Ehrmann meant it, would involve the disappearance of Judaism or, more precisely, the integration of Jews and non-Jews. Wittels appealed to the universal ideals when he used the term *Verjudung* in *Der Taufjude*. Though his suggesting of the transformation of the world in the Jewish image was a clear statement of partisan preference as well as an invitation to misrepresentation, he defined the ultimate purpose of the task: The Jews must unite, they must prevail, because "the spirit of the Jews is the spirit of progress, freedom, and the future."[29]

Wittels's conception of the Jewish spirit as the spirit of humanity indicates the final humanitarian goal toward which he and other German Jews of the time aspired. Though many Jews mimicked the fashionable terms of separation to assert their independence and autonomy, they wished, above all, to affirm the liberal, or Nietzschean, ideal of the whole. Wittels deliberately emphasized his metaphorical use of the term "blood." He believed the Jews were distinguished by their "blue blood," which infused into them the culture of freedom and progress.[30]

Freud and Rank also regarded their allegiance to Judaism as an allegiance to the ideals of progress and humanity. In his 1926 address to the B'nai B'rith, Freud maintained that to be a Jew is to be independent, prepared for the struggle, and uncompromising about the truth. Frequently, he encouraged Jewish pride in other members of his circle only to bring to the surface the feelings of determination and purpose. As he wrote Abraham in 1907, at the beginning of their correspondence, "The fact that things will be difficult for you as a Jew will have the effect, as it has with all of us, of bringing out the best of which you are capable." At the same time, he advised Max Graf (1875-1958), an early follower, not to waver from the Jewish commitment in the face of anti-Semitism. Do not baptize your son, he implored. "Develop in him all the energy he will need for that struggle. Do not deprive him of that advantage."[31] His support of other Jews outside the movement stressed values transcending local Jewish concerns. In a commemorative book (1911) for an organization supporting Jewish students in Vienna with limited financial means, Freud defined the significance of the charitable group, in typically universal terms. "It seems appropriate to support anything which is concerned not just with privation, but with knowledge."[32] Though Freud appreciated the B'nai B'rith's providing him warm, fraternal fellowship and an escape from the discouraging influences of anti-Semitism, he preferred the society's emphasis on humanity to the more narrow regard for the Jewish plight. Freud's association of Jewish values with ethical purpose prompted him to reject explicitly Roback's views of psychoanalysis. Writing to Roback in 1930, he expressed his disappointment with the tendency to read Jewish "mystical leanings" into the science.[33] Freud believed that instead of limiting the scope of psychoanalysis, the Jewish consciousness imparted to the science a dynamism aimed at benefiting all mankind.

Like Freud and Wittels, Rank felt that Jews were distinguished by a unique appreciation of mankind's regenerative resources. He defined the essence of Judaism as a primitive, sexual force that produced natural and creative energy. Moreover, he believed that, due to an early acquisition of a consciousness of natural life forces, Jews were in the best position for helping others. Similar to the way his psychoanalytic colleagues conceived the relationship between Jews and non-Jews, Rank's conception of the strong helping the weak implied a relationship of relative, not absolute, superiority. Rank regarded the Jews as unique because he believed that the rest of mankind had not yet appreciated the human sources of vital life. The distinction he made between the redeemed Jews and the unredeemed non-Jews referred not to a cultural antithesis, but to different stages along the continuum of inner maturity that anticipated the eventual universal affirmation of irreducible nature.

Just as the desire for social reconciliation was lost in the non-Jewish reading of Jewish expressions of pride and superiority, the implication that ethnic or national groups were hopelessly divided was lost in the Jewish translation of the current racial terms. As one of the founders of Wien observed in 1935, the emphasis on Jewish pride at the turn of the century did not reduce the intensity of a wish which motivated Jews, in the 1860s and 1870s, to assimilate to German culture — the desire for the elimination of all barriers between citizens of the state. He noted: "For the majority of those brothers who enjoyed wide respect, the position toward Judaism was that of complete assimilation. . . . Judaism meant to these brothers a conduct of life in the highest ethical sense of the Prophets." Indeed, an expression of this wish for social integration had appeared in the first printed report of the activity of Wien, which covered the period from October 1895 to June 1897. The author of this report remarked that the society was determined "to elevate all Jews to such a level of culture, education, breeding [*Gesittung*], and ethical conduct that for them the way [would] be open for the brotherhood of all mankind and for the eternal peace of man."[34]

The emphasis on the whole was the passion and purpose of the Jewish psychoanalytic pioneers. Freud's turn to a metapsychology in 1895-96 expressed the desire for developing a comprehensive theory of man. As he later said, such a theory would establish a "common ground of irreligion and humanity." He regarded the unconscious, "the general basis of psychical life" and his most important leveling concept, as the central feature of the metapsychology.[35] Wittels's "lofty passion of the oppressed" referred to a search for equality and justice, just as Rank's early endeavor in psychoanalysis — he too called it a "passion" — was "to comprehend the whole."[36] On April 13, 1905, Rank wrote in his diary, "The life of each man is so complicated. But one seldom takes the trouble to recognize the connections." A few months later, he developed his fundamental principle of the whole, the concept of *Allsexualität*. This term described the original and indivisible psychical impulse as well as the source of needs variously expressed in the developed organism.[37]

Jews who adopted the consciousness of a national resurgence as well as the current expressions of pride, solidarity, and superiority did not abandon their search for social reconciliation. Rather, the expressions of national power provided them with a vanguard mode for seizing the goal of their emancipation.

Erik Erikson observed that the dynamic quality of emancipation involved not only the determination to confront society, but certain "defensive adjustments," the exploitation of the very terms society had used against the minority. "Positive identity is also defined by negative images."[38] Jews freely expressed their sense of national freedom in the most provocatively separatistic terms of the day, but they utilized the current images to organize and give impetus to their shared humanitarian ideals. Instead of establishing the separation of Jews from non-Jews, Jewish pride intensified the Jewish struggle for social reconciliation. As Ehrmann asserted, Jews were "the champions of the ideal of humanity."[39]

To many close to the psychoanalytic movement today, an argument asserting the genuineness of the early analysts' humanitarian intentions appears to be superfluous or too serious a response to the anti-Semitic myth of "secret Jewish interests." This is the opinion of Ernst Federn (1914-), the son of one of Freud's earliest, longest, and most admired followers, as well as a leading advocate of psychoanalysis. He has maintained that the forces which brought the early analysts together were the powerful ideas of honesty and tolerance, not anything particularly Jewish.[40] The view that Federn expresses is one that is shared almost unanimously by those connected with the movement.

The proponents of the psychoanalytic movement maintain the characteristically scientific or artistic point of view that the concerns of psychoanalysis are universal or "pure," that is, unfettered by special interests. They frequently regard the question of the Jewish involvement in the early circle as a basic challenge to the movement's better intentions. This stress on the purity of the movement itself reflects a sensitivity to anti-Semitic accusations that have shadowed the movement since its inception.

The attempt to universalize the psychoanalytic movement at the expense of neglecting its Jewish origins has done a disservice to the cause which the supporters of the movement have sought to promote, for the understating of the Jewish sources of psychoanalysis has cut them off from the dynamic currents that gave rise to the movement. The Jewish consciousness of the early analysts created a basis for self-respect, independence, and courage as well as a basis for mutual encouragement. Most important, the positive assertion of Jewish inner and collective strength affirmed, in the strongest way available to the early analysts, the ideals of the Enlightenment or of Nietzschean cultural revitalization. As Wittels argued in *Der Taufjude,* Jewish pride not only encouraged moral integrity, but also restored the conviction of a "life purpose." Wittels himself derived from Jewish affirmation an exhilaration that renewed his struggle for justice and freedom. Rank's conception of the "Jewish task" invigorated his search for the social whole as well. As early as the mid-1880s, Freud's affirmation of Jewish pride inspired courage in him and an appreciation for fellow supporters. His association with the B'nai B'rith a decade later augmented this tendency by providing him with an example of strength through unity. More than as a sympathetic environment, the Jewish society as a study group receptive to his scientific discoveries and as a source of Freud's following prefigured the psychoanalytic movement itself. Because of the German-Jewish disposition toward humanitarian ideals, the feeling of Jewish pride crystallized both the vision of and the struggle for social wholeness.

Of course, the strong assertion of Jewish pride frequently obscured the objective of social reconciliation for many inside and outside the psychoanalytic circle. The superior Jewish self-conception and the feeling of mistrust for the non-Jew distracted Jews within the circle from the psychoanalytic appeal to universality. Indeed, the affirmations of Jewish pride contributed to national and racial tensions in turn-of-the-century Vienna. In addition, the visibility of the Jews in the psychoanalytic society as well as the expression of Jewish solidarity and superiority gave the critics of the movement many opportunities for achieving their purposes. They have exploited the manifestations of Jewish involvement to debunk the movement, disparage Jews, or both. However erroneous their views, the critics succeeded in sustaining an effective polemic against psychoanalysis.

Though the supporters of the movement have taken the opposing position by defending the movement's purity, they commit the same error their critics have committed by separating the humanitarian goals from the Jewish sources of psychoanalysis. The Jewish component is as inconsequential to them as the universal interests are insincere to the movement's detractors. These false distinctions between particular and universal interests diminish the creative role of Jewish pride within Freud's circle. Until the essential balance between sectarianism and universalism is taken into account, no estimation of the formation of the movement can be complete.

NOTES

1. Fritz Wittels, *Die Sexuelle Not* (Vienna, Leipzig: C. W. Stern, 1907). Jung is cited in *Minutes of the Vienna Psychoanalytic Society,* ed. Herman Nunberg and Ernst Federn, trans. M. Nunberg (New York: International Universities Press, 1962, 1967, 1974, 1975), vol. 2, 82n (hereafter cited as *Minutes,* followed by the volume and page numbers).

2. Fritz Wittels, "[A.A.] Brill — the Pioneer," *The Psychoanalytic Review,* 35 (1948), 397.

3. *Minutes* 2, 53-58, 85-87; Wittels, "Brill," 397.

4. Fritz Wittels, *Sigmund Freud: His Personality, His Teachings, and His School,* trans. Eden and Cedar Paul (New York: Dodd, Mead, 1924), 7.

5. Fritz Wittels, *Der Taufjude* (Vienna, Leipzig: M. Breitensteins Verlagsbuchhandlung, 1904), 13-32.

6. Ibid., 32.

7. Ibid., 35-39.

8. Besides Paul Federn (1871-1950) and, of course, Freud, Hitschmann remained in the Vienna movement longer than anyone else, from 1905 to 1938. For data on Hitschmann's lectures, see *Festschrift anlässlich des fünfundzwanzigjährigen Bestandes des israel. Humanitätsvereines 'Eintracht' (B'nai B'rith) Wien 1903-1928* (Vienna: Selbstverlage des Vereines, 1928), 131-35. For data after 1928, see *B'nai B'rith Mitteilungen für Österreich,* 30 (March 1930), 141; 30, 10 (December 1930), 383; 31 (June 1931), 246; 32 (April

1932), 141; 33 (February 1933), 80; and 35 (April 1935), 82. The journal of the 'B'nai B'rith in Austria, printed from 1897 to 1938, under different titles, will henceforth be cited as *BBJ.*

9. *Festschrift 'Eintracht,'* 118.

10. *Jahresbericht der Jüdisch-akademischen Lesehalle in Wien, über das Vereinsjahr 1897* (Vienna: Verlag der Jüdisch-akademischen Lesehalle, 1897), 13. The Jahresbericht recorded "L. Sadger" as the author of this lecture. This is a misprint. The lecture was a pathography of Heinrich von Kleist, a favorite theme of I. Sadger's in the psychoanalytic study circle. *Minutes* 1-4. In 1909, Sadger published a book on Kleist. During the 1900-1 term, Sadger taught a course at the Lese- und Redehalle jüdische Hochschüler. *Jüdisches Volksblatt,* March 1, 1901, 5.

Like the B'nai B'rith Wien, the Lese- und Redehalle jüdische Hochschüler attracted Jews who later contributed to the development of the psychoanalytic movement. Wittels lectured to the student group in 1900-1. *Jüdisches Volksblatt,* March 1, 1901, 5. Moreover, the student society had a similar relationship with Freud as the B'nai B'rith had, though the Redehalle's relationship was less intense. In 1904, the Redehalle elected Freud to its honor committee. Freud returned the recognition by contributing to the financial support of the student society. *Jahres-Bericht der Lese- und Redehalle jüdischer Hochschüler in Wien, über das Vereinsjahr 1904* (Vienna: Verlag der Lese- und Redehalle jüdischer Hochschüler in Wien, 1905), 51, 61. The student organization thus appears to have been fertile ground for the germination of the psychoanalytic movement. As the B'nai B'rith inspired a following of Freud's from Freud's generation, the Redehalle inspired a following from the younger generation.

11. Lou Andreas-Salomé, *In der Schule bei Freud: Tagebuch eines Jahres 1912-1913,* ed. Ernst Pfeiffer (Zurich: Max Niehans Verlag, 1958), 67. The quote represents Andreas-Salomé's paraphrasing of Tausk's views on the Jews in the psychoanalytic movement. She recorded this conversation with Tausk in her journal on January 11, 1913. There are other indications of strong Jewish commitment in the psychoanalytic movement before World War I, but less convincing than those discussed in the text. Leopold Königstein was active in the B'nai B'rith and one of Freud's closest friends during this period, but he had only the slightest formal connection with the movement. The musicologist Max Graf (1873-1958), also close to Freud and one of the first to join Freud's circle (1902), expressed strong Jewish allegiance only after the war, when he founded the Institut für jüdische Musikforschung. See Salomon Wininger, ed., *Grosse jüdische National-Biographie mit mehr als 8000 Lebensbeschreibungen namhafter jüdischer Männer und Frauen aller Zeiten und Länder: Ein Nachschlagewerk für das jüdische Volk und dessen Freunde* (Czernowitz: "Arta," 1925-1931), vol. 2.

12. Sigmund Freud and Karl Abraham, *A Psycho-Analytic Dialogue: The Letters of Sigmund Freud and Karl Abraham 1907-1926,* ed. Hilda C. Abraham and Ernst L. Freud; trans. Bernard Marsh and Hilda C. Abraham (New York: Basic Books, 1965), 34: May 3, 1908 (hereafter cited as *Dialogue*).

13. Sigmund Freud and Carl Jung, *The Freud/Jung Letters: The Correspondence between Sigmund Freud and C. G. Jung,* ed. William McGuire; trans. Ralph Manheim and R. F. C. Hull (Princeton: Princeton University Press, 1974), 145: May 3, 1908. On Freud's early expression of ambivalence over Jung, see ibid., 218-20, and Vincent Brome, *Freud and His Early Circle* (New York: William Morrow, 1968), 82-83.

14. On Freud, see *Dialogue,* 64, 139: December 6, 1908, May 13, 1913; Wittels, *Der Taufjude,* 38, 40; Otto Rank, "Das Wesen des Judentums" (MS., The Otto Rank Collection at Columbia University, December 13, 1905), 3.

15. Wittels, *Der Taufjude,* 37, 40. The diary passage in which Rank's thought appeared reads: "Our [i.e., the European people's] entire knowledge, including philosophy, comes from the Jews. Much of what we now proclaim as originally-conceived wisdom, the Jews knew 4,000 years ago. Nietzsche says somewhere that Euorpe is not yet ripe for the

Indian culture. This comes closest to the truth." Rank, "Tagebücher" (MSS., The Otto Rank Collection at Columbia University, 1902-5), I, 7: July 20, 1903; henceforth cited as "Tagebücher," followed by the volume number of the diaries, the page(s), and the date of the diary inscription. This positive estimation of the Jews anticipated his much more elaborate treatment in "Das Wesen des Judentums."

16. On Weininger and on Beer-Hofmann, see Chapter 1.

17. Arthur Schnitzler, *The Road to the Open*, trans. Horace Samuel (New York: Alfred A. Knopf, 1923), 249-52; idem, *Professor Bernhardi*, trans. Hetty Landstone (New York: Simon and Schuster, 1928), 78-79.

18. Ernest Jones, *Free Associations: Memories of a Psycho-Analyst* (New York: Basic Books, 1959), 208-12; idem, *The Life and Work of Sigmund Freud* (New York: Basic Books, 1953, 1955, 1957), vol. 2, 43-44; henceforth cited as *Life*, followed by the volume and the page numbers. Had the assignment for writing the authoritative biography of Freud gone not to Jones, but to Siegfried Bernfeld (1892-1953), as many close to the movement believed it had, or should have, the confusion over the meaning and extent of Jewish pride in the psychoanalytic movement, to which Jones unwittingly contributed, might have been resolved. An active member of the movement from 1915 on, and the first to conduct extensive historical research on Freud, Bernfeld was emminently familiar with Jewish national aspirations. After World War I, he founded and became the first leader of the Verband der jüdischen Jugend Österreichs, the Austrian Jewish Youth Movement. During this time, he published material on the promise of youth for the future of the Jewish people, which led to the organization of a Jewish institute for research on adolescence and education. Like the psychoanalytic movement he supported, it was a movement by, but not strictly for, Jews, self-consciously nationalistic, but directed toward humanitarian goals. See Willi Hoffer, "Siegfried Bernfeld and 'Jerubbaal': An Episode in the Jewish Youth Movement," *Leo Baeck Institute Yearbook*, 10 (1965), 150-67, and George Mosse, "The Influences of the Völkisch Idea on German Jewry," *Studies of the Leo Baeck Institute*, ed. Max Kreutzberger (New York: Frederick Ungar, 1967), 110-11. See also Philip Lee Utley, "Siegfried Bernfeld: Left-Wing Youth Leader, Psychoanalyst, and Zionist, 1910-April 1918" (Doctoral diss., University of Wisconsin-Madison, 1975).

19. A. A. Roback, *Jewish Influence in Modern Thought* (Cambridge, Mass.: Sci-Art Publishers, 1929), 171-97. This section of Roback's chapter "Is Psychoanalysis a Jewish Movement?" appeared earlier, under the same title, in honor of Freud's seventieth birthday in *B'nai B'rith Magazine*, 40 (1926), 198-99, 201, 238-39.

20. See *Life* 1, 330n. Dühring used the term *Verjudung* in *Die Judenfrage als Rassen-Sitten- und Kulturfrage* (Karlsruhe, Leipzig: Reuther, 1881); see, e.g., 59. In an unpublished manuscript written c. 1938, Richard Bermann (1883-1939), Freud's Jewish contemporary and brief acquaintance (c. 1901-3), lamented the view, in Catholic Vienna around the turn of the century, that psychoanalysis represented the "Sexualexcess eines perversen Juden." "Die Fahrt auf dem Katarakt: Autobiographie ohne einen Helden" (MS., Memoir Collection #191 of the Leo Baeck Institute, New York, n.d.), 33. For later examples of such slander, see Elisabeth Spigl, "Das Wiener Judentum der Achtziger Jahre in Literatur und Presse" (Diss., Vienna, 1943), and Friedrich Walter, *Wien: Die Geschichte einer deutschen Grossstadt an der Grenze* (Vienna: Verlag Adolf Holzhausens Nachfolger, 1940-44), vol. 3, 409-10.

21. See, for example, Hans Kohn, *Karl Kraus, Arthur Schnitzler, Otto Weininger: Aus dem jüdischen Wien der Jahrhundertwende* (Tübingen: J. C. B. Mohr, 1962), 69.

22. See Jacob Wassermann, *My Life as German and Jew*, trans. S. N. Brainin (New York: Coward-McCann, 1933), 83-86.

23. Jones, *Free Associations*, 208-12.

24. *Dialogue*, 34: May 3, 1908; Sigmund Freud, *The Standard Edition of the Complete Psychological Works of Sigmund Freud*, ed. and trans. James Strachey (London: The Hogarth Press, 1953-1974), 19, 222.

25. H. Stuart Hughes, *Consciousness and Society: The Reorientation of European Social Thought 1890-1930* (New York: Vintage Books, 1958), 65-66.

26. See Carl Schorske, "The Transformation of the Garden: Ideal and Society in Austrian Literature," *American Historical Review*, 72 (July 1967), 1283-1320.

27. Jacob Katz, *Out of the Ghetto: The Social Background of Jewish Emancipation, 1770-1870* (Cambridge: Harvard University Press, 1973), 51, 78-79. See Uriel Tal, *Christians and Jews in Germany: Religion, Politics, and Ideology in the Second Reich, 1870-1914*, trans. Noah Jonathan Jacobs (Ithaca and London: Cornell University Press, 1975), and M. Kreutzberger, "The German-Jewish Utopia of Social Emancipation," *Emancipation and Assimilation Studies in Modern Jewish History*, ed. Jacob Katz (Westmead, England: Gregg International Publishers, 1972), for other studies of the asymmetric perceptions of the Enlightenment held by Germans and German Jews.

28. Solomon Ehrmann, "Über die Function des Judenthums innerhalb der Menschheit und der B. B. innerhalb des Judenthums." *BBJ*, 4 (January 1902), 104.

29. Wittels, *Der Taufjude*, 39-40.

30. Ibid., 40.

31. On Freud's advice to Abraham, see *Dialogue*, 9: October 8, 1907; his advice to Graf is recounted in Max Graf, "Reminiscences of Professor Sigmund Freud," trans. Gregory Zilboorg, *Psychoanalytic Quarterly*, 11 (1942), 473.

32. *Denkschrift des Vereines zur Unterstützung mittelloser israelitischer Studierender in Wien aus Anlass seines fünfzigjährigen Bestandes 1861-1911*, ed. Guido Fuchsgelb (Vienna: Selbstverlage des Vereines, 1911), 27.

33. Sigmund Freud, *The Letters of Sigmund Freud 1873-1939*, ed. Ernst L. Freud; trans. Tania and James Stern (London: The Hogarth Press, 1961), 393-94: February 20, 1930.

34. Karl Klemperer, "Erinnerungen an die ersten Jahre der 'Wien,' " *BBJ*, 35 (November-December 1935), 200; *BBJ*, 1 (October 1897), 24-25.

35. Joseph Wortis, *Fragments of an Analysis with Freud* (Indianapolis: Bobbs-Merrill, 1963), 144; Sigmund Freud, *The Interpretation of Dreams*, trans. James Strachey (New York: Avon Books, 1967), 651.

36. Otto Rank, *Der Künstler: Ansätze zu einer Sexual-Psychologie*, 3d ed. (Vienna, Leipzig: Hugo Heller und Cie, 1918), 2.

37. "Tagebücher," IV, 9: April 13, 1905. Rank referred to the concept *Allsexualität* in "Die Barttracht" (MS., The Otto Rank Collection at Columbia University, July 26, 1905), 1. He developed the concept in *Der Künstler*, 23-25 and in "Tagebücher," IV, 29: May 31, 1905.

38. Erik Erikson, *Identity, Youth, and Crisis* (New York: W. W. Norton, 1968), 21-25, 299-304.

39. Ehrmann, 103.

40. Conversations with Ernst Federn in Vienna, October 1974-July 1975. For his views on the psychoanalytic movement, see Ernst Federn, "Gibt es noch eine psychoanalytische Bewegung?" (MS., Based on a lecture given by the author to the Vienna Psychoanalytic Society, June 1973); idem, "Epilogue" to "Thirty-Five Years with Freud: In Honor of the Hundredth Anniversary of Paul Federn, M.D.," *Journal of the History of the Behavioral Sciences*, 8 (January 1972), 46-47; idem, "Einige Bemerkungen über die Schwierigkeiten eine Geschichte der Psychoanalyse zu schreiben," *Jahrbuch der Psychoanalyse*, 7 (1974), 21.

APPENDIX A

LECTURES FREUD PRESENTED TO THE B'NAI B'RITH, 1897-1917

Appendix A is divided into two parts. The first part lists, for the first time, the 21 lectures Freud delivered to the B'nai B'rith from 1897, the year he joined the society, to 1917, the last year he gave an address to the brotherhood. The second part is a reconstruction of each lecture based on the facts of the lectures and their correspondence with the published works. Even though the lectures from 1897 to 1902, and the lecture "Wir und der Tod" (1915), are also discussed in Chapter 3, discussion of them is included here to form a complete survey in one section of Freud's B'nai B'rith lectures.

PART 1

December 7 and 14, 1897. "Traumdeutung"[1] ("Interpretation of Dreams")*

February 3, 1899. "Zur Psychologie des Vergessens" ("The Psychology of Forgetting")

February 4, 1900. "Das Seelenleben des Kindes" ("The Psychic Life of the Child")

April 24, 1900. " 'Fécondité' von Émile Zola" ("*Fertility* by Émile Zola")

February 26, 1901. "Zufall und Aberglaube" ("Chance and Superstition")*

Fall 1901. "Ziele und Zwecke des Ordens B'nai B'rith" ("Goals and Purposes of the B'nai B'rith Order," introduction to a series of discussions)

Between January 14 and March 4, 1902. "Die Stellung der Frau zu unserer Vereinigung" ("The Role of the Woman in our [B'nai B'rith] Union," introduction to a series of discussions)

April 30, 1902. "Über Träume" ("On Dreams")

---

*Given to the B'nai B'rith before appearing as an article in a professional journal or as part of a book.

Between March 11 and December 30, 1901. "Émile Zola"

April 16, 1904. "Über den physiologischen Schwachsinn des Weibes (Dr. Möbius)" (*"The Physiological Feeble-Mindedness of the Woman* by Dr. [Paul J.] Möbius")*

1904. "Hammurabi"

1905. "Über die Physiologie des Unbewussten" ("The Physiology of the Unconscious")

March 19, 1907. "Psychologie im Dienste der Rechtspflege" ("Psychology in the Service of the Administration of Justice")

November 2, 1907. "Über den Witz" ("On Jokes")

1908. "Kindertaufen" ("The Baptism of Children")

1911. "Das Hamlet-Problem"

November 4, 1913. "Was Ist Psychoanalyse?"*

February 16, 1915. "Wir und der Tod" ("We and Death")*

February 15, 1916. "La Révolte des Anges" (*"The Revolt of the Angels* [by Anatole France] ")

1917. "Phantasie und Kunst" ("Phantasy and Art")

PART 2

December 7, 1897. "Traumdeutung" ("Interpretation of Dreams")
December 14, 1897. "Traumdeutung" ("Interpretation of Dreams")

> "Two lectures by Brother Dozent Dr. Freud about the interpretation of dreams. The lecturer, beginning with the familiar physiological causes of dreams, discussed the psychology of dream life and established the principles of a self-contained theory. In the conclusion of his ingenious interpretation, he characterized the great significance of his scientific theory; he said: Whoever is occupied with the dreams of

---

*Given to the B'nai B'rith before appearing as an article in a professional journal or as part of a book.

man and understands their true meaning peers into the secrets of the human soul as into a crater imbedded within the earth's dark interior."[2]

February 3, 1899. "Zur Psychologie des Vergessens" ("The Psychology of Forgetting")

Freud began his first serious exploration of parapraxes four months before his talk to the brotherhood. In August 1898 he wrote Fliess, "I have at last understood a little thing that I have long suspected. You know how you can forget a name and substitute part of another for it." During the last week in September, Freud wrote a paper entitled "The Psychical Mechanism of Forgetfulness." It appeared in the December issue of a medical monthly, and eventually formed the basis of the first chapter of *The Psychopathology of Everyday Life* (1901). Most likely, Freud relied on the published article printed a few weeks earlier for his B'nai B'rith lecture. In this article, Freud discussed the emergence of threatening or repressed thought into the process of name recollection, which produced the phenomenon of memory lapses.[3]

February 4, 1900: "Das Seelenleben des Kindes" ("The Psychic Life of Child")

After completing his essay on forgetfulness in late 1898, Freud continued to explore the phenomenon of parapraxis, particularly the psychological sources of memory lapses. Already, on January 1, 1899, Freud alluded to the distortion of memories due to experiences of earliest childhood. By the end of May, Freud sent in his manuscript on "Screen Memories" for publication.[4] It was published in September and later incorporated into the fourth chapter of *The Psychopathology of Everyday Life* (1901). Freud used a line from the published article to entitle his lecture, suggesting that the lecture, like the article, showed how the "psychical functioning of children" serves to distort the actual content of frightening childhood events, but in a symbolic way so that the analyst through interpretation of the screened memory can recover the original content as well as the sources of repression.[5]

April 24, 1900. " 'Fécondité' von Émile Zola" (*Fertility* by Émile Zola")

Freud's interest in Zola emerged years before this lecture, in the interpretation of the Revolutionary dream (Count Thun) and in a letter to Fliess in 1898. However, evidence of his fascination for this particular work appeared only years later, when in 1907 Freud listed "ten good books" in response to a colleague's inquiry. At this time, Freud frequently commented on the eccentric themes in Zola's novels at the meetings of the psychoanalytic society. To Freud, Zola's work disclosed classical symptoms of an obsessional neurosis. This expression of interest explains Freud's immediate attraction to the novel in 1900. Fécondité (*Fertility*) was a wild celebration of the large family and procreation generally. Almost every chapter began, "Two years passed and Mathieu and Marianne had another child." An equally repetitive theme involved the censuring of sexual relations which did not result in procreation.[6] For the analyst the book vividly clarified obsessional behavior and, in the absolution from wrong-doing in the act of procreation, expressed sexual guilt. Freud's review may have anticipated his paper on the resemblance between obsessive actions and religious practices, written in 1907 when he renewed his interest in the French author, for Zola intended his novel to be the first of an evangelical cycle. Zola deliberately named the hero "Mathieu" after the author of Christian gospel.

February 26, 1901. "Zufall und Aberglaube" ("Chance and Superstition")

> This was the third talk on the topic of slips and lapses, and the third time a B'nai B'rith lecture preceded the publication of corresponding observations. Freud regarded parapraxes as good preliminary material for introducing nonmedical people to psychoanalysis. Three of his *Introductory Lectures* (1916-17), for example, were devoted to the subject. After he lectured on screen memories to the brotherhood in February 1900, Freud left the subject of parapraxes aside until the following fall, when he began to collect material for the "psychology of every-day life." On February 15, 1901, he reported to Fliess, "I shall finish with the every-day psychology during the next few days." The last chapter of *The Psychopathology of Everyday Life* was entitled "Determinism, Belief in Chance and Superstition: Some Points of View." This particular lecture clearly incorporated this material. The chapter elucidated the psychological significance of superstitions and the force of the unconscious, which determines seemingly unintentional, accidental occurrences.[7]

Fall 1901. "Ziele und Zwecke des Ordens B'nai B'rith" ("Goals and Purposes of the B'nai B'rith Order, Introduction to a series of discussions)

Between January 14 and March 4, 1902. "Die Stellung der Frau zu unserer Vereinigung" ("The Role of the Woman in our [B'nai B'rith] Union," introduction to a series of discussions)

> Freud's remarks on the goals and purposes of the B'nai B'rith came at a time when the brotherhood was involved in a volatile debate over the manner of reconciling the society's sectarian interests and its universal ideals. Freud would have encouraged his fellow brothers to go beyond the self-centered activities of Jewish charity toward a championing of democratic and humanitarian ideals. The discussion which Freud introduced prompted Ehrmann's significant reponse, "The Function of Judaism within Mankind and the B.B. within Judaism" (1902).[8]

April 30, 1902. "Über Träume" ("On Dreams")

This was the first of two papers Freud gave to a B'nai B'rith audience outside Vienna. He delivered it to "Moravia," a lodge in Brünn.[9] Freud apparently felt dreams were, like parapraxes, effective material for introducing his ideas to a lay audience. Five years earlier, he succeeded in impressing the brothers of Wien with a discussion on the same subject. This time, Freud had available to him not only a completed and published account of the results of his investigations, but a 40-page précis which he contributed to the first number of a medical serial. The essay, "The Dream," appeared a year before the lecture.[10]

Between March 11 and December 30, 1902. "Émile Zola"

Freud's interest in Zola included an appreciation of the Frenchman's heroic rejection of incompetent and tyrannical authority. Twice in 1898 he lauded the expression of revolt in Zola's *Germinal* and *La terre* as well as his battle against the exponents of monarchy and anti-Semitism during the dramatic Dreyfus affair. Jews strongly identified with Zola at the time. One recalled, "A Jewish lad in Vienna could not help but write a passionate letter to a friend about [Dreyfus'] unwarranted persecution. . . . Émile Zola stood up and declared: J'accuse!"[11] The fact that Zola died on September 29, 1902, and the simple title of the talk suggest Freud's desire to commemorate the man's accomplishments. As in the previous reference to Zola, this theme also permitted the analytic mind to explore the patricidal impulse in Zola's life, such as the struggle against "feeble-minded" authority, as Freud found in *La terre,* against "the degeneracy of France," as Freud referred to Zola's struggle in a letter to Fliess, or against obsolescence and repression in society, as other contemporary Jewish analysts perceived the fight against anti-Semitism.[12]

April 16, 1904. "Über den physiologischen Schwachsinn des Weibes (Dr. Möbius)" ("*The Physiological Feeble-Mindedness of the Woman* by Dr. [Paul J.] Möbius")

This was the first of three times Freud responded to Möbius' work, published in 1900 — a controversial demonstration that women were biologically less intelligent than men. In this " 'Civilized' Sexual Morality and Modern Nervous Illness" (1908), and again, twenty years later, in *The Future of an Illusion,* Freud flatly denied the biological basis of intellectual inferiority and instead asserted that the inferior intellect of women could be traced back to sexual suppression which inhibited curiosity generally.[13]

1904. "Hammurabi"

Though none of the sources identifies a more specific date of this lecture, the journal of the B'nai B'rith referred to this lecture in early 1905, suggesting that Freud delivered it sometime in the fall of 1904.[14] This was undoubtedly the first time Freud discussed at length the significance of the Hebrew prophet Moses. Many years later, he published "The Moses of Michelangelo" (1914) and *Moses and Monotheism* (1939). When Freud visited Rome for the first time in September 1901, he was inspired by Michelangelo's statue of Moses. From the statue, Freud gained insight into the prophet's inner strength and controlled passion.[15] A few months later, a team of French archeologists uncovered a large stone in the acropolis of Susa in the Near East that had inscribed upon it a codex dictated by a "sun god" to King Hammurabi, the powerful Babylonian leader of the eighteenth century B.C. The discovery caused an immediate sensation in intellectual and theological circles throughout Europe. The inscription contained the first collection of laws then known to antedate those of the Bible. Scholars immediately noted the strong parallels between the codex and chapters in the second book of Exodus. The parallel led them to believe that Moses, who lived four centuries later, had adopted his laws from the codex and thus had given to the Hebrews of Egypt a foreign code of laws.[16]

Freud made a similar observation in his 1914 paper on Moses. Citing Exodus 32:7, the rage of Moses at the sight of the Golden Calf, Freud concluded that many parts of the Bible have been "clumsily put together from various sources. . . . It is well known that the historical parts of the Bible dealing with the Exodus, are crowded with still more glaring incongruities and contradictions" than the Golden-Calf story. To Freud, this justified Michelangelo's deviation from scripture in portraying "a different Moses," one, Freud added, "superior to the historical or traditional Moses. . . . He added something new and more than human to the figure."[17] The codex discovery was thus a credible subversion of the dogmatic claims of the Bible as well as a significant confirmation of Freud's skeptical attitude. At the same time, the document made it possible to preserve the integrity of Moses' achievements from the degrading references to his character, such as those in the story of the Golden Calf.

1905. "Über die Physiologie des Unbewussten" ("The Physiology of the Unconscious")

The title is too vague to determine the content of this speech with the relatively high degree of certainty made possible by the titles of the other lectures. However, it appears that this lecture reflected Freud's current efforts at explaining unconscious processes through the analysis of the characteristics and effects of jokes (*Jokes and Their Relation to the Unconscious,* 1905), a subject that would have especially appealed to the brotherhood since many of the anecdotes used to illustrate the joke book described Jewish circumstances.[18] Freud probably derived the material for this lecture from part six of the book on jokes, "The Relation of Jokes to Dreams and the Unconscious." This part showed the link between jokes and the unconscious and the possibility created by this link of interpreting the work of the unconscious.[19]

March 19, 1907. "Psychologie im Dienste der Rechtspflege" ("Psychology in the Service of the Administration of Justice")

In June 1906 Freud gave a lecture to an audience of young lawyers on determining the truth of statements made in court.[20] In December, he published the text of this lecture in a journal of criminology under the heading "Psychoanalysis and the Establishment of the Facts in Legal Proceedings." The B'nai B'rith address almost certainly duplicated the contents of this publication. In the published version, Freud discussed the use of psychoanalysis in ascertaining the innocence or guilt of an accused person.[21]

November 2, 1907. "Über den Witz" ("On Jokes")

Freud delivered this lecture to the two B'nai B'rith societies in Prague.[22] He apparently drew on his investigations into the psychoanalytical meaning of jokes and probably illustrated his argument with Jewish jokes as he did in *Jokes and Their Relation to the Unconscious*. At the time he delivered the address, Freud was preparing a public lecture for delivery a month later on phantasy and creative writing as wish fulfillment ("The Creative Writer and Day Dreaming").[23] The B'nai B'rith lecture thus reflected Freud's current preoccupations with interpreting play.

1908. "Kindertaufen" ("The Baptism of Children")[24]

(The title of this lecture is too vague to determine its contents from the published sources.)

1911. "Das Hamlet-Problem"

Freud's first and most important published discussion of the psychological significance of Shakespeare's drama appeared in a footnote to chapter five of *The Interpretation of Dreams* (1899-1900). Freud offered an explanation of Hamlet's hesitation in taking revenge on the murderer of his father. Hamlet's repressed patricidal impulses and his repressed incestuous love for his mother unconsciously prevented him from retaliating.[25] After 1900, Freud frequently referred to the drama as an example of both the oedipus complex and the degree to which these impulses are disguised.[26] In 1911, a number of Freud's followers, stimulated by the publishing opportunities created by the establishment of a psychoanalytic monograph series in 1907 and two psychoanalytic journals in 1909-10, as well as by the prospect of a third journal (1912), expressed an interest in analyzing the Hamlet complex. Ernest Jones published his analysis of Hamlet's oedipus complex in 1910 for the tenth number of the series. The following year, another member of Freud's circle wrote the article "Zum Hamletproblem." As general editor of these publications and as the one who encouraged Jones to publish his contribution,[27] Freud was in close contact with the germinating interest in Hamlet. The expression of this interest probably prompted Freud to deliver his interpretation of the drama to the B'nai B'rith. This address represents his only complete analysis of Hamlet.

November 4, 1913. "Was Ist Psychoanalyse?"

In September and October 1913, tensions between Freud and Carl Jung became severe. Freud was deeply offended by what appeared to him as a defection when Jung pointed out the differences between him and Freud at a conference in August and at the Munich psychoanalytic conference on September 5-8. For his part, Jung wrote a bitter letter to Freud on October 27, 1913, reproaching Freud for secretly doubting his "bona fides." He informed Freud that he could no longer collaborate with him on the psychoanalytic journal *Jahrbuch* and announced his resignation from the editorship.[28] Immediately, Freud embarked on defending and defining the science of psychoanalysis. The results of this work appeared in "On Narcissism" and in "The History of the Psychoanalytic Movement," both published in 1914. Freud's B'nai B'rith lecture was most likely his first effort at defining psychoanalysis in light of Jung's stirring challenge. In response to Jung, Freud offered the concept of narcissism as an alternative to Jung's nonsexual libido and asserted that the first task of psychoanalysis was to explain neurosis, for which the concepts of repression, sexuality, and the unconscious were indispensable.[29]

February 16, 1915. "Wir und der Tod" ("We and Death")

This lecture — the only one that actually exists — shows the seriousness of Freud's efforts at presenting to the brotherhood his work on developing psychoanalytic theory. The argument of this lecture for the existence and repression of the death wish is substantially the same one that appeared a few months later in the psychoanalytic journal *Imago,* as the second part of "Thoughts for the Times on War and Death."[30] The important differences between the two papers are procedural: In the B'nai B'rith lecture, Freud spoke directly and sympathetically to his Jewish audience. He even proposed to call his lecture, "We Jews and Death," in order to show how Jews, like everyone else, can succumb to aggressive drives, or can dampen curiosity, by fearing or denying death. Freud's effort to interest the Jewish society in his psychoanalytic research again shows his desire to engage the brotherhood in his investigations into the central, dynamic relationship between unconscious impulses and their repression.

February 15, 1916. "La Révolte des Anges" (*"The Revolt of the Angels* [by Anatole France]")

Freud entitled his lecture after the name of a book written by Anatole France in 1914. As he related to Hanns Sachs, Freud was particularly impressed with two parts of the novel, the part where France described civilization as an internal struggle for power, and the end of the book where the author portrayed Satan as refusing to perpetuate the cruelty and narrowmindedness of political ambition.[31] Satan believed that only reason could overcome vainglory, destruction, and jealousy. "We have destroyed Ialdabaoth, our tyrant, if in ourselves we have destroyed ignorance and fear. . . . Victory is the mind, and it is in ourselves and in ourselves alone that we must attack and destroy Ialdabaoth."[32]

1917. "Phantasie und Kunst" ("Phantasy and Art")[33]

(The title of this lecture is too vague to determine its contents from the published sources.)

NOTES

1. Dates and titles of the lectures were found in: *Vierteljahrsberichte* (October 1897-April 1904) and *Zweimonats-Berichte* (June 1904-1921) *für die Mitglieder der österr. israel. Humanitätsvereine 'B'nai B'rith';* Wilhelm Knöpfmacher, *Entstehungsgeschichte und Chronik der Vereinigung 'Wien' B'nai B'rith in Wien 1895-1935* (Vienna: Verlag der israelitischen Humanitätsvereine 'B'nai B'rith für Österreich in Wien, 1935); Wilhelm Jerusalem, *Festschrift zur Feier des fünfundzwanzigjährigen Bestandes* (Vienna: Selbstverlag des Vereines, 1920); "Festsitzung der 'Wien' anlässlich des 70. Geburtstages Br. Univ. Prof. Doktor Sigmund Freud," *B'nai B'rith Mitteilungen für Österreich*, 26 (May 1926), 101-38; Marie Bonaparte, Anna Freud, and Ernst Kris, eds., *The Origins of Psycho-Analysis: Letters to Wilhelm Fliess, Drafts and Notes: 1887-1902*, trans. Eric Mosbacher and James Strachey (New York: Basic Books, 1954), hereafter cited as *Origins;* papers and notes in the library of the B'nai B'rith, Vienna. When sources conflicted, information was derived from the journal of the B'nai B'rith (*BBJ*), or, when such information was lacking, from Knöpfmacher, the most reliable of the other sources.

2. *BBJ*, 1 (February 1898), 67.

3. *BBJ*, 2 (December 1899), 156. See *Origins,* 260-62, 264-65, 328: August 28, 1898, September 22 and 27, 1898, and February 14, 1901. See also Sigmund Freud, *The Standard Edition of the Complete Psychological Works of Sigmund Freud*, ed. and trans. James Strachey (London: The Hogarth Press, 1953-1974), vol. 3, 289-97. (Hereafter cited as *SE* followed by the volume and page number.)

4. *Origins,* 270-71: January 3, 1899; *Origins,* 281: May 28, 1899.
5. *BBJ,* 3 (April 1900), 52; *SE* 3, 303-22.
6. *BBJ,* 3 (1900), 38. See Sigmund Freud, *The Letters of Sigmund Freud 1873-1939,* ed. Ernst L. Freud, trans. Tania and James Stern (London: The Hogarth Press, 1961), 278: to Hugo Heller, 1907 (cited hereafter as *Letters*), and *Minutes of the Vienna Psychoanalytic Society,* ed. Herman Nunberg and Ernst Federn, trans. M. Nunberg (New York: International Universities Press, 1974), 103, 204: January 13 and April 7, 1909. See also Émile Zola, *Fécondité* (Paris: Charpentier-Fasquelle, 1907).
7. *BBJ,* 4 (January 1902), 107; *Origins,* 325, 328: October 14, 1900, February 15, 1901; *SE* 6, 239-79.
8. See Solomon Ehrmann, "Über die Function des Judenthums innerhalb der Menschheit und der B.B. innerhalb des Judenthums," *BBJ,* 4 (January 1902), 98-105.
9. *BBJ,* 5 (October 1902), 62.
10. Ernest Jones, *The Life and Work of Sigmund Freud* (New York: Basic Books, 1953), vol. 1, 362 (hereafter cited as *Life*). James Strachey, the translator of Freud's works into the English edition *SE,* translated "Über den Traum" as "On Dreams"; see *SE* 5, 631ff.
11. *BBJ,* 5 (March 1903), 104. Freud praised Zola in *The Interpretation of Dreams* (New York: Avon Books, 1967), 247 and 250-51n (hereafter cited as *Dreams*), and in *Origins,* 245; February 9, 1898. The Revolutionary dream took place in early 1898. The Jew who commended Zola's courage was Richard Bermann (1883-1939), in "Die Fahrt auf dem Katarakt: Autobiographie ohne einen Helden" (Unpub. ms.: Memoir Collection #191 of the Leo Baeck Institute, n.d.), 13.
12. See pp. 259-63. For a discussion of the connection between Zola and the oedipal revolt in *The Interpretation of Dreams,* see Alexander Grinstein, *On Sigmund Freud's Dreams* (Detroit: Wayne State University Press, 1968), 111-24.
13. *BBJ,* 7 (October 1904), 38; *SE* 9, 199; *SE* 21, 48.
14. *BBJ,* 8, nos. 1 and 2 (1904), 12.
15. *Life* 2, 20; *SE* 13, 220-21.
16. See Friedrich Delitzsch, *Babel und Bibel* (Leipzig: J. C. Hinrichs, 1902). This lecture on the common religious heritage of the Near East sparked the controversy. See also *Jüdisches Volksblatt,* March 25, 1904, 5; Samuel Fuchs, "Hammurabi," *Jewish Encyclopedia* (1907 ed.), 198-200.
17. *SE* 13, 230-33.
18. *BBJ,* 9, no. 1 (1906), 9. See *Origins,* 211: June 12, 1897.
19. *SE* 8, 159-180.
20. *Life* 2, 13.
21. Knöpfmacher, 50; *SE* 9, 99-114.
22. *BBJ,* 11, 1 (1908), 23, 25.
23. *SE* 9, 145, 153.
24. Knöpfmacher, 52.
25. Knöpfmacher, 59; *Dreams,* 298-99; see *Origins,* 224: October 15, 1897.
26. See "Psychopathic Characters on the Stage" (1905-6), *SE* 7, 309-10; the fourth of Freud's "Five Lectures on Psycho-Analysis" (1909), *SE* 11, 47; "Leonardo da Vinci and A Memory of His Childhood" (1910), *SE* 11, 137.
27. *Life* 2, 64.
28. Sigmund Freud and Carl Jung, *The Freud/Jung Letters: The Correspondence between Sigmund Freud and C. G. Jung,* ed. William McGuire, trans. Ralph Manheim and R. F. C. Hull (Princeton: Princeton University Press, 1974), 550; *Life* 2, 98.
29. *BBJ,* 17, nos. 1 and 2 (1914), 42; *SE* 14, 73-104; ibid., 42-66.
30. "Wir und der Tod," *BBJ,* 18, no. 1 (1915), 41-51; see *Imago,* 4, no. 1 (1915), 1-21, and *SE* 14, 274-302.
31. Knöpfmacher, 71. Hanns Sachs, *Freud: Master and Friend* (Cambridge, Mass.: Harvard University Press, 1944), 105.

32. Anatole France, *The Revolt of the Angels*, trans. unknown (New York: Dodd, Mead, 1914), 348.

33. Knöpfmacher, 71.

APPENDIX B

OTTO RANK: A CHRONOLOGY

DATES IN THE FAMILY HISTORY (1849-84)

1849. Father (Simon Rosenfeld, 1849-1927) born in Kobersdorf in the Burgenland, February 22.

1856. Mother (Karoline Fleischner, 1856-1935) born in Hausbrünn, Moravia, December 10.

1880. Simon and Karoline marry in Vienna at the israelitische Cultusgemeinde, August 31.

1881. Brother (Paul, 1881-1921) born May 30.

1882 or 1883. Sister dies a few months after her birth.

RANK'S PREPSYCHOANALYTIC PERIOD (1884-1905)

1884. Rank (1884-1939) born in Vienna, April 22. Lives in Vienna's second district, the Leopoldstadt.

c. 1890-c. 1894. Volksschule (in the Czerningasse, the second district).

c. 1894-98. Bürgerschule.

1898-99. Rank works at the Firma Ludwig Wilhelm as a locksmith's apprentice.

1899-1903. Attends the Maschinenbau-Abteilung der höheren Gewerbeschule.

1899-1902. Absorbing interest in the theater.

1900-1. Reacts to what he calls "oppressive fetters" — breaks with father.
Wants to become actor.
Uses name "Rank" for first time.
Brother enters the field of law.

1902. Interest in theater wanes.
    c. October. Begins to write poetry.

1903. Ends technical education. Works for a few more years in machine factories.
    First year of evidence of de facto name change (Rosenfeld to Rank).
    Begins "Tagebücher" in January (completed in 1905); search for "enlightenment" and for knowledge.
    "Tagebuchblätter einer Totgeborenen" (possibly written earlier).
    March. Leaves Jewish confession (*Confessionsloskeit*).
    November. "Begins Götzen,"; first act completed in early 1904.

1904. February. Naturalized as an Austrian citizen — regards himself a *Schriftsteller* (author).
    June. "Der Freund."
    October. First reading of Freud's *Interpretation of Dreams.*
    November. "Träume und Versuche ihrer Deutung."

1905. February. Begins work on *Der Künstler* (published in 1907) and *Der Inzestmotiv* (published in 1912).
    April. Introduced to Freud by Alfred Adler.
    April. Second reading of *The Interpretation of Dreams.*
    May. Writes the manuscript on the reinterpretation of Freud's Frau Doni dream.
    July. "Die Barttracht."
    August. Ends his "Tagebücher."
    October. Enters the k.k. Staatsgymnasium im XVIII Wiener Gemeindebezirke. Diploma in 1908.
    December. "Das Wesen des Judentums."
    Moves away from parents' home to the ninth district (possibly in early 1906).

EARLY YEARS IN FREUD'S CIRCLE (1906-13)

1906. Joins Freud's circle, the Psychological Wednesday Society — assumes role as society's salaried secretary.
    Completes draft of *Das Inzestmotiv.*

1907. *Der Künstler* is published.
    (First signs of dissension within Freud's circle.)

1908. (April. First international psychoanalytic convention in Salzburg.)
    June. Receives diploma from gymnasium.

October. Enters the University of Vienna (until 1912): major field — philosophy; minor field — German language.
October. Converts to Roman Catholicism.
November. Begins legal procedures for changing name to Rank.

1909. *Der Mythus von der Geburt des Helden*
March. Officially changes name to Rank.
November. Application for state stipend (for university education) rejected.

1910. First year of extensive writing; four published pieces and many reviews appear in the two new psychoanalytic journals, *Jahrbuch* (1909-14) and *Zentralblatt* (1910-12).
(March-April. The Nuremburg Convention.)

1911. (September: Weimar Convention. October: Adler resigns from Freud's circle.)
11 published pieces, including *Die Lohengrinsage,* his doctoral thesis (1912).

1912. (November. Wilhelm Stekel resigns from the Vienna Psychoanalytic Society.)
16 published pieces, including *Das Inzestmotiv* and (with Hanns Sachs) "Entwicklung und Ansprüche der Psychoanalyse."
Edits (with Sachs) the psychoanalytic journal of the arts, *Imago.*
Receives doctorate from the University of Vienna. Thesis is the first anywhere on the subject of psychoanalysis.

1913. Becomes one of five members of "the committee," the group in the psychoanalytic circle that declared steadfast loyalty to Freud's theories; Rank: "I was in the deepest of all."
15 published pieces, including "Die Nacktheit in Sage und Dichtung" and (with Sachs) "Die Bedeutung der Psychoanalyse für die Geistes-wissenschaften."
Edits (with Ernest Jones and Sandor Ferenczi) the *Internationale Zeitschrift fur (ärztliche) Psychoanalyse* (1913-16).

MAJOR DATES IN CAREER AND FAMILY (1914-41)

1914-16. Enters World War I. Stays close to Vienna.
Continues to publish extensively for psychoanalytic journals (e.g., 13 published pieces in 1914).

1916-18. Lieutenant in the Austrian army. Stationed in Cracow. Writes for and edits the *Krakauer Zeitung,* the official military journal.

1918. October. Returns to Jewish confession.
November. Marries Betty Münzer.

1919. Manages the new international psychoanalytic publishing house in Vienna.

1920. Despite no medical training, begins to practice psychoanalytic therapy. Style at first is close to Sandor Ferenczi's. Freud sends several patients.

1921. Only child, Helene Marianna (1921-), is born.
Brother dies.

1924. "Entwicklungsziele der Psychoanalyse" (with Ferenczi)
Das Trauma der Geburt

1924-26. Breaks with Freud's circle. Rank: "Analysis . . . killed what it analyzed. . . . Psychoanalysis . . . became pontifical, dogmatic. . . . I became interested in the artist."

1926. *Technik der Psychoanalyse (Will Therapy)*

1926-34. Lives in Paris.

1927. Father dies.

1932. *Art and the Artist.*

1934-39. Lives in the United States (becomes U.S. citizen).
Teaches at the Graduate School of Jewish Social Work (New York) and at the Pennsylvania School of Social Work (Philadelphia).

1935. Mother dies.
1938 or 1939. Divorces Betty Münzer.
1939. August. Second wife, Estelle Buel.
(September. Freud dies.)
October. Rank dies.

1941. *Beyond Psychology.*

APPENDIX C

TRANSLATION OF OTTO RANK'S "DAS WESEN DES JUDENTUMS" ("THE ESSENCE OF JUDAISM")

"Have not many nations greater than ourselves disappeared?[1] Or do you want to bear in the future the miserable existence of the eternal Jew who cannot die? Subservient as he is to every developing people, the eternal Jew has buried the Egyptians, the Greeks, and the Romans" — Gottfried Keller.[2]

Human knowledge is based on the same principle as the light of the planets. Just as the streams of light from certain fixed stars which rotate far away from us reach us only after thousands of years, so emerges enlightened knowledge after an equally long evolution of our unconscious. It radiates with the same intensity as it did along its once distant path.

In my work, *The Artist: Essays in Sexual Psychology,* I have defined this gradual consciousness of the unconscious as the pivotal moment in the cultural development of every people, and have demonstrated that this process is brought about through an unceasing sexual repression. This repression propels the organism from an originally *unconscious* state of *"total sexuality"*[3] to the *conscious* state of isolated sexuality,[4] until finally the organism reaches the neurotic state of *anti-sexuality,* a *disturbance of consciousness.* The great historically preeminent nations are therefore characterized by a development from this original state to the state of hysteria. It is between these poles, however, where the entire cultural activity of the human race has taken place up till now. If a people have become "hysterical" after reaching the highest state of sexual repression, passivity would become the prominent feature. This nation would become masochistic and seek out a sadistic, natural people, primitive in its sexuality, in the desire to be overwhelmed. In the end, it would demand its own demise and hurl itself to its own destruction. Each nation followed one another this way and as a consequence, elevated itself to always higher spheres of consciousness, until the point is reached in a people, whose unrelenting hysteria could effectively *make the collective unconscious conscious,* where the highest form of the consciousness of *"overmen"* prevails. Since in a single people, sexual repression does not evolve uniformly, but rather, all transitional stages from perversity to neurosis exist together at the same time, the various stages do not follow one another in a precise line of development. Every individual represents a different stage of the process of repression.

The *Jews* assume an unusual position in this process. In consequence of a protracted and fundamentally "normal" sexual existence, which derived from the early stages of their development, they have been able to preserve themselves for a long time in a relatively favorable stage of the repression process. Like the woman, they have remained "unchanged." The possibility for this was given to them by their direct relation to "nature," to primitive sexuality. They have yet to experience the metamorphosis from a "lower" organism to the state of isolated sexuality. Their myth contained in the Old Testament expresses this fact: it describes the Jews as "the first men" to have created the woman. Generally, their religion, which they constructed thousands of years ago, appropriate to a stage in the repression process still prominent to this day, preserves the greatest part of the people in psychic balance. Where the religion is insufficient to do this, Jews resort to wit; for, they do not have their own "culture."[5] They are, so to speak, women among the people and must above all join themselves to the masculine life-source if they are to become "productive." A similarly lagging cultural development or sexual repression can be found in any people, for example, in the Indians, whose affairs derive from the distant past and who have preserved themselves to this day. Only a relatively young people, for example, the Teutons, are much more culturally developed. Thus, *the essence of Judaism is its stress on primitive sexuality.* In my aforementioned work, I indicated that the essence of the artist was a sharply limited but an intense ("abnormal") repression of sexuality. From this it is clear why the most important artists of the last century, *Schopenhauer and Nietzsche,* among others, have been for the most part hostile toward Jews. *Their anti-Semitism has been nothing more than an expression of the denial of sexuality.* The *friendly* attitude of "gifted" men, like Nietzsche, toward the Jews is an expression of the will to *combat* sexual repression. This "psychic" foundation of the hatred of the Jews can also explain the anti-Semitism which the Jews themselves frequently express.

For, through a painful suppression, in which the Jews resigned themselves to a parasitic existence* among the people with whom they were living, and through merging with these people, repression of sexuality mounted among the "cultivated" Jews as well. While the other people gradually evolved from the highest stress on sexuality to a normal balance, then to becoming artists and finally to neurosis, the Jews achieved this outcome suddenly and without transition. Just as the developing culture of the other people was directed toward resisting hysteria as long as possible and had produced out of this resistance the highest cultural achievements — art and philosophy — so did the nature of the "culture-less" Jew resist neurosis in its own way. It directed the people to a number of specifically Jewish professions, which are simple, sensible

---

*The psychic-parasitic existence of the Jews has its biological analogy in the parasites, of which the sexual component makes up the most considerable part of the body.

attempts at preventing nervous illness and which always pursue only practical ends. Moreover, we were attracted to a few extreme cases, for each choice of profession depends on the "bent of the psyche." Instantly the Jews became artists, journalists. They soon brought these kinds of the "cure" into such high respect that today the newspaper, the most common and most circulated means of "discharging affect" (resisting hysteria), stands among the leading cultural achievements. Indeed, the Jews had to carry on like the artist, only in a positive sense, for weak individuals discharge affect in response to a high degree of sexual repression. Jews created the *match-maker* profession.[6] When later this proved to be in many cases an insufficient cure for both sexes mutually, they became *physicians.* For, the Jews thoroughly understand the *radical* cure of neurosis better than any other people, even better than the artistically and sublimely talented Greeks with their powerful tragedies. They brought matters to such a point that they could help others, since they have sought to preserve themselves from the illness. This[7] is not the least part of their task, which they had to sustain with an almost pathological determination throughout the ages, in spite of the numerous difficulties involved.

NOTES

1. "Das Wesen des Judentums," December 13, 1905. The essay was initialed O.R. Translated by Dennis B. Klein.

2. Gottfried Keller (1819-90), the Swiss novelist, drew the attention of Freud and Eduard Hitschmann, as well as of Rank. Hitschmann wrote a psychoanalytic study of Keller for *Imago* in 1915.

3. "*Allsexualität*" was a neologism of Rank's. The term meant total gratification or the complete fulfillment of impulses emanating, without distortion, from an original and indivisible source. Rank invented the term to distinguish between an organism in the stage of complete gratification and organisms in varying stages of partial gratification.

4. "*Monosexualität.*" In the first chapter of *Der Künstler* ("Die Sexuelle Grundlage"), Rank inserted the stage of "*Vielsexualität*" between the stages of "*Allsexualität*" and "*Monosexualität*" in the linear process of biological and cultural repression. According to the theory he elaborated in the published work, the human organism deviated from the primal state of existence when it came into contact with the outer world (reality). Pleasure, formerly derived from the sources of unrestrained inner emanations, increasingly depended upon the dissipation of tension caused by the conflict between the inner and outer worlds. In the process, the libido learned the most economic routes of gaining pleasure in this way. The stage of *Monosexualität* expressed a high degree of fixation, where only certain instincts, isolated or "preferred" over repressed or "neglected" instincts in the expedient method of the libido, were gratified.

5. According to Rank, "*Kultur*" was an advanced stage of the repression process, where a spontaneous rebellion against repression occurred and soon defined human behavior. Cultural achievements served the function of discharging repressed affect and were accompanied by increasing degrees of consciousness. Thus, before the Jews assimilated to society, they had existed in the early, "natural" state and thus lacked a "culture."

6. "Beruf des Heiratsvermittlers." In the thirteenth chapter of *Geschlecht und Charakter* (*Sex and Character,* 1904), Otto Weininger attacked the Jews for their lack of individuality and for their absorption in sexual matters. This explained to him their

involvement in matchmaking. "The Jews are thoroughly matchmakers [*Heiratsvermittler*]. It is due to their disposition toward matchmaking that Jews fail to comprehend asceticism. Matchmaking is the ultimate breakdown of limits; and the Jew is the one *par excellence* who breaks down limits." *Geschlecht und Charakter* (Vienna, Leipzig: Wilhelm Braumüller, 1904), 423-24. Having once accepted Weininger's polemic as an expression of his own contempt, Rank reversed Weininger's tone in his Jewish essay. He believed that instead of being destructive, sexuality and matchmaking were the foundations of an elevated state of existence, one undisturbed by repression or asceticism. Rank regarded matchmaking as a positive expression of naturalness.

7. The demonstrative article seems to refer to the previous sentence: the task of the Jews is to "help others." But the clause at the end of the sentence which the article introduces indicates that the Jewish task is to "preserve themselves from the illness" of neurosis. Instead of being ambiguous, the article makes an important connection. In his notion of phylogenetic progression, nothing existed in isolation. Everything influenced the development of other things. Self-preservation thus meant a preservation of a state of natural human existence, and thus transcended the self. Rank pointed to this connection between self-preservation and the universal task in a paper he and Hanns Sachs wrote seven years later. They argued that religion was more than an expression of discharged affect. "Because of its capacity for discharging affect, religion is endowed with an extremely important task." It serves as a "custodian for every important cultural achievement. . . . It is obligated to neutralize the dangerous anti-social forces [of repression], and consequently to preserve what is ethical." "Entwicklung und Ansprüche der Psychoanalyse," *Imago*, 1 (March 1912), 15-16. In the passage at the end of the Jewish essay, Jewish self-preservation implied the task of restoring mankind to health.

BIBLIOGRAPHY

Abrahamsen, David. *The Mind and Death of a Genius.* New York: Columbia University Press, 1946.

"Adresse des Lesevereins der deutschen Studenten Wiens an den Professor Dr. Th. Billroth (überreicht am 15. December 1875)." In Theodor Billroth, *Prof. Dr. Th. Billroths Antwort auf die Adresse des Lesevereines der deutschen Studenten Wiens.* Vienna: Verlag von Carl Gerolds Sohn, 1875.

Altmann, Alexander. "The New Style of Preaching in Nineteenth-Century German Jewry." In *Studies in Nineteenth-Century Jewish Intellectual History,* edited by Alexander Altmann, pp. 65-116. Cambridge: Harvard University Press, 1964.

Andreas-Salomé, Lou. *The Freud Journal of Lou Andreas-Salomé.* Translated by Stanley A. Leavy. New York: Basic Books, 1964.

_____ . *In der Schule bei Freud: Tagebuch einer Jahres 1912/1913.* Edited by Ernest Pfeiffer. Zurich: Max Niehans Verlag, 1958.

Arendt, Hannah. *The Origins of Totalitarianism.* New York: Harcourt, Brace & Co., 1951.

Arkel, Dirk van. *Anti-Semitism in Austria.* Leiden: Diss. Rijksuniversiteit, 1966.

Aron, Willy. "Notes on Sigmund Freud's Ancestry and Jewish Contacts." *YIVO Annual of Jewish Social Science,* 57, no. 11 (1957), 286-95.

Ascher, Arnold. "Ehren-Vizegrosspräsident Dr. Wilhelm Knöpfmacher − 80 Jahre." *B'nai B'rith Mitteilungen für Österreich,* 33 (June 1933), 219-23.

_____ . "Grosspräsident Dr. Edmund Kohn." *B'nai B'rith Mitteilungen für Österreich,* 29 (June 1929), 185-89.

Bakan, David. *Sigmund Freud and the Jewish Mystical Tradition.* Princeton: D. van Nostrand, 1958.

Beer-Hofmann, Richard. "Jaákobs Traum." In *Gesammelte Werke,* edited by Otto Kallir, pp. 16-84. Frankfurt a/M: S. Fischer Verlag, 1963.

_____. *Der Tod Georgs.* In *Gesammelte Werke,* pp. 523-624.

_____. "Verse." In *Gesammelte Werke,* 1653-76.

Bein, Alex. *Theodor Herzl: A Biography.* Translated by Maurice Samuel. Philadelphia: The Jewish Publication Society of America, 1940.

Bergmann, Martin S. "Moses and the Evolution of Freud's Jewish Identity." *The Israel Annals of Psychiatry and Related Sciences,* 14 (March 1976), 3-26.

Bermann, Richard A. "Die Fahrt auf dem Katarakt: Autobiographie ohne einen Helden." Manuscript, Memoir Collection #191, Leo Baeck Institute, New York, n.d.

Bernays, Anna Freud. "My Brother, Sigmund Freud." *American Mercury,* 51 (November 1940), 335-42.

Bernfeld, Siegfried. "Sigmund Freud, M.D. 1882-1885." *International Journal of Psychoanalysis,* 32, no. 3 (1951), 204-17.

Bernfield, Siegfried, and Suzanne Cassirer Bernfeld. "Freud's First Year in Practice, 1886-7." *Bulletin of the Menninger Clinic,* 16 (March 1952), 37-49.

Beurle, Karl. *Beiträge zur Geschichte der deutschen Studenschaft Wiens.* Vienna: Lesk u. Schwidernoch, 1893.

Billroth, Theodor. *Über das Lehren and Lernen der medicinischen Wissenschaften an den Universitäten der deutschen Nation nebst allgemeinen Bemerkungen über Universitäten: Ein culturhistorische Studie.* Vienna: Carl Gerolds Sohn, 1876.

_____. *Prof. Dr. Th. Billroths Antwort auf die Adresse des Lesevereines der deutschen Studenten Wiens.* Vienna: Verlag von Carl Gerolds Sohn, 1875.

Birnbaum, Nathan. *Die nationale Wiedergeburt des jüdischen Volkes in seinem Lande, als Mittel zur Lösung der Judenfrage: Ein Appell an die Guten und Edlen aller Nationen.* Vienna: J. Dux, 1893.

Birnbaum, Nathan, ed. *Selbst-Emanzipation: Zeitschrift für die nationalen, socialen, und politischen Interessen des jüdischen Stammes.* Vienna: Bukert, 1885-86, 1890-93.

Bloch, Chaim. "Theodor Herzl and Joseph S. Bloch: An Unknown Chapter of Zionist History Based on Verbal Statements and Written Notes." *Herzl Year Book,* 1 (1958), 154-64.

Bloch, Joseph Samuel. *Israel and the Nations.* Translated by Leon Kellner. Berlin, Vienna: Benjamin Harz, 1927.

―――. *My Reminiscences.* Vol. 1. Translated by A. R. Smith. Vienna, Berlin: R. Löwit, 1923.

―――. *Der nationale Zwist und die Juden in Österreich.* Vienna: Verlag von M. Gottlieb, 1886.

B'nai B'rith Mitteilungen für Österreich, 1924-38.

Braun, Ludwig. "Br. Sigmund Freud." *B'nai B'rith Mitteilungen für Österreich,* 36 (September-October 1936), 119-27.

―――. "Festrede am 70. Geburtstage des Grosspräsidenten Ehrmann." *B'nai B'rith Mitteilungen für Österreich,* 25 (January 1925), 53-67.

―――. "Die Persönlichkeit Freuds und seine Bedeutung als Bruder." *B'nai B'rith Mitteilungen für Österreich,* 26 (May 1926), 118-31.

―――. "Trauerrede zum Andenken an den Grosspräsidenten Br. Dr. Edmund Kohn." *B'nai B'rith Mitteilungen für Österreich,* 29 (June 1929), 192-99.

Braunthal, Julius. *Victor and Friedrich Adler: Zwei Generationen Arbeiterbewegung.* Vienna: Verlag der Wiener Volksbuchhandlung, 1965.

Braun-Vogelstein, Julie. "Besprechung am 23. Februar 1959, 8.30 p.m. zwischen Dr. [Kurt] Eissler und Frau Julie Braun-Vogelstein." Manuscript, The Julie Braun-Vogelstein Nachlass (New York City), 1959.

―――. Interview by Kurt Eissler, executive secretary of the Sigmund Freud Archives, New York, January 5, 1954. Manuscript, The Julie Braun-Vogelstein Nachlass (New York City), 1954.

Breuer, Josef. "Curriculum Vitae." Manuscript, Archiv. der Akademie der Wissenschaften in Wien, 1923.

Broch, Hermann. *Hofmannsthal und seine Zeit: Eine Studie.* Munich: R. Piper u. Co. verlag, 1964.

Brome, Vincent. *Freud and His Early Circle.* New York: Wm. Morrow & Co., 1968.

Buber, Martin. "Geleitwort" to *Gesammelte Werke* by Richard Beer-Hofmann, edited by Otto Kallir, pp. 5-12. Frankfurt a/M: S. Fischer Verlag, 1903.

Cahnmann, Werner J. "Adolf Fischhof and His Jewish Followers." *Leo Baeck Institute Yearbook,* 4 (1959), 111-39.

_____ . "The Fighting Kadimah." *Chicago Jewish Forum,* 17 (Fall 1958), 24-27.

Castle, Eduard. "Jung-Österreich und Jung-Wien: Die neue Generation um Hermann Bahr." In *Deutsch-österreichische Literaturgeschichte: Ein Handbuch zur Geschichte der deutsche Dichtung in Österreich-Ungarn, von 1890 bis 1918,* edited by Eduard Castle et al., vol. 4, 1649-1702. Vienna: Verlag von Carl Fromme, 1937.

Charmatz, Richard. *Österreichs innere Geschichte von 1848 bis 1895.* 2 vols. Leipzig, Berlin: B. G. Teubner, 1918.

Cranefield, P. F. "Josef Breuer's Evaluation of His Contribution to Psychoanalysis." *International Journal of Psychoanalysis,* 39 (1958), 319-22.

Cuddihy, John Murray. *The Ordeal of Civility: Freud, Marx, Levi-Strauss and the Jewish Struggle with Modernity.* New York: Basic Books, 1974.

Denkschrift des Vereines zur Unterstützung mittelloser israelitischer Studierender in Wien aus Anlass seines fünfzigjährigen Bestandes 1861-1911. Edited by Guido Fuchsgelb. Vienna: Selbstverlage des Vereines, 1911.

Dubnow, S. M. *Die neueste Geschichte des jüdischen Volkes.* 3 vols. Berlin: Judischer Verlag, 1929.

Dühring, Eugen Karl. *Die Judenfrage als Rassen- Sitten- und Kulturfrage.* Karlsruhe, Leipzig: Reuther, 1881.

Ebner-Eschenbach, Marie von, and Josef Breuer. *Marie von Ebner-Eschenbach- Dr. Josef Breuer: Ein Briefwechsel, 1889-1916.* Edited by Robert A. Kann. Vienna: Bergland Verlag, 1969.

Eder, Karl. *Der Liberalismus in Altösterreich Geisteshaltung, Politik und Kultur.* Vienna, Munich: Verlag Herold, 1955.

Ehrmann, Solomon. "Betrachtungen über den Stand der 'B'nai B'rith' am Ende des Jahrhunderts." *Vierteljahrsbericht für die Mitglieder der österr. israel. Humanitätsvereine 'B'nai B'rith,'* 2 (December 1899), 137-49.

_____ . "In diesen Tagen..." Speech. In *B'nai B'rith Mitteilungen für Österreich,* 26 (May 1926), 102-3.

_____ . "Meine persönlichen Beziehungen zu Sigmund Freud." *B'nai B'rith Mitteilungen,* 26 (May 1926), 132-34.

_____ . "Der s.w. Verbandspräsident Br. Prof. Dr. S. Ehrmann." *Zweimonats-Bericht für die Mitglieder des österr-israel. Humanitätsvereine 'B'nai B'rith,'* 14, no. 3 (1911), 139-40.

_____ . "Über die Function des Judenthums innerhalb der Menschheit und der B. B. innerhalb des Judenthums." *Vierteljahrsbericht,* 4 (January 1902), 98-105.

_____ . "Was Wir Wollen." *B'nai B'rith Mitteilungen,* 24 (December 1924), 9-10.

_____ . "Was Wir Wollen." *Vierteljahrsbericht,* 1 (October 1897), 3-7.

Ellenberger, Henri F. *The Discovery of the Unconscious: The History and Evolution of Dynamic Psychiatry.* New York: Basic Books, 1970.

Erikson, Erik. *Identity, Youth, and Crisis.* New York: W. W. Norton, 1968.

Federn, Ernst. "Einige Bemerkungen über die Schwierigkeiten eine Geschichte der Psychoanalyse zu schreiben." *Jahrbuch der Psychoanalyse,* 7 (1974), 9-22.

_____ . "Epilogue" to "Thirty-Five Years with Freud: In Honour of the Hundredth Anniversary of Paul Federn, M.D." *Journal of the History of the Behavioral Sciences,* 8 (January 1972), 45-53.

_____ . "Gibt es noch eine psychoanalytische Bewegung?" Manuscript, Based on a lecture given by the author to the Vienna Psychoanalytic Society, June 1973.

Festschrift anlässlich des fünfundzwanzigjährigen Bestandes des israel. Humanitätsvereines 'Eintracht' (B'nai B'rith) Wien 1903-1928. Vienna: Selbstverlage des Vereines, 1928.

Festschrift des k.k. Erzherzog Ranier- Real-Gymnasiums im II. Gemeinde-Bezirke in Wien Früher: Leopoldstädter kommunal- Real- u. Obergymnasium aus Anlass seines fünfzig Jahre andauernden Bestehens. Vienna: Verlag der Anstalt, 1914.

"Festsitzung der 'Wien' anlässlich des 70. Geburtstages Br. Univ. Prof. Doktor Sigmund Freud." *B'nai B'rith Mitteilungen für Österreich,* 26 (May 1926), 101-38.

Fournier, August. *Erinnerungen.* Munich: Drei Masken Verlag, 1923.

Fraenkel, Josef. "Mathias Acher's Fight for the 'Crown of Zion.'" *Jewish Social Studies,* 16 (April 1954), 115-34.

_____ , ed. *The Jews of Austria: Essays on Their Life, History, and Destruction.* 2d ed. London: Vallentin, Mitchell, 1967, 1970.

France, Anatole. *The Revolt of the Angels.* New York: Dodd, Mead, 1914.

Frankfurter, S. "Wesen und Aufgaben des Bundes B.B." *B'nai B'rith Mitteilungen für Österreich,* 34 (October 1934), 220-31.

Franz, Georg. *Liberalismus: Die deutschliberale Bewegung in der habsburgischen Monarchie.* Munich: Verlag Georg D. W. Callwey, 1955.

Freud, Martin. *Glory Reflected: Sigmund Freud – Man and Father.* London: Angus and Robertson, 1957.

_____. "Who Was Freud?" In *The Jews of Austria: Essays on Their Life, History, and Destruction,* edited by Josef Fraenkel, 197-211. London: Vallentin, Mitchell, 1970.

Freud, Sigmund. "Briefe an Arthur Schnitzler." *Neue Rundschau,* 66, 1 (1955), 95-106.

_____. *Briefe 1873-1939,* edited by E. L. Freud. Frankfurt a/M; S. Fischer Verlag, 1960.

_____. " 'Civilized' Sexual Morality and Modern Nervous Illness." *The Standard Edition of the Completed Psychological Works of Sigmund Freud.* Translated and edited by James Strachey, vol. 9, 179-204. London: The Hogarth Press, 1953-1974.

_____. "The Creative Writer and Day Dreaming." *Standard Edition,* vol. 9, 142-54.

_____. "Five Lectures on Psycho-Analysis." *Standard Edition,* vol. 11, 3-55.

_____. "Future of an Illusion." *Standard Edition,* vol. 21, 3-56.

_____. German original of speech to members of the B'nai B'rith Lodge. *B'nai B'rith Mitteilungen für Österreich,* 26 (May 1926), 103-5.

_____. *The Interpretation of Dreams.* Translated by James Strachey. New York: Avon Books, 1967.

_____. *Jokes and Their Relation to the Unconscious. Standard Edition,* vol. 8.

_____. "Jugendbriefe Sigmund Freud." *Neue Rundschau,* 80 (1969), 678-93.

_____. "Leonardo da Vinci and a Memory of His Childhood." *Standard Edition,* vol. 11, 59-137.

_____. *Letters of Sigmund Freud 1873-1939.* Edited by Ernst L. Freud; translated by Tania and James Stern. London: The Hogarth Press, 1961.

_____. *Moses and Monotheism. Standard Edition,* vol. 23.

_____. "The Moses of Michelangelo." *Standard Edition*, vol. 13, 108-36.

_____. "On Narcissism: An Introduction." *Standard Edition*, vol. 14, 67-102.

_____. "On the History of the Psycho-Analytic Movement." *Standard Edition*, vol. 14, 3-66.

_____. *The Origins of Psycho-Analysis: Letters to Wilhelm Fliess, Drafts and Notes: 1887-1902.* Edited by Marie Bonaparte, Anna Freud, and Ernst Kris; translated by Eric Mosbacher and James Strachey. New York: Basic Books, 1954.

_____. "The Psychical Mechanism of Forgetfulness." *Standard Edition*, vol. 9, 99-114.

_____. "Psycho-Analysis and the Establishment of the Facts in Legal Proceedings." *Standard Edition*, vol. 9, 99-114.

_____. "Psychopathic Characters on the Stage." *Standard Edition*, vol. 7, 304-10.

_____. *The Psychopathology of Everyday Life. Standard Edition*, vol. 6.

_____. "The Resistance to Psycho-Analysis." *Standard Edition*, vol. 19, 213-24.

_____. "Screen Memories." *Standard Edition*, vol. 3, 303-22.

_____. "Some Early Unpublished Letters of Freud." Translated by Ilse Schrier. *International Journal of Psycho-Analysis*, 50, pt. 4 (1969), 419-27.

_____. Statement to the B'nai B'rith Wien. *B'nai B'rith Mitteilungen für Österreich*, 35 (November-December 1935), 193.

_____. "Thoughts for the Times on War and Death." *Standard Edition*, vol. 14, 274-302.

_____. "To Members of the B'nai B'rith Lodge." In *Letters of Sigmund Freud 1873-1939*, edited by Ernst L. Freud; translated by Tania and James Stern, pp. 367-68. London: The Hogarth Press, 1961.

_____. "Wir und der Tod." *Zweimonats-Bericht für die Mitgleider der österr. israel. Humanitätsvereine 'B'nai B'rith,'* 18, no. 1 (1915), 41-51.

_____. "Zeitgemässes über Krieg und Tod." In *Gesammelte Schriften*, vol. 10, 315-46. Zurich: Internationaler Psychoanalytischer Verlag, 1925.

Freud, Sigmund, and Carl Jung. *The Freud/Jung Letters: The Correspondence between Sigmund Freud and C. G. Jung.* Edited by William McGuire; translated by Ralph Manheim and R. F. C. Hull. Princeton: Princeton University Press, 1974.

Freud, Sigmund, and Karl Abraham. *A Psycho-Analytic Dialogue: The Letters of Sigmund Freud and Karl Abraham 1907-1926.* Edited by Hilda C. Abraham and Ernst L. Freud; translated by Bernard Marsh and Hilda C. Abraham. New York: Basic Books, 1965.

_____. *Sigmund Freud-Karl Abraham: Briefe 1907-1926.* Edited by Hilda C. Abraham and Ernst L. Freud. Frankfurt a/M: S. Fisher Verlag, 1965.

Fuchs, Albert. *Geistige Strömungen in Österreich 1867-1918.* Vienna: Globus-Verlag, 1949.

Fürth, Rudolf. "Gedenkrede Trauerfeier zum Andenke an den Ehren-Gross-präsidenten Dr. Wilhelm Knöpfmacher." *B'nai B'rith Mitteilungen für Österreich,* 37 (November/December 1937), 146-50.

Furtmüller, Carl. "Alfred Adler: A Biographical Essay." In *Alfred Adler: Superiority and Social Interest, a Collection of Later Writings,* edited by Heinz L. Ansbacher and Rowena R. Ansbacher, pp. 330-95. Evanston, Ill.: Northwestern University Press, 1964.

Gay, Peter. *Freud, Jews and Other Germans: Masters and Victims in Modernist Culture.* New York: Oxford University Press, 1978.

Gedenkschrift: Die Lesevereine der deutschen Hochschüler an der Wiener Universität. Vienna: Im Selbstverlage des Lese- und Redevereins des deutschen Hochschüler in Wien 'Germania,' 1912.

Gedo, John E., and Ernest Wolf. "Die Ichthyosaurusbriefe." *Psyche* (Stuttgart), 24 (October 1970), 785-97.

Gicklhorn, Josef, and Renée Gicklhorn. *Sigmund Freuds akademische Laufbahn im Lichte der Dokumente.* Vienna, Innsbruck: Verlag Urban and Schwarzenberg, 1960.

Gicklhorn, Renée. "Eine Episode aus S. Freuds Mittelschulzeit." *Unsere Heimat,* 36 (1965), 18-24.

Gold, Hugo. *Geschichte der Juden in Wien.* Tel Aviv: Olamenu, 1966.

Graf, Max. "Reminiscences of Professor Sigmund Freud." *Psychoanalytic Quarterly,* 11 (1942), 465-76.

Grinstein, Alexander. *On Sigmund Freud's Dreams.* Detroit: Wayne State University Press, 1968.

Grollman, Earl A. *Judaism in Sigmund Freud's World.* New York: Bloch Publishing Co., 1965.

Grunwald, Max. *Geschichte der Wiener Juden bis 1914 (Festschrift)*. Vienna: Selbstverlag der israelitischen Kultusgemeinde, 1926.

―――. *Vienna*. Philadelphia: The Jewish Publication Socety of America, 1936.

Häusler, Wolfgang. "Toleranz, Emanzipation und Antisemitismus: Das österreichische Judentum des bürgerlichen Zeitalters (1782-1918)." In *Das österreichische Judentum: Voraussetzungen und Geschichte*, edited by Nikolaus Vielmetti, pp. 83-140. Vienna: Jugend u. Volk, 1974.

Hammerschlag, Samuel. "Das Programm der israelit. Religionsschule in Wien." In *Bericht der Religionsschule der israelitischen Cultusgemeinde in Wien über die Schuljahre 1868 und 1869*. Vienna: Im Selbstverlage der israel. Cultusgemeinde, 1869.

Heer, Friedrich. "Freud, the Viennese Jew." In *Freud, the Man, His World, His Influence*, edited by Jonathan Miller; translated by W. A. Littlewood, pp. 2-20. Boston: Little, Brown, 1972.

―――. *Land im Strom der Zeit: Österreich Gestern, Heute, Morgen*. Vienna, Munich: Verlag Herold, 1958.

Heller, Judith Bernays. "Freud's Mother and Father." *Commentary*, 21 (May 1956), 418-21.

Herzl, Theodor. *The Complete Diaries of Theodor Herzl*. Edited by Raphael Patai; translated by Harry Zohn. New York: Herzl Press and Thomas Yoseloff, 1960.

―――. *The Jewish State: An Attempt at a Modern Solution of the Jewish Question*. Revised and translated by Jacob Alkow. New York: American Zionist Emergency Council, 1946.

Hirschler, Sigmund. "Toast auf die neueingetretener Mitglieder." In *Zur Erinnerung an die General-Versammlung des Vereines für fromme und wohlthätige Werke: Chevra-Kadischa am 10. Adar 5633/9. März 1873*, pp. 30-32. Vienna: Im Selbstverlage des Vereines, 1873.

Hitschmann, Eduard. "Sigmund Freud und seine Lehre." *B'nai B'rith Mitteilungen für Österreich*, 26 (May 1926), 106-18.

Hoffer, Willi. "Siegfried Bernfeld and 'Jerubbaal': An Episode in the Jewish Youth Movement." *Leo Baeck Institute Yearbook*, 10 (1965), 150-67.

Hughes, H. Stuart. *Consciousness and Society: The Reorientation of European Social Thought, 1890-1930*. New York: Vintage Books, 1958.

Jahrbuch der k.k. Universität Wien. Vienna: Selbstverlag der k.k. Universität, 1891-95.

Jahresbericht der Jüdisch-akademischen Lesehalle in Wien. Vienna: Verlag der Jüdisch-akademischen Lesehalle, 1897.

Jahresberichte der akademischen Lesehalle in Wien. Vienna: Selbstverlag der akademischen Lesehalle, 1871-80.

Jahresberichte der israelitischen Cultusgemeinde in Wien. Vienna: Selbstverlage der israelitischen Cultusgemeinde in Wien, 1906, 1911, 1917.

Jahres-Berichte der Lese- und Redehalle jüdischer Hochschüler in Wien. Vienna: Verlag der Lese- und Redehalle jüdischer Hochschüler, 1905, 1907.

Jahresberichte des Leopoldstädter Communal-Real-und Obergymnasiums in Wien. Vienna: Verlag des Leopoldstädter Real- und Obergymnasiums, 1866-1873.

Jahresberichte des Lesevereines der deutschen Studenten Wiens. Vienna: Selbstverlag des Lesevereines der deutschen Studenten Wiens, 1872-1878.

Jeiteles, Israel. *Die Kultusgemeinde der Israeliten in Wien mit Benützung des statistischen Volkszählungsapparates vom Jahre 1869.* Vienna: L. Rosner, 1873.

Jerusalem, Wilhelm. *Festschrift zur Feier des fünfundzwanzigjährigen Bestandes.* Vienna: Selbstverlag des Vereines, 1920.

Johnston, William M. *The Austrian Mind: An Intellectual and Social History 1848-1938.* Berkeley: University of California Press, 1972.

Jones, Ernest. *Free Associations: Memories of a Psycho-Analyst.* New York: Basic Books, 1959.

_____. *The Life and Work of Sigmund Freud,* 3 vols. New York: Basic Books, 1953, 1955, 1957.

Jüdisches Volksblatt, 1899-1914.

Kainz, Friedrich. "Jung-Österreich und Jung-Wien: Arthur Schnitzler und Karl Schönherr." In *Deutsch-österreichische Literaturgeschichte: Ein Handbuch zur Geschichte der deutsche Dichtung in Österreich-Ungarn, von 1890 bis 1918,* edited by Eduard Castle et al., vol. 4, 1745-1804. Vienna: Verlag von Carl Fromme, 1937.

Kann, Robert A. "German Speaking Jewry during Austria-Hungary's Constitutional Era (1867-1918)." *Jewish Social Studies,* 10 (July 1948), 239-56.

_____. *The Multinational Empire: Nationalism and National Reform in the Habsburg Monarchy 1848-1918,* 2 vols. New York: Columbia University Press, 1950.

Katz, Jacob. "Die Entstehung der Judenassimilation in Deutschland und deren Ideologie." In *Emancipation and Assimilation: Studies in Modern Jewish History*, edited by Jacob Katz, pp. 195-276. Westmead, England: Gregg International Publishers, 1972.

_____. *Out of the Ghetto: The Social Background of Jewish Emancipation, 1770-1870*. Cambridge: Harvard University Press, 1973.

Katz, Julius. "Zweck und Bedeutung des Comités für geistige Interessen." *Vierteljahrsberichte für die Mitglieder der österr. israel. Humanitätsvereine 'B'nai B'rith,'* 4 (April 1902), 146-52.

Klemperer, Karl. "Erinnerungen an die ersten Jahre der 'Wien,' " *B'nai B'rith Mitteilungen für Österreich,* 35 (November-December 1935), 199-204.

Knöpfmacher, Wilhelm. *Entstehungsgeschichte und Chronik der Vereinigung "Wien" B'nai B'rith in Wien 1895-1935*. Vienna: Verlag Verband der israelitischen Humanitätsvereine 'B'nai B'rith' für Österreich in Wien, 1935.

_____. "Kritische Bemerkungen." *Vierteljahrsbericht für die Mitglieder der österr. israel Humanitätsvereine 'B'nai B'rith,'* 1 (October 1898), 152-56.

König, Karl. "Dr. Josef Breuer 1842-1925." *Wiener klinische Wochenschrift,* 69 (April 19, 1957), 280-84.

Kohn, Edmund. "IV. Festrede aus Anlass des zehnjährigen Bestandes der 'Wien.' " *Zweimonats-Bericht für die Mitgleider der osterr. israel. Humanitätsvereine 'B'nai B'rith,'* 8, no. 6 (1905), 201-20.

_____. "Bruder Freud." *B'nai B'rith Mitteilungen für Österreich,* 26 (May 1926), 136-38.

Kohn, Hans. "Eros and Sorrow: Notes on the Life and Work of Arthur Schnitzler and Otto Weininger." *Leo Baeck Institute Yearbook,* 6 (1961), 152-69.

_____. *Karl Kraus, Arthur Schnitzler, Otto Weininger: Aus dem jüdischen Wien der Jahrhundertwende*. Tübingen: J. C. B. Mohr (Paul Siebeck), 1962.

_____. "Das kulturelle Problem des modernen Westjuden." *Der Jude,* 5 (August-September 1920), 281-97.

Kraus, Karl. "Er ist doch e Jud." In *Untergang den Welt durch schwarze Magie*, pp. 331-38. Munich: Kösel-Verlag, 1960.

_____. *Eine Krone für Zion*. Vienna: Verlag von Moriz Frisch, 1898.

_____. "Pro Domo et Mundo." In *Beim Wort Genommen*, pp. 818-304. Munich: Kösel-Verlag, 1955.

Kreutzberger, M. "The German-Jewish Utopia of Social-Emancipation." In *Emancipation and Assimilation: Studies in Modern Jewish History*, edited by Jacob Katz, pp. 91-110. Westmead, England: Gregg International Publishers, 1972.

Kris, Ernst. "Introduction." In *The Origins of Psycho-Analysis: Letters to Wilhelm Fliess, Drafts and Notes: 1887-1902*, edited by Marie Bonaparte, Anna Freud, and Ernst Kris; translated by Eric Mosbacher and James Strachey, pp. 1-47. New York: Basic Books, 1954.

Krull, Marianne. *Freud und sein Vater: Die Entstehung der Psychoanalyse und Freuds ungelöste Vaterbindung*. Munich: C. H. Beck, 1979.

Lesky, Erna. *Die Wienermedizinische Schule im 19. Jahrhundert*. Graz: H. Böhlau, 1965.

Lessing, Theodor. *Der jüdische Selbsthass*. Berlin: Zionistischer Bücher-Bund, 1930.

Liptzin, Solomon. *Germany's Stepchildren*. Philadelphia: The Jewish Publication Society of America, 1944.

———. *Richard Beer-Hofmann*. New York: Bloch Publishing Co., 1936.

———. "Richard Beer-Hofmann." In *The Jews of Austria: Essays on Their Life, History, and Destruction*, edited by Josef Fraenkel, pp. 213-19. London: Vallentin, Mitchell, 1970.

———. "Richard Beer-Hofmann: a Biographical Essay." In *Jacob's Dream*, by Richard Beer-Hofmann, pp. 1-26. New York: Johannespresse, 1946.

McGrath, William J. *Dionysian Art and Populist Politics in Austria*. New Haven and London: Yale University Press, 1974.

———. "Student Radicalism in Vienna." *Journal of Contemporary History*, 2 (July 1967), 183-201.

M. P. "Die Kämpfe in den Lesevereinen." *Gedenkschrift: Die Lesevereine der deutschen Hochschüler an der Wiener Universität*, 31-48. Vienna: Im Selbstverlage des Lese- und Redevereines des deutschen Hochschüler in Wien 'Germania,' 1912.

Magris, Claudio. *Der habsburgische Mythos in der österreichischen Literatur*. Translated from Italian by Madeleine von Pasztory. Salzburg: Otto Müller Verlag, 1966.

Marrus, Michael R. *The Politics of Assimilation: A Study of the French Jewish Community at the Time of the Dreyfus Affair*. Oxford: Oxford University Press, 1971.

May, Arthur J. *The Hapsburg Monarchy 1867-1914*. New York: W. W. Norton & Co., 1968.

Mayer, Sigmund. *Eine jüdischer Kaufmann 1831-1911: Lebenserinnerungen*. Leipzig: Verlag von Duncker u. Humblot, 1911.

―――. *Die Wiener Juden: Kommerz, Kultur, Politik 1700-1900*. Vienna, Berlin: R. Löwit Verlag, 1917.

Meyer, Hans Horst. "Josef Breuer 1842-1925." *Neue österreichische Biographien*, vol. 5, 30-47. Vienna: Amalthea Verlag, 1928.

Minutes of the Vienna Psychoanalytic Society. 4 vols. Edited by Herman Nunberg and Ernst Federn; translated by M. Nunberg. New York: International Universities Press, 1962, 1967, 1974, 1975.

Molisch, Paul. *Politische Geschichte der deutschen Hochschulen in Österreich von 1848 bis 1918*. Vienna, Leipzig: Wilhelm Braumüller, 1939.

Moser, Jonny. *Von der Emanzipation zur antisemitischen Bewegung: Die Stellung Georg Ritter von Schönerers und Heinrich Friedungs in der Entwicklungsgeschichte des Antisemitismus in Österreich (1848-1896)*. Vienna: Diss. Universität Wien, 1962.

Mosse, George. "The Influences of the Völkisch Idea on German Jewry." *Studies of the Leo Baeck Institute*, edited by Max Kreutzberger, pp. 83-114. New York: Frederick Ungar, 1967.

Neumann, Julius. "Ein Programmvortrag." *Vierteljahrsbericht für die Mitglieder der österr. israel. Humanitätsverein 'B'nai B'rith,'* 6 (December 1903), 103-11.

Nietzsche, Friedrich. *The Birth of Tragedy and the Genealogy of Morals*. Translated by Francis Goeffing. Garden City, N.Y.: Doubleday & Co., 1956.

―――. *Thus Spoke Zarathustra*. In *The Portable Nietzsche*, translated by Walter Kaufmann, pp. 103-439. New York: Viking Press, 1966.

―――. *Twilight of the Idols*. In *The Portable Nietzsche*, pp. 463-564.

―――. *Schopenhauer as Educator*. Translated by James W. Hillesheim and Malcolm R. Simpson. Chicago: Henry Regnery Co., 1965.

Nin, Anais. *The Diary of Anais Nin*. Vol. 1, *1931-1934;* vol. 2, *1934-1939*. Edited by Gunther Stuhlmann. New York: Harcourt Brace Jovanovich, 1966, 1967.

Obergruber, Rudolf. *Die Zeitschriften für jüdische Kulturinteressen im 19. Jahrhundert in Wien*. Vienna: Diss. Universität Wien, 1941.

Pollock, George H. "The Possible Significance of Childhood Object Loss in the Josef Breuer-Bertha Pappenheim (Anne O.)-Sigmund Freud Relationship." *Journal of the American Psychoanalytic Association,* 16 (October 1968), 711-39.

Pulzer, Peter G. J. "The Austrian Liberals and the Jewish Question, 1867-1914." *Journal of Central European Affairs,* 23 (July 1963), 131-42.

_____. "The Development of Political Anti-Semitism in Austria." In *The Jews of Austria: Essays on Their Life, History and Destruction,* edited by Josef Fraenkel, pp. 429-43. London: Vallentin, Mitchell, 1970.

_____. *The Rise of Political Anti-Semitism in Germany and Austria.* New York: John Wiley and Sons, 1964.

Rabinbach, Anson G. "The Migration of Galician Jews to Vienna, 1857-1880." *Austrian History Yearbook,* 11 (1975), 44-54.

Rainey, Reuben McCorkle. "Freud As Student of Religion: Perspectives on the Background and Development of His Thought." Doctoral diss. Columbia University, 1971.

Rank, Otto. Analysis of Writings, 1906-1930. Manuscript, Otto Rank Collection at Columbia University, 1930.

_____. "Die Barttracht: Eine Studie." Manuscript, Otto Rank Collection, July 20, 1905.

_____. "Curriculum Vitae." Manuscript, Niederösterreichisches Landesarchiv, November 15, 1909.

_____. "Der Freund: Eine Novelle." Manuscript, Otto Rank Collection, June 6, 1904.

_____. "Götzen: Vier Acte aus dem Schauspiel des Lebens." Manuscript, Otto Rank Collection, November 1903.

_____. "Im October vorigen Jahres. . . " Manuscript, Otto Rank Collection, May 12, 1905.

_____. *Das Inzestmotiv in Dichtung und Sage: Gründzuge einer Psychologie des dichterischen Schaffens.* Vienna: Deuticke, 1912.

_____. *Der Künstler: Ansätze zu einer Sexual-Psychologie.* Vienna, Leipzig: Hugo Heller und Cie, 1907; 3d ed., 1918.

_____. *Die Lohengrinsage: Ein Beitrag zu ihrer Motivgestaltung und Deutung.* Leipzig, Vienna: Verlag von Franz Deuticke, 1911.

———. "Die Nacktheit in Sage und Dichtung." *Imago,* 2 (1913), 267-301, 409-46.

———. Sketchbooks, source for "Tagebücher." Manuscripts, Otto Rank Collection, October 8, 1903-August 24, 1905. 5 vols.

———. "Tagebuchblätter eines Totgeborenen." Manuscript, Otto Rank Collection, n.d.

———. "Tagebücher." Manuscripts, Otto Rank Collection, January 1, 1903-August 21, 1905. 5 vols.

———. "Träume und Versuche ihrer Deutung." Manuscript, Otto Rank Collection, November 24, 1904.

———. *The Trauma of Birth.* London: Routledge and Kegan Paul, 1929.

———. "Das Wesen des Judentums." Manuscript, Otto Rank Collection, December 13, 1905.

Rank, Otto, and Hanns Sachs. "Entwicklung und Ansprüche der Psychoanalyse." *Imago,* 1 (March 1912), 1-16.

Rechenschafts-Bericht des im Jahre 1764 organizierten Vereines für fromme und wohlthätige Werke Chewra-Kadischa über die Verwaltungsjahre 1892, 1893, 1894. Vienna: Im Selbstverlage des Vereines, 1895.

Roazen, Paul. *Freud and His Followers.* New York: Alfred A. Knopf, 1975.

Roback, A. A. *Jewish Influence in Modern Thought.* Cambridge, Mass.: Sci-Art Publishers, 1929.

Robert, Marthe. *From Oedipus to Moses: Freud's Jewish Identity.* Translated by Ralph Manheim. Garden City, N.Y.: Anchor Books, 1976.

Rosenmann, M[oses]. *Dr. Adolf Jellinek: Sein Leben und Schaffen, Zugleich ein Beitrag zur Geschichte der israelitischen Kultusgemeinde Wien in der Zweiten Hälfte des neunzehnten Jahrhunderts.* Vienna: Jos. Schlesinger Verlag, 1931.

Rothman, Stanley, and Philip Isenberg. "Freud and Jewish Marginality." *Encounter,* 43 (December 1974), 45-54.

Sablik, K. "Sigmund Freud und die Gesellschaft der Ärzte in Wien." *Wiener klinische Wochenschrift,* 80 (February 9, 1968), 107-10.

Sachs, Hanns. *Freud: Master and Friend.* Cambridge: Harvard University Press, 1944.

Sajner, Josef. "Sigmund Freuds Beziehungen zu seinem Geburtsort Freiberg (Príbor) und zu Mähren." *Clio Medica*, 3 (1968), 167-80.

Scheuer, Oscar Franz. *Burschenschaft und Judenfrage: Der Rassenantisemitismus in der deutschen Studentenschaft*. Berlin: Verlag Berlin-Wien, 1927.

_____. *Die geschichtliche Entwicklung des deutschen Studententums in Österreich mit besonderer Berücksichtigung der Universität Wien von ihrer Gründung bis zur Gegenwart*. Vienna, Leipzig: Verlag von Ed. Beyers Nachf., 1910.

Schnitzler, Arthur. *My Youth in Vienna*. Translated by Catherine Hutter. New York: Holt, Rinehart & Winston, 1970.

_____. *Professor Bernhardi: Comedy in Five Acts*. Translated by Helly Landstone. New York: Simon and Schuster, 1928.

_____. *The Road to the Open*. Translated by Horace Samuel. New York: Alfred A. Knopf, 1923.

Scholem, Gershom. *On Jews and Judaism in Crisis: Selected Essays*. Edited by Werner J. Dannhauser. New York: Schocken Books, 1976.

Schorske, Carl E. "Politics and the Psyche in fin de siècle Vienna: Schnitzler and Hofmannsthal." *American Historical Review*, 66 (July 1961), 930-46.

_____. "Politics in a New Key: An Austrian Triptych [Schönerer, Lueger, Herzl]." *Journal of Modern History*, 39 (December 1967), 343-86.

_____. "The Transformation of the Garden: Ideal and Society in Austrian Literature." *American Historical Review*, 72 (July 1967), 1283-1320.

Schur, Max. *Freud: Living and Dying*. New York: International University Press, 1972.

Simon, Ernst. "Sigmund Freud, the Jew," translated by Aubrey Hodos. *Leo Baeck Institute Yearbook*, 2 (1957), 270-305.

Simon, Walter B. "The Jewish Vote in Austria." *Leo Baeck Institute Yearbook*, 16 (1971), 97-121.

Singer, Isidore. *Berlin, Wien und der Anti-Semitismus*. Vienna: D. Löwy, 1882.

Sokolow, Nahum. *History of Zionism 1600-1918*. 2 vols. London: Longmans, Green, 1919.

Spigl, Elisabeth. *Das Wiener Judentum des achtziger Jahre in Literatur und Presse*. Vienna: Universität Wien, 1943.

Spitzer, Daniel. *Wiener Spaziergänge.* 7 vols. Vienna, Leipzig: Verlag von Julius Klinikhardt, 1879-94.

Stanescu, Heinz. "Young Freud's Letters to His Rumanian Friend, Silberstein," translated by J. Meron. *Israel Annals of Psychiatry and Related Disciplines,* 9 (December 1971), 195-207.

Statuten der Jüdisch-akademischen Lesehalle in Wien. Vienna: Bergmann, 1896.

Steiner, Rudolf. *Mein Lebensgang.* Dornach, Switzerland: Philosophisch-Anthroposophischer Verlag, 1932.

Suttner, Bertha V. *Lebenserinnerungen.* Berlin: Verlag der Nation, 1969.

Taft, Julia Jesse. *Otto Rank: A Biographical Study Based on Notebooks, Letters, Collected Writings, Therapeutic Achievements, and Personal Associations.* New York: The Julian Press, 1958.

Tal, Uriel. *Christians and Jews in Germany: Religion, Politics and Ideology in the Second Reich, 1870-1914.* Translated by Noah Jonathan Jacobs. Ithaca, London: Cornell University Press, 1975.

Tartakower, Arieh. "Jewish Migratory Movements in Austria in Recent Generations." In *The Jews of Austria: Essays on Their Life, History, and Destruction,* edited by Josef Fraenkel. London: Vallentine, Mitchell, 1970.

Thompson, Clara. *Psychoanalysis: Evolution and Development.* New York: Grove Press, 1950.

Tietze, Hans. *Die Juden Wiens: Geschichte-Wirtschaft-Kultur.* Leipzig, Vienna: E. P. Tal Co. Verlag, 1933.

Toury, Jacob. *Die politischen Orientierungen der Juden in Deutschland: Von Jena bis Weimar.* Tübingen: J. C. B. Mohr (Paul Siebeck), 1966.

Treitschke, Heinrich von. "Unsere Aussichten." In *Deutsche Kämpfe Neue Folge Schriften zur Tagespolitik.* Leipzig: S. Hirzel Verlag, 1896.

Urban[tschitsch], Rudolf von. *Myself Not Least.* London, New York: Jarrolds, 1958.

Viereck, George S. *Glimpses of the Great.* London: Duckworth, 1930.

Vierteljahrsberichte für die Mitglieder der österr. israel. Humanitätsvereine 'B'nai B'rith,' October 1897-April 1904.

Vital, David. *The Origins of Zionism.* London: Oxford University Press, 1975.

Walter, Friedrich. *Wien: Die Geschichte einer deutschen Grossstadt an der Grenze.* 3 vols. Vienna: Verlag Adolf Holzhausens Nachfolger, 1940-44.

Wassermann, Jacob. *My Life As German and Jew.* Translated by S. N. Brainin. New York: Coward-McCann, 1933.

Weininger, Otto. *Geschlecht und Charakter.* Vienna, Leipzig: Wilhelm Braumüller, 1904.

―――. *Sex and Character.* London: William Heinemann, 1906.

―――. *Über die letzten Dinge.* 3d ed. Edited by Moriz Rappaport, 1912. Vienna: Wilhelm Braumüller, 1904.

Weinzierl, Erika. "Die Stellung der Juden in Österreich seit dem Staatsgrundgesetz von 1867." *Zeitschrift für die Geschichte der Juden,* 5, nos. 2/3 (1968), 89-96.

Wiener, Max. "The Ideology of the Founders of Jewish Scientific Research." *YIVO Annual of Jewish Social Science,* 5 (1950), 184-96.

Wininger, Salomon, ed. *Grosse jüdische National-Biographie mit mehr als 8000 Lebensbeschreibungen namhafter jüdischer Männer und Frauen aller Zeiten und Länder: Ein Nachschlagewerk für das jüdische Volk und dessen Freunde.* 7 vols. Czernowitz: "Arta," 1925-36.

Wittels, Fritz. "Brill – The Pioneer." *The Psychoanalytic Review,* 35 (1948), 394-98.

―――. *Die Sexuelle Not.* Vienna, Leipzig: C. W. Stern, 1907.

―――. *Sigmund Freud: His Personality, His Teachings, and His School.* Translated by Eden and Cedar Paul. New York: Dodd, Mead, 1924.

―――. *Der Taufjude.* Vienna, Leipzig: M. Breitensteins Verlagsbuchhandlung, 1904.

Wortis, Joseph. *Fragments of an Analysis with Freud.* Indianapolis: Bobbs-Merrill, 1963.

Zohn, Harry. "Three Austrian Jews in German Literature: Schnitzler, [Stefan] Zweig, Herzl." In *The Jews of Austria: Essays on Their Life, History, and Destruction,* edited by Josef Fraenkel, pp. 67-82. London: Vallentin, Mitchell, 1970.

―――. *Wiener Juden in der deutschen Literatur.* Tel Aviv: Olamenu, 1964.

Zohner, Alfred, "Literarische Zeit- und Streitschriften." In *Deutschösterreichische Literaturgeschichte: Ein Handbuch zur Geschichte der deutsche*

Dichtung in Österreich-Ungarn, Von 1890 bis 1918, vol. 4, edited by Edward Castle et al., pp. 1703-14. Vienna: Verlag von Carl Fromme, 1937.

Zohner, Alfred, Carola Seligmann, and Eduard Castle. "Jung-Österreich und Jung-Wien: 'Café Griensteidl.' " In *Deutsch-österreichische Literaturgeschichte*, pp. 1714-36.

Zola, Émile. *Fécundité*. 2d ed. Paris: Charpentier-Fasquelle, 1907.

Zur Erinnerung an die General-Versammlung des Vereines für fromme und wohlthätige Werk: Chewra-Kadischa am 10. Adar 5633 (9. März 1873). Vienna: In Selbstverlage des Vereines, 1873.

Zweig, Stefan. *The World of Yesterday: An Autobiography*. New York: The Viking Press, 1945.

Zweimonats-Berichte für die Mitglieder der österr. israel. Humanitätsvereine 'B'nai B'rith,' June 1904-21.

INDEX

Abraham, Karl, 93, 94, 142, 148
Acher, Mathias, 20
Adler, Alfred, 121, 126
Adler, Victor, 13, 52, 53
Akadmische Lesehalle, 7, 54
Allsexualität, 149
anti-Semitism, 29, 148; and assimilation, 8-9, 13-14, 15; and B'nai B'rith, 75, 83, 84; of Catholics, 12; cultural/racial, 10, 53; and Freud, 48-62, 70-73, 96; and German organizations, 54; and liberalism, 8-9, 12-13; and nationalism, 9-10, 13, 49, 51; pervasiveness of, 144; political/popular support of, 11; racial, 54; and Rank, 130-31; as term, 54; and Zionism, 22, 83
Apollonian spirit, 115, 116
archetype, Moses as, 94, 140
art: psychoanalytic view of, 104-8; as renewal, 116-18; and repression, 106; and sexuality, 128
Artist, The (Rank), 103
assimilation, Jewish: and anti-Semitism, 8-9, 13-14, 15; of Freud, 40-49, 53, 58, 70, 104; as ideology, 6; and legal rights, 4-5; and nationalism, 49-52, 55; and personal vulnerability, 41; of Rank, 104; and Zionism, 30
Austrian Jews, 2-16, 42, 80
Austria Reform Association, 9
"Autobiographie" (Rank), 112

"Beard as Dress, The"(Rank), 129
Beer-Hofmann, Richard, 14, 15, 24, 31, 32, 142, 147

Berlin, Wien und der Anti-Semitismus (Singer), 13
Bermann, Heinrich, 25, 27
Bernays, Martha, 40, 44, 55, 56, 57, 60
Bernhardi, 26, 27
Bill of Rights, Viennese (1867), 7
Billroth, Theodor, 50-53
Binswanger, Ludwig, 93
Birnbaum, Nathan, 17-21
Birth of Tragedy from the Spirit of Music, The (Nietzsche), 111, 114, 115
Bloch, Joseph Samuel, 18-21, 24
B'nai B'rith, 69, 140, 147, 148; and anti-Semitism, 75, 83, 84; and Freud, 72, 74, 77, 84-96, 138; and psychoanalysis, 69-96; in Vienna, 75-84; welfare programs of, 81 (*see also* Wien)
Braun, Heinrich, 49
Braun, Ludwig, 84, 85, 86
Breuer, Josef, 11, 57, 58, 59, 72, 82, 126
Brunner, Sebastian, 3
Bürgerministerium, 4

Café Griensteidl, 14
Camelias (Beer-Hofmann), 14
Catholics: anti-Semitism of, 12; cultural/political supremacy of, 2; loyalty to Rome of, 9; in reform movement, 11
"Chance and Superstition" (Freud), 90
Charcot, Jean-Martha, 57, 61
Chevra-Kadischa, 58, 82
Christian Socialist Party, 11, 70

193

cocaine, 56
compulsive neurosis, 40
Concordat of 1855, 2
constitutional rights and liberal tradition, 2
creativity, 128
Crown for Zion, A (Kraus), 30

daimon, 114
Death of Georgs, The (Beer-Hofmann), 31
death wish, 92
Deutscher Klub, 10
Deutsch-österreichischer Leseverein, 54
Deutsche Wochenschrift, 12, 19
Diaspora, 18
Dionysian spirit, 115, 116
Dora case, 75
dreams: and Freud, 70-73, 88, 90, 94, 126, 128, 132, 141-51; psychic foundation of, 70-71; and Rank, 109, 118-19, 121-27
"Dreams and Attempts to Interpret Them" (Rank), 122
Dreyfus, Alfred, 8, 90
Dühring, Eugen Karl, 10, 13, 17, 144

ego: preservation of, 123, 130; revenge of, 124
Ehrmann, Solomon, 48, 73, 77, 78, 79, 81-84, 93, 147
Eintracht, 87, 140
"Émile Zola" (Freud), 90
enfranchisement, 5
Enlightenment and Jews, 2-5, 7, 14, 16, 17, 27, 78, 146, 150
Erikson, Erik, 150
"Essence of Judaism, The" (Rank), 103

February Patent, 2, 4, 5
Fécondité (Zola), 89
Federn, E., 150
Fliess, Wilhelm, 61, 72, 73, 74, 87-90
Fluss, Emil, 46, 47, 50
Franz, Georg, 4
Franz Josef, Emperor, 2, 70

Frau Doni dream, 126, 128, 132
Frei, Josef, 117
French Jews, 8
Freud, Emanuel, 55
Freud, Jacob, 42
Freud, Martin, 60, 72
Freud, Sigmund, 9, 10, 14, 24, 32, 104, 139, 142, 145; and anti-Semitism, 48-62, 70-73, 96; assimilation of, 40-49, 53, 58, 70, 104; and B'nai B'rith, 72, 74, 77, 84, 85-96, 138, 144, 147; childhood of, 42, 43, 46; and dreams, 2, 70-73, 88, 90, 94, 128, 132, 141-51; Jewish identification of, 57-62; and liberalism, 44-45; and nationalism, 47, 49, 62; and psychology of movement, 40-62; and Rank, 105-8, 121, 124, 126-28; and reform, political, 47-48; and tradition, religious, 47 (see also individual works)
Friedjung, Heinrich, 12, 13
"Friend, The" (Rank), 119, 120
friendship, essence of, 119-20
"Function of Judaism within Mankind and of the B.B. with Judaism, The" (Ehrmann), 81

Ganzjude, 85
Gemütlichkeit, 11
General Hospital, 54, 56, 58, 59, 76, 96
genius, ideal of, 117
German Jews, 7, 8, 12-13, 17, 18, 20, 22, 24, 32, 40-62
Germinal (Zola), 90
Gesellschaft der Ärzte, 61
Gewissen Wiens, 7
"Goals and Purposes of the B'nai B'rith Societies" (Freud), 74
"Götzen" (Rank), 113, 114, 116, 120, 128
Graf, Max, 148
Grenzboten, 3

Hammerschlag, Samuel, 42-45, 58, 59, 72

Hannibal, 70, 71, 72, 94, 142
Ha-Shahar, 17
Heilkünstler, 129, 132
Herzl, Theodor, 6, 7, 12, 13, 15, 21, 22, 23, 24, 27, 28, 30, 31, 139
Hitschmann, Eduard, 74, 84, 87, 140
Holubek, Franz, 10, 13, 18
Holy Fellowship, 58
Hughes, H. Stuart, 145, 146
Humanitätsfond, 81
Humanitätsvereine, 82
Hungarian Jews, 51

identity, positive, 150
"Idols" (Rank), 112
Imago, 91, 92, 105
Immigration, Jewish, 50-54, 81
incest and repression, 106
individuality and society, 117
International Psychoanalytic Association, 94
Internationale Zeitschrift für Psychoanalyse, 105
Internationaler Psychoanalytischer Verlag, 144
Interpretation of Dreams, The (Freud), 44, 71, 88, 105, 121, 122, 124, 126, 139
Introductory Lectures (Freud), 90
Inzestmotiv, Das (Rank), 106

"Jacob's Dream" (Beer-Hofmann), 31
Jacques, Heinrich, 6
Jellinek, Adolf, 4, 6, 7, 13, 14, 18, 21, 43
Jesus, 2
Jewish Academic Reading Room, 24
Jewish Question as a Racial, Moral and Cultural Question, The (Dühring), 10
Jewish State, The (Herzl), 21, 22, 24, 28, 31
Jokes and Their Relation to the Unconscious (Freud), 71
Jones, Ernest, 93, 142, 143
Joseph II, 5
Judah Maccabee, 18

Jüdische akademische Lesehalle, 73, 88
Jüdische Selbsthass, Der (Lessing), 29
Jüdische Volkspartei, 20
Jüdischer Volksverein, 20
Jüdisches Volksblatt, 20
Jung, Carl, 93, 94, 138, 142, 143
Jung-Wien circle, 14

Kadimah, 17-20, 58
Katz, Jacob, 146
Kind, Das (Beer-Hofmann), 14
Klein, Melanie, 107
Kneipen, 54
Knöpfmacher, Wilhelm, 46-47, 73, 77, 80, 81
Kohn, Edmund, 76, 79, 81, 83
Kohn, Hans, 29
Koller, Carl, 56, 57, 59, 72, 96
Königstein, Leopold, 61, 70, 72, 74, 82, 87
Kraus, Karl, 23, 29, 30, 31
Kris, Ernst, 72
Kulturdeutsche, 8
"Künstler, Der" (Rank), 105, 106, 125, 126, 128, 129, 132
Kuranda, Ignaz, 3

Leo XIII, Pope, 70
Leseverein der deutschen Studenten Wiens, 47, 51, 52, 53, 54, 77
Lessing, Theodor, 29, 44, 78
liberalism, 21, 28; and anti-Semitism, 8-9, 12-13; Freud and religion, 44-45, 48, 60; and Jewish expression, 3-5; and legal rights, 3; and Nietzsche, 111, 112; and reform, 6-7; and subjective states, 146
Libertas, Burschenschaft, 54
Linzer Programm, 10
Liptzin, Solomon, 28
Lohengrinsage, Die (Rank), 105
Lueger, Karl, 11, 15, 70, 72

Magris, Claudio, 13, 25
Mahler, Gustav, 118
maternal separation, 107
Mattathias, 20

Memorial on the Status of the Jews in Austria, 6
Meynert, Theodor, 61
Mittelstand, 9, 10
Mosaic law, 45
Moses and Monotheism (Freud), 94
Moses as archetype, 94, 140
"Moses of Michelangelo, The" (Freud), 94

"Nacktheit in Sage und Dichtung, Die" (Rank), 106
Napoleon, 120
Nathan the Wise (Lessing), 44
Nathonssohn, Amalia, 42
nationalism, 47; and anti-Semitism, 9-10, 13, 49, 51; and assimilation, 49-52, 55; and autonomy, 20; and Freud, 47, 49, 62; and Zionism, 22-23, 30
Nazis, 11, 15, 144
Neue Freie Presse, 7, 15, 22, 53
Neue Zeit, Die, 4, 21
neurosis, 40, 103, 145; obsessional, 140; preoedipal basis of, 107; radical cure for, 118-33; and repression, 128; and unconscious, 127-28
Nietzsche, Friedrich: and liberal culture, 111, 112; and Rank, 104, 108-21, 124, 128-32
Nin, Anaïs, 107
Nothnagel, Hermann, 69, 70
Nurdeutsche, 8

obsessional behavior, 90, 140
"Obsessive Actions and Religious Practices" (Freud), 90
oedipal triad, 106
Old Testament, 43
"On Dreams" (Freud), 90
Ostdeutsche Post, 3
Österreichische Wochenschrift, 19
Österreichische-israelitsche Union, 19
Ostjuden, 9, 12, 17, 48

Palestine, resettlement in, 18
parricide, repression of memory of, 92

Passover, 42, 45
patricide, 106
patriotism of Jews, 6-7
Pinsker, Leon, 18
Plener, Ernst von, 5
Professor Bernhardi (Schnitzler), 1, 16, 25, 143
"Psychic Life of the Child, The" (Freud), 74, 89
"Psychical Mechanism of Forgetfulness, The" (Freud), 71, 89
psychoanalysis: as art, 104-8, 125; and B'nai B'rith, 69-96; and German Jews, 32; humanitarian claims of, 143; and intuition, 132; as movement, 62, 145 (*see also* Freud, Sigmund; Rank, Otto)
Psychological Wednesday Society, 90
"Psychology of Forgetting, The" (Freud), 88
Psychopathology of Everyday Life, The (Freud), 71, 89, 90
Purim, 42

Quarterly Report, 81, 88

Rank, Otto, 9, 31, 32, 103-33, 139, 141, 144, 148, 149; and anti-Semitism, 130-31; and assimilation, 104; childhood of, 108-10; and child psychology, 121; on creativity, 128; and dreams, 109, 118-19, 121-27; and Jewish task, 150; and neurosis, radical cure for, 118-33; and Nietzsche, 104, 108-21, 128-32; rebellion of, 110-12; surname change of, 110 (*see also individual works*)
Reading and Discourse Room of Jewish University Students, 24
Reading Society of the German Students of Vienna, 10
Rechtsstaat, 7, 16
Redehalle, 24
regression of death wish, 92
Reichsrat, 11, 19, 21
Reigen (Schnitzler), 14, 15

repression: and art, 106; and collective malaise, 106; and incest, 106; and neurosis, 128; and parricide memory, 92; and sexuality, 103, 106, 130, 142; sources of, 89
"Resistances to Psychoanalysis, The" (Freud), 145
Rie, Oskar, 72, 74, 87, 140
Road to the Open, The (Schnitzler), 1, 12, 14, 15, 16, 25, 142
Roazen, Paul, 105
Roback, A.A., 143, 144, 148
Rohling, August, 10, 14, 18, 19
Rosenfeld, Karoline Fleischner, 108
Rosenfeld, Otto (*see* Rank, Otto)
Rosenfeld, Paul, 108-9
Rosenfeld, Simon, 108
Rosenmann, Moriz, 4
Rousseau, 78

Sachs, Hans, 95, 105
Sadger, Isidor, 140
Saujud, 56
Schmerling, Anton von, 3, 5
Schmidt, Erich, 54
Schnirer, Moritz, 17
Schnitzler, Arthur, 1, 4, 7, 12, 14, 24-28, 30, 31, 142, 143
Scholem, Gershom, 8
Schönerer, Georg von, 10, 13
Schopenhauer, 124, 130
Schopenhauer as Educator (Nietzsche), 111, 112, 114, 115
Schorske, Carl, 14
"Screen Memories" (Freud), 71, 89
Self-determination, 16-28
Sex and Character (Weininger), 29, 30
Sexual Need, The (Wittels), 138
sexuality: and creativity, 128; guilt over, 90; and Jewishness, 129-32; repression of, 103, 106, 130, 142
Sigismund as name, 46, 49
Silberstein, Eduard, 45, 48
Singer, Isidor, 13
Smolenskin, Perez, 17, 18
Social Democratic Party, 13
socialism, 47-48

"Society for the Awakening and Promotion of Individuality . . . , The," 116
Society of German Students, 54
Society of Physicians, 61
Society of Psychiatry and Neurology, 71
Solferino, battle of, 3
Specht, Richard, 118
Sperl Gymnasium, 48
Spinoza, 83
Spitzer, Daniel, 7, 14, 27
Staatsgrundgesetz, 4, 139
Story of King David (Beer-Hofmann), 31
Studies on Hysteria (Freud and Breuer), 126
suicide, 40-41

Taaffe, Count, 7, 10
Talmud, 10, 19, 42
Talmud Jew, The (Rohling), 10, 18
Taufjude, Der (Wittels), 138, 139, 140, 142, 148, 150
Tausk, Victor, 140
terre, La (Zola), 90
"Thoughts for the Times on War and Death" (Freud), 91
Thus Spake Zarathustra (Nietzsche), 114, 119
Toleranz-Edikt (1782), 5
transference, 72
Trauma of Birth, The (Rank), 107
Treitschke, Heinrich von, 12
Twilight of the Idols (Nietzsche), 111, 112, 114

Über die letzen Dinge (Weininger), 117-18
unconscious, 121, 125; and neurosis, 127-28
Union, 21
universities, Jews in, 70
University of Vienna, 11, 12, 17, 21, 24, 47, 49, 129
unverschämte Antisemiten, 144
Urbantschitsch, Rudolf, 93

Vaterland, 8

Verjudung, 144, 147, 148
Vienna, 2-16; B'nai B'rith in, 75-84
Vienna Medical School, 50
Vogelsang, Karl Freiherr von, 8, 11
völkisch, 10
Volksblatt, 20
Voltaire, 78

Wagner, R., 105, 115, 118, 120, 121, 125, 128
Waidhofer Verband, 54
Walter, Friedrich, 144
Wassermann, Jacob, 8, 28, 32
"We and Death" (Freud), 91, 92
Wiener Kirchenzeitung, 3
Weininger, Otto, 29, 30, 32, 117-18, 142
Weiss, Nathan, 40-42, 54, 55, 56, 58
Weltprocess, 118
Wergenthin, Georg von, 25

"Wesen des Judentums, Das" (Rank), 129
Wilhelmine Empire, 8
Wien, 74, 77, 79, 81, 83, 84, 86, 87, 91, 149
Wittels, Fritz, 138, 139, 140, 142, 144, 148, 150
Wochenschrift, 20

Yom Kippur, 45, 60

Zielbewusstsein, 141
Zionism, 20; and anti-Semitism, 22, 83; and assimilation, 30; goals of, 27; and mission, 31; and national identity, 23; and nationalism, 22-23, 30
Zola, Émile, 89, 90
Zucker, Herr, 71, 72
Zweig, Stefan, 11, 16, 25, 27, 31